A Study of English
Sentences with Inanimate Subjects

英语
无灵主语句研究

何明珠 著

·广州·

版权所有　翻印必究

图书在版编目（CIP）数据

英语无灵主语句研究/何明珠著.—广州：中山大学出版社，2019.12

ISBN 978-7-306-06804-0

Ⅰ.①英…　Ⅱ.①何…　Ⅲ.①英语—句法—研究　Ⅳ.①H314.3

中国版本图书馆 CIP 数据核字（2019）第 293257 号

出 版 人：	王天琪
策划编辑：	熊锡源
责任编辑：	熊锡源
封面设计：	曾　斌
责任校对：	井思源
责任技编：	何雅涛
出版发行：	中山大学出版社
电　　话：	编辑部 020 - 84110779，84110283，84111997，84110771
	发行部 020 - 84111998，84111981，84111160
地　　址：	广州市新港西路 135 号
邮　　编：	510275　传　真：020 - 84036565
网　　址：	http://www.zsup.com.cn　E-mail:zdcbs@mail.sysu.edu.cn
印　刷　者：	广州市友盛彩印有限公司
规　　格：	787mm×1092mm　1/32　9 印张　235 千字
版次印次：	2019 年 12 月第 1 版　2019 年 12 月第 1 次印刷
定　　价：	40.00 元

如发现本书因印装质量影响阅读，请与出版社发行部联系调换

序

何明珠教授嘱我为他即将出版的专著写几句话，我心中十分忐忑，自感分量太轻，是何教授真诚的鼓励，让我斗胆提笔。

初识何教授，应该是在十八年前，当时的他在英语无灵主语现象研究方面，在国内已卓有建树，这些年来他一直在这方面勤耕不辍，持续深化，形成系统，其实已集大成。学术研究，可以大题小做，也可小题大做，而我偏向于将何教授的研究归到小题大做之列。我认为他成功的关键在于他在学术方向上的选择极富主见，而且一旦认准了方向就会无比专注地钻研，这恐怕也是任何学术成功之人的普适之路。

时下关于建立翻译学这一独立学科（或至少是"亚科学"）的讨论很是活跃，命题繁多，智略深湛。不少有关中西译论比较互补和翻译多元研究（诸如翻译与文化研究、翻译与语言学、翻译与接受美学、翻译与女性主义、翻译与后殖民主义、翻译与解构主义等）的危言谠论，读来令人耳目一新（陆谷孙，2001），何教授显然也从对国外译论的研讨中获益不少。在理论的探讨上，他拒绝照搬照抄和"西方理论迷信"，以艰苦的翻译实践和在实践中所积累的切身体悟和感悟为立足，对各关联学科理论智慧吸取加工、提炼整合。在本书中所涉及的语言及译论问题众多，可见他是既浸淫于传统，又有很大超越的。由于考虑到读者群体水平的不同，很多时候都是作者刻意用最简练实用的话语表现出来的。

　　无灵主语是英语研究中一个古老而又新生的话题，在多年的教研实践中，我每年都会花三到四周的时间给研究生或本科生讲授这一专题，我跟他们说掌握好这一语言现象，会让自己的英语写作和翻译水平有质的提高。通过大量的实例演练，学生们也认可了我的说法，甚至有学生跟我说，如果真的能够把英语的无灵主语现象琢磨透了，毕业时会对自己的英语水平底气十足。当然，也有学生发现，英语无灵主语的巧妙使用对动词的选取要求甚高，问我有何诀窍。学生的思考让我非常欣慰，我回答说，如果真的能够在英语无灵主语句的使用上做到巧用动词，那表明英语学习已臻较高水准，因为它需要学生具备相当系统的英语语言功底——从词汇到句法再到语篇。也就是说，在翻译或写作中，英语无灵主语句使用是否纯熟是检验英语表达是否地道的一个重要参照。

　　在无灵主语句中，通常折射一定生命内涵的动词被"挪用"于不具生命的主语，因此，这样的句式就自然而然地抹上了拟人色彩。除了表达顿趋活泼外，此种句型往往新意拂面，结构严谨，言简意丰。

　　以无灵名词作主语的句子，在汉语中，古已有之。如：

　　　　独怜幽草涧边生，上有黄鹂深树鸣。春潮带雨晚来急，野渡无人舟自横。——唐·韦应物《滁州西涧》

　　"春潮带雨晚来急，野渡无人舟自横"两句中的"春潮"和"舟"，也属无灵名词，但是，它们偏偏使用了通常只有有灵主语才使用的动词，如"带"和"自横"。

遗憾的是，英语的无灵主语句比比皆是；而汉语的无灵主语句则寥若晨星。

英汉对比，句子主语何以如此悬殊？何以存在如此鲜明的差异呢？揭示思维模式，是翻译的功能之一。

翻开中国哲学史，老子、孔子、孟子所宣讲的"处世之道""治学之道"是中国哲学的立足点。老子开宗明义地提出"人是万物之主体"，庄子在《齐物论》中也提出"万物与我为一"。历史长河，浩瀚久远，汉民族的思维方式也就这样年复一年地受其熏陶，汉民族的语言心理也这样日复一日地受其影响，国人对人称主语句式的使用和接受发展到"心有灵犀一点通"的地步，"人称主语"的有无，已经无关紧要。它的省略令行文或言辞更趋简洁，而丝毫不影响彼此交流。

问题回到英语，情况就大不一样了。英语句法严谨，不似汉语表达那样的疏放流散。设想，假如把英语句子的主语都框死在"人称主语"的樊篱中，那么，英语将顿趋乏味黯然（毛荣贵，2005）！

英语无灵主语句的使用非但能给文学翻译增光添彩，还能在非文学翻译中起到非常显著的提高译文质量的作用。这些我们在以前的研究中有过探讨，此处不再赘述。

何教授对英语无灵主语的研究是非常透彻和系统的。读罢这部大作，使人眼前依稀浮想出这样一幅图景：在无灵主语研究这块葱郁的园田里，一位勤勉执着的学者，或于蒙蒙细雨中，或于炎炎烈日下，头戴斗笠，挥动银锄，弯腰耕作，秋收冬藏。皇天不负有心人，辛勤的劳作终于换来沉甸甸的收获。更为难得的是，他非常无私地与后学分享自己的治学之道。

若能在研究英语无灵主语句的同时结合传统翻译原则、

标准与策略等，探讨其间的关联性、制约性、互动性和调节性，那么，该书对我国传统译论的继承和创新就会做出更大的贡献，而这又正是翻译方向研究生学科理论思维能力培养和训练中所亟须的（曾利沙，2006）。即便如此，笔者仍敢断言，该研究融专题性、趣味性、鉴赏性与学术性于一体，在语言学习、英语写作与翻译研究之间架起了一座桥梁，在文化"译出"增长幅度逐渐超过"译入"的今天，该研究的作用不可小视。也期盼何教授沿着这条康庄大道阔步前行并期待他在将来取得更丰硕的成果。

范武邱

2019 年夏识于通泰梅岭

目　　录

第一章　研究综述 …………………………………… 1
 1. 英语无灵主语句研究综述（上） ………… 2
 2. 英语无灵主语句研究综述（下） ………… 12

第二章　成因、类型与汉译研究 ……………… 21
 3. 英语无灵主语句的理解与翻译 ………… 22
 4. 英语无灵主语句与英汉思维特征对比 ……… 35
 5. 英语无灵主语句的隐含逻辑语义关系分析 ……… 41
 6. 英语无灵主语句的认知突显分析 ………… 58
 7. 英语无灵主语句的隐喻性与生命性认知探源 ……… 67
 8. 英语无灵主语句的生成机制与表现形式再探 …… 81
 9. 生命性与英语无灵主语句的类型分析 ……… 96
 10. 英语无灵主语句的汉译策略与方法探讨 ……… 110

第三章　应用研究 …………………………………… 130
 11. 英语无灵主语句与汉式英语 …………… 131
 12. 英语书面与口头语篇中的无灵主语句对比分析
　　…………………………………………… 143
 13. 英语无灵主语句谚语研究 ………………… 162
 14. 中美大学生英语作文中无灵主语句使用情况
　　对比分析 ………………………………… 175

第四章　探讨与商榷 ········· 195
　　15. 论英语无灵主语句的分析与解释基础 ········· 196
　　16. 生命性与无灵主语句的拟人效果 ········· 201
　　17. 年轻人做学问不可毛糙 ········· 208

Appendix ········· 215
　　18. English Sentences with Inanimate Subjects:
　　　　A Metaphorical Perspective ········· 216

参考文献 ········· 261

第一章

研究综述

English sentences with inanimate subjects

1. 英语无灵主语句研究综述(上)①

1.1　名称与定义溯源

对英语无灵主语句这一语言现象的研究，最初大多散见于国外的英语语法与词汇研究著作（Jespersen, 1933: 154 - 158; 1951: 235 - 237; Lewis, 1949; Leech and Svartvik, 1974: 24 - 26; Comrie, 1981; Quirk, 1985: 1020 - 1029）和国内的英汉语法比较与翻译著作（钱歌川，1981: 1 - 2；张今、陈云清，1981；陈定安，1991）中，但使用的名称各不相同。国外用得较多的是 impersonal style/subject 或 inanimate subject，而国内使用的名称却多种多样，有必要在此来一次追根溯源。

国内最早的专题研究始于钱歌川先生，其《英文疑难详解》一书对 200 个英语语法与词汇疑难问题进行了详细分析与解答，而摆在首位的就是对无灵主语句的探讨，所使用的名称则是"无生物主语"。这一名称后来虽有人继续使用，但使用范围并不广。国内最早使用"无灵主语"这一名称的是张今和陈云清两位先生，他们在《英汉比较语法纲要》一书中对此进行了深入研究。笔者借助中国知网（CNKI），使

---

① 本节内容原载于《西安外国语大学学报》2011 年第 2 期。

1. 英语无灵主语句研究综述（上）
English sentences with inanimate subjects

用不同关键词，检索了研究这一语言现象的期刊文章，得出如下结果（检索时间：2010年5月4日）：

表1-1 不同关键词的检索结果

关键词	无生物主语	无生命主语	非人称主语	物称主语	无灵主语
相关文章（篇）	9	26	8	22	66
跨越年限	1985—2003	1985—2007	1983—2007	1983—2007	1990—2009

以上数据虽然可能存在重复或漏检的情况，也许还会有一些出入，但总的方向是明确的，读者可以随时上网验证。由于"非人称主语"与"物称主语"同义，"物称"又常与"人称"对应使用，因此，"物称主语"出现在论文题目中的频率高于"非人称主语"，但二者在文中却基本上是互换使用的，因而可将其合二为一。如此看来，"无生命主语"与"物称主语"或"非人称主语"的使用频率基本相当，而近年来"无灵主语"的使用却非常广泛。

为什么会这样呢？这得从几位主要作者早期在外语类核心或重要期刊上发表论文时所使用的名称说起。连淑能（1983；1993：29-32；2002：40-46）是最早从事这一研究且持续时间较长的学者之一。他在《翻译通讯》和《山东外语教学》上发表论文的题目分别是《英语含非人称主语句子的汉译》和《英语的"物称"与汉语的"人称"》，但在文中却有这样的叙述："汉语重人称（或'有灵'，animate），英语重物称（或'无灵'，inanimate）。"并反复使用了"无灵主语""有灵动词"等名称。冯树鉴（1990：64-66；1991：10-15；1995：9-11）分别在《大学英语》《英语知识》及《科技英语学习》上发表论文的题目是《谈谈无灵主语句的汉译》《无生命名词作主语时的译法》以及《无灵名词作主语时的汉译》，并在文中不断使用了"有灵名词""无灵名词""有灵主语""无灵主语"等名称。刘树阁（1994：68－72；1995：65－66）分别在《郑州工学院学报（社科版）》与《现代外语》上发表文章的题目是《有灵动词与无生物主语——浅析英语无生物主语句子的理解与翻译》与《英语无生命主语句子的理解与翻译》，文中也交叉使用了"有灵动词""无灵动词""无生命名词""无生命主语"等名称。正是因为这些早期作者"举棋不定"，才有上述长时间不同名称共存的现象。另外，自1990年冯树鉴以《谈谈无灵主语句的汉译》为题发表论文开始，陆续有丁玉伟（1995：59－60）、喻家楼与胡开宝（1997：52－54）、陈晓静与李英垣（2000：62－65）、席建国与马苏勇（2002：126－132）等以"（英语）无灵（主语）句"为标题或关键词分别在《山东外语教学》《外国语》《湖州师院学报》《四川外语学院学报》发表论文；何明珠（2003a：51－55；2003b：75－77；2005a：11－14；2005b：87－90；2005c：403－409；2007：26－29；2009a：88－91；2009b：37－39）先后在《外语教学》《外语与外语教学》等多家学报上发表以"英语无灵主语句"为题的系列论文8篇。这可能是近年"无灵主语"这个名称广泛使用的原因之一。此外，这一名称本身还有言简意明、不含歧义的优点。既然人们乐意使用这个名称，而名称又是个约定俗成的东西，采用"无灵主语"这个名称来探讨这一语言现象势所必然。

　　英语无灵主语句之所以能长期激发研究者的兴趣是因其具有独特性。这种独特性或特征则集中反映在其定义中。杨永林（1986：21－26）最早为英语无灵主语句下了定义：

"英语非人称主语句即为:非人称主语后续表示感觉、知觉、意识、情感、动作等意味的人称动词所构成的英语句式。"他从修辞角度划分了两类无灵主语句:"英语非人称主语句所表现的修辞手法主要有两种。一是拟人化;二是借代格。"此外,他还区分了无生命主语(non-life subjects)句与非人称主语(subjects of impersonal sentences)句:"无生命主语句既可后续人称动词(personal verbs)做谓语,亦可后续非人称动词(impersonal verbs)做谓语。而非人称主语句只有满足了非人称主语后续表示感觉、知觉、意识、情感、动作等意味的人称动词这一条件时,才能成立。显而易见,非人称主语句正确的英语说法应是'impersonal subject sentences',而不该是'non-life subject sentences'。"后来,何明珠(2003a: 51-55)从英语无灵主语句的隐喻性角度下了这样的定义:"英语无灵主语句(English sentences with inanimate subjects)是指用不具备生命意义的实体(如实物、抽象概念和动作名词等)作主语,用表达物质过程或心理过程的动词作谓语的句子。"这一定义既可避免无生命主语句与非人称主语句之间的无谓区分,又可将"The execution of the prisoner preceded the president's arrival."之类的句子纳入英语无灵主语句的研究范围之内。当然,随着研究的深入,也许会有更好的定义出现。

1.2 研究内容概述

长期以来,国内对英语无灵主语句的研究主要集中在英汉对比与翻译这两大方面。对比的目的是为了更好地理解,而理解的目的则在于更好地翻译,这几乎成了研究英语无灵主语句的定式,对上述检索到的期刊文章进行初步分析与统计也能证明这一点。不过，对比的角度或对比的方法不同就会涉及不同的研究内容，获得不同的见解或得出不同的研究结论，因而这必然能够从不同视角加深对英语无灵主语句的认识。现将相关主要研究内容与成果概述如下。

1.2.1 通过英汉主语对比，研究英语无灵主语句

英汉主语对比研究必然涉及英语无灵主语句这一语言现象。牛保义（1994：49－53）就英汉主语的特性、意义类型以及语法功能这三个方面进行了对比，认为"英语主语概念严谨、涵盖清晰、词类单一、语法功能强，对全句关系密切，是句中不可缺少的重要成分。汉语主语概念泛、涵盖宽、种属多、语法功能弱，对全句不具有密切关系，是具有明显话题性的成分"。马秉义（1995：55－59）对英汉主语差异作了初步探讨，并指出这两者之间有六方面不同：①英汉主语概念不同；②英语的形式主语与汉语的省略主语不同；③英语的代词主语与汉语的名词主语不同；④英语的无生物主语与汉语的生物主语不同；⑤英汉主语位置不同；⑥英汉主谓搭配不同。王满良（1999：87－95）与黄昆海（2002：26－28）也做了类似的研究，但马文和黄文与英语无灵主语句研究关系更密切。此外，还有不少就某一具体类别主语进行的英汉比较研究，如魏志成（1997：48－55）论及了"英汉时间主语比较及翻译"，牛保义（2008：1－6）进行了"英汉语工具主语句的象征关系研究"。这些研究都能加深对英语无灵主语句的认识。

1.2.2 通过英汉表达方式的对比，研究英语无灵主语句

英汉表达方式对比是早期英语无灵主语句研究的主要内

1. 英语无灵主语句研究综述(上)
English sentences with inanimate subjects

容,面广量大,只能择其要者,略作概述。上文提到早期研究英语无灵主语句都是以汉译这类句子为目的,自然就少不了英汉表达法的对比。钱歌川(1981:1-2)的滥觞之作如此,连淑能(1983,1993:29-32)、杨永林(1986:21-26)与刘树阁(1995:65-66)等研究者也不例外。他们都认为,英语重物称(或无灵)、汉语重人称(或有灵)这一特点主要表现在英汉主谓的不同搭配上:英语的无灵主语常与有灵谓语搭配使用,而汉语的无灵主语则不能与有灵谓语搭配。他们还对英语无灵主语进行分类研究并分别探讨相应的汉译方法。杨文将英语无灵主语细分为十类:时间名词型、地点名词型、动作状态名词型、事物名词型、情感及心理活动名词型、身体部位名词型、动作表情名词型、谚语型、惯用型以及外来型。刘文则将英语无灵主语句分为三类:①以时间和地点名词做主语,以 see, witness, find 等动词做谓语的句子;②以表示生理、心理状况的名词或表示某种遭遇的名词做主语,以 fail, desert, escape, seize, visit, strike 等动词做谓语的句子;③以具有行为和动作意义的名词做主语,以含有使役意义的动词做谓语的句子。王竹(1997:22-25)在探讨英汉句子表达方式差异时列出了如下五点:①英语重形合,汉语重意合;②英语动静有分,汉语多用动态词;③英语句子成分的位置多变换,汉语句子成分的位置多固定;④英语多被动,汉语多主动;⑤英语重物称,汉语重人称。赵明(1999:14-16)在讨论英汉翻译中的"有灵"与"无灵"时指出,除了汉译英语无灵主语句时要注意转换有灵和无灵表达方式外,在汉译英语"转移修饰"词语和"指物名词+of+指人名词"结构时也要对有灵和无灵表达方式进行调整。此外,从句法结构对比(张今、陈云清,1981;王寅,1993)和修辞手段对比(冯树鉴,

1990：64－66；胡曙中，1993）角度对英语无灵主语句进行研究的成果同样非常丰富。

1.2.3　通过英汉思维的对比，研究英语无灵主语句

语言与思维密不可分。英汉思维对比研究的成果对探讨英语无灵主语句具有重要指导意义。连淑能（2002：40－46）论述了中西思维方式的十大关系：伦理性与认知性、整体性与分析性、意向性与对象性、直觉性与逻辑性、意象性与实证性、模糊性与精确性、求同性与求异性、后馈性与超前性、内向性与外向性、归纳性与演绎性。这些截然相反的思维方式不仅能有效地解释汉语有灵主语和英语无灵主语普遍存在各自语言中的原因，还能指明这一语言现象在英汉互译过程中的转换途径。毛忠明（2002：67－71）对英语主语的思维研究深刻揭示了英语无灵时间主语句、工具主语句和抽象主语句的存在理据及其汉译方法。张海涛（1999：21－23）与陈晓静和李英垣（2000：62－65）也是通过英汉思维特征对比来研究英语无灵主语句及其汉译的。魏在江（2006：92－96）则从中西思维方式对比的视角，通过对张培基先生的译文评析，探讨汉译英过程中如何将汉语人称主语转变成英语物称主语。此外，潘文国（1997）论述了英汉语言心理上的对比问题，试图推导出隐藏在不同表达方式后面的心理和文化背景，这对英语无灵主语句的研究更具指导意义。唐青叶（2004：39－43，2009：62－65）的英语双向成对心理动词研究对探讨英语无灵主语句很具启发性。

1.2.4　借助隐喻理论，研究英语无灵主语句

进入21世纪以来，随着国内认知语言学与隐喻研究的

不断深入，人们开始借助隐喻理论从认知和隐喻的角度对英语无灵主语句的生成机制进行研究。何明珠（2003a：51-55；2005a：11-14；2005b：87-90；2009b：37-39）运用认知语言学家莱考夫（Lakoff）的"概念隐喻"理论、系统功能语法学家韩礼德（Halliday）的"语法隐喻"理论以及认知语法学家兰盖克（Langacker）的"认知突显"理论，对英语无灵主语句的生成机制进行了多角度分析，阐明了英语无灵主语句的隐喻性特征。同类研究还有左自鸣（2004：107-120）、翁义明（2005：87-89）、孙兴文（2006：125-130）、孙锐（2008：97-99）等。

1.3 问题思考与前景展望

以上概述表明，经过30多年的长期探索，英语无灵主语句的研究范围已有较大拓展，研究成果也越来越丰富。从发表在相关期刊上的文章数量来看，英语无灵主语句研究已成为近期英汉对比语言学的一个热门话题。然而，综观近年发表的相关论文，仍然存在不少问题。一是论文数量虽多，但质量过硬并有独到见解的文章却不多，能在外语类核心期刊上发表的则更是少之又少。例如，在中国期刊网上检索2007年发表的有关英语无灵主语句的文章就有十几篇，但在外语类核心期刊上却找不到一篇。这些文章的内容都大同小异，缺乏创新。二是少数作者治学不严谨，成文很仓促，即使发表出来的文章也还存在不少差错。例如，2007年发表在《科技英语学习》第2期上的一篇短文，全文总共只有14个例句，其中8个被发现存在疏漏和瑕疵。三是有些年轻作者根本没有进行过相关研究，只是发现这类文章较多，又容易看懂，于是找来几篇稍作整合，更换标题，就署上自己的名字而发表。这样一来，文不对题的情况时有发生。例如，有一篇发表在某高等函授学报上的文章，标题是《浅谈汉语非人称主语句的英译》，而用作例句的 29 个汉语句子中，20 个是明明白白的人做主语的句子；3 个是省略了主语的句子；2 个是使用了拟人修辞格的句子；只剩 4 个可以算作非人称主语的句子。细看才知道该作者只是把别人论述英语非人称主语句汉译时的英语例句与汉语译文的排列顺序颠倒过来就算完事，连别人按英语非人称主语所做的归类也原原本本照搬。再如，有一篇题为《英语无灵主语句的认知语言学诠释》的文章，载某高校学报。通读全文却找不到任何与认知语言学相关的原理，不知作者如何可以称之为英语无灵主语句的认知语言学诠释。此类文不对题现象绝非孤例。因此，端正学风是进行一切学术研究的前提。

鉴于当前英语无灵主语句研究存在上述严重问题，笔者认为要想将研究深入下去并取得实实在在的成果，就必须在端正学风的基础上拓展研究内容与创新研究方法。就研究内容的拓展来说应该包括：①继续从不同视角、运用不同科学原理探索英语无灵主语句的形成原因和生成机制；②继续从英汉对比的角度深入探讨英汉无灵与有灵主语句的异同并全面系统地描写相关英汉互译技巧；③借助语料库等现代科学手段进行英语无灵主语句的分布研究；④加大英语无灵主语句在英语写作与英汉互译教学中的研究力度；⑤突破英语无灵主语句的句子结构研究局限，综合研究其词法、语法、篇章、修辞、语用、文体等功能。就研究方法的创新而言应该注意：①正确处理归纳和描写语言现象与揭示和阐释语言规律的关系；②综合运用不同学科知识并大胆采用不同学科如语义学、语用学、认知语言学、系统功能语言学、心理语言学、语料库语言学、文本类型学、统计学等的研究方法；

1. 英语无灵主语句研究综述（上）
English sentences with inanimate subjects

③重视理论依托与理论框架的构建，因为缺乏理论指导的研究，难以取得有用的研究成果；④坚持微观研究和宏观研究相结合、定量研究和定性研究相搭配以及个案分析和综合研究相补充等原则。

总之，英语无灵主语句，表面上看，只不过是一种造句方式或句子类型，是微观层面上的一种语言现象，但要对其进行全面、系统、深入的研究，则要涉及词汇学、语义学、语用学、修辞学、文体学、对比语言学、翻译学、心理语言学、认知语言学、系统功能语言学、语料库语言学、思维学、统计学等许多学科所关注的问题。因此，英语无灵主语句研究既有很大的理论意义和实践价值，又极具挑战性，需要坚实的语言学理论基础和锲而不舍的钻研精神才能取得新的研究成果。唯有不断拓展研究内容、创新研究方法，通过由此及彼、以小见大、综合融通、全面系统的语言探索途径，方能开创英语无灵主语句研究的美好前景。

2. 英语无灵主语句研究综述（下）

2.1 引言

上节综述探讨了从20世纪80年代到21世纪初的30年间英语无灵主语句研究状况，本节继续对最近10年（2009—2019）的研究情况进行探讨。

笔者于2019年7月25日在中国知网（CNKI）上，以"无灵主语"为关键词，用"模糊"检索方式，将起止时间定为2010至2019年，在"期刊"栏目下，检索到相关期刊文章54篇；与此同时，笔者用同样的关键词与同样的检索方式，不设起止时间，在"博硕士"栏目下，检索到相关硕士论文34篇。本综述就以这两类论文为研究素材进行定量与定性分析。

为了与上节综述衔接，在分类研究之前，有必要对研究对象的名称作简要说明。笔者在"期刊"栏目下检索时，除使用"无灵主语"作为关键词检索到54篇文章外，还用其他关键词进行了检索，结果见表2–1。

2. 英语无灵主语句研究综述（下）
English sentences with inanimate subjects

表2-1 不同关键词的检索结果

关键词	无生物主语	无生命主语	非人称主语	物称主语	无灵主语
相关文章（篇）	0	4	11	3	54
跨越年限	2010—2019	2010—2019	2010—2019	2010—2019	2010—2019

表2-1显示，国内用不同名称表达同一概念的情况有所好转。虽然"无生命主语""非人称主语"与"物称主语"这些名称仍有人使用，但相比而言，"无灵主语"这个名称已被广泛接受和采用。

2.2 期刊论文综述

本节将围绕上述54篇期刊论文从发表时间、期刊类别、论文作者与研究内容四个方面进行分析。

2.2.1 发表时间

上述54篇论文发表时间的分布情况如表2-2所示。

表2-2 论文发表的时间分布情况

年份	2010	2011	2012	2013	2014	2015	2016	2017	2018	2019	合计
篇数	6	9	11	9	6	5	1	3	2	2	54

表2-2显示，近十年相关研究的高潮出现在头三年（2011—2013）间，从2014年起，开始回落，但一直没有间断。2019年仍处在年中，应该还有增加的可能，因此既有逐

年减少的势头，又有渐渐回升的迹象。

2.2.2 期刊类别

上述 54 篇论文中有 30 篇发表在大学学报上，其余 24 篇发表在相关学术期刊上。由于期刊的种类很多，档次不同，归属有别，很难准确分类，因此除核心期刊外，只能粗略地按期刊出版周期分为若干类别。由于大学学报大多都是双月刊，少数是月刊或季刊，因此只分本科学报与专科学报两类（见表 2-3）。

表 2-3 论文发表的期刊分布情况

期刊类别	核心期刊	季刊	双月刊	本科学报	月刊	专科学报	半月刊	旬刊	合计
篇数	5	3	5	24	6	3	5	3	54

这里的核心期刊包括《语言与翻译》《西安外国语大学学报》《外国语文》与《英语研究》4 种；季刊是指《语言教育》与《外文研究》2 种；双月刊包括《当代外语研究》与《语文学刊》等；月刊是指《现代语文》与《大学教育》等；旬刊包括《科技风》《价值工程》与《中外企业家》3 种。

如表 2-3 所示，54 篇论文中发表在高层次学术期刊与低档次综合刊物上的都不多，大部分都集中发表在本科大学学报上。

2.2.3 论文作者

分析上述 54 篇论文作者的基本情况，发现如下三个现象：一是除少数由导师指导的在读研究生之外，其余作者都是大学外语教师；二是除 4 位作者发表了两篇以上论文之外,其余都是单篇论文作者;三是除少数几位作者具有高级职称或博士学位外,其余都是只有讲师及以下职称或硕士及以下学位的教师。

2.2.4 研究内容

上述 54 篇论文中,有 24 篇涉及翻译研究,数量最多,接近总数的一半;有 11 篇涉及英语写作教学研究,数量次之;有 9 篇是关于思维方式或英汉思维方式对比分析的文章;有 8 篇涉及英语无灵主语或无灵主语句的生成机制、句法特征与语用功能等应用方面的研究;还有 2 篇涉及朝鲜语与拉丁语的无灵主语研究(参见表 2-4)。

表 2-4 论文涉及的研究内容分布情况

研究内容	翻译研究	写作研究	思维研究	成因、特征、功能等研究	其他外语研究
论文篇数	24	11	9	8	2
所占比率	44%	20%	17%	15%	4%

翻译研究涉及的范围很广。王雪莹(2014)从心智意识角度探讨了无灵主语在翻译过程中的意象转换途径;张志祥(2018)在"语言结构顺应"视域下研究了利用英语无灵主语句翻译汉语导游词的可能性;吴小芳(2012)讨论了如何用英语无灵主语句翻译汉语无主句;王晓俊(2014)通过对相关汉语名作与英语名译的比较分析,阐明了使用英语无灵主语句的翻译效果;胡明涛(2013)探讨了许渊冲古诗英译过程中利用无灵主语句所创造出来的意境美;童肆琴(2013)对英语无灵主语句在《红楼梦》两个英译本的使用情况进行了分析;王素娥(2016)分析了刘士聪散文翻译中

利用非人称主语"反客为主"的作用；郑雅（2015）等以英语小说汉译为例，讨论无灵主语与有灵主语转换的文章不少；最近，于心荟和卫洁（2019）还讨论了汉英同声传译中的人称主语与物称主语的转换问题。凡此种种，不一而足。

相关的写作研究也很丰富。何明珠（2012，2013）对口头与书面语篇中的英语无灵主语句进行了个案研究、对中美大学生英语作文中无灵主语句的使用情况进行了对比分析；楚建伟和高云（2014）探讨了通过语法隐喻教学与无灵主语句运用来提高学生的英语书面语语体意识；常虹（2012）通过包括无灵主语句使用情况在内的写作测试对英汉对比教学进行了实证研究；长孙馥蓉（2011）对大学英语写作教学中的名词化与无灵主语句也进行了探讨。

相关思维方式、思维习惯与思维差异的研究也不少。张哲（2011）讨论了如何通过英语无灵主语句的教学培养学生的英语思维方式和习惯；赵景梅（2015）通过对比英汉句法特征（包括无灵主语与有灵主语）分析了中西思维差异；刘锦（2012）探讨了中英思维方式差异（包括人称与物称）对英汉翻译的影响。

有关英语无灵主语句的形成原因、生成机制、句法特征、语用功能以及相关应用研究也在不断深化。何明珠（2011，2013）从生命性概念的跨域映射方式入手，进一步探讨了英语无灵主语句的隐喻性根源以及生命性与隐喻性之间的关系，对英语无灵主语句谚语进行了深入研究；王燕华与黄培希（2010）对学生英语写作中无灵主语句的产生机制进行了分析；霍明杰（2014）在心智哲学的意向性理论视角下，对英语无灵主语句进行了深入而系统的研究；吴小芳（2012）从概念转喻的角度对英语无灵主语句的成因作了进一步阐释；张寒冰（2019）最近也从生命度等级的角度对英语无灵主语句进行了深入分析。

对照上节综述中的"问题思考与前景展望"部分,发现第一个问题仍然存在,即质量过硬、见解独到、能在外语类核心期刊上发表的论文仍然不多;第二与第三个问题已基本解决,治学不严、学风不正的现象已基本克服,错误成堆、胡乱拼凑的文章已基本消失。因此,未来的目标就是要提高研究水平,确保研究质量。要达到这一目标,还是要继续"拓展研究内容与创新研究方法"。例如,虽然已有少量实证研究,但借助语料库语言学研究方法进行英语无灵主语句的分布研究还阙如;利用网络技术与大数据手段,对不同层次英语学习者的无灵主语句使用情况进行的实证研究还未出现;突破句子结构分析局限的应用性综合研究仍不多见。总之,英语无灵主语句研究的全面纵深发展有赖于进一步扩大眼界,在坚实的语言学理论基础上进行跨学科宏观与微观研究。

2.3 硕士论文综述

值得注意的是,从 2004 年起,英语无灵主语句研究逐渐成为国内英语专业硕士论文的热门选题。本节将围绕上述 34 篇硕士论文从提交时间、选题特点与研究内容三个方面进行分析。

2.3.1 提交时间

上述 34 篇硕士论文的提交时间如表 2-5 所示。

表 2-5 硕士论文提交时间情况

年份	04	06	08	10	11	13	14	15	16	17	18	19	合计
篇数	2	1	1	1	2	2	3	5	4	4	6	3	34

表 2-5 显示，有关英语无灵主语句研究的硕士论文从 2013 年起逐年稳步增加，2018 年达到高潮，多达 6 篇。因写作本综述所进行的上网检索时间是 2019 年 7 月 25 日，估计本年度的相关数目还会增大。

2.3.2 选题特点

分析上述 34 篇硕士论文的选题，发现一个明显的特点：在 2004—2013 这 10 年间提交的 9 篇硕士论文，全部都是研究论文，而在 2014—2019 这 6 年间提交的 25 篇硕士论文中，只有 2 篇研究论文，其余 23 篇都是翻译实践报告。进一步分析发现：11 篇研究论文的提交者来自 11 所不同的大学，而在 23 篇翻译实践报告的提交者中存在来自同一所大学的现象，最多的有 7 人来自同一所大学。

2.3.3 研究内容

上述 11 篇硕士研究论文中，涉及翻译研究的 4 篇，有关思维方式对比研究的 3 篇，探讨无灵主语句生成机制的 3 篇，以及相关应用研究的 1 篇。虽然这些硕士论文各方面都仍显稚嫩，但不乏闪光之点或独到之处，现择要分述如下。

曾文华（2004）对英汉衔接差异进行了分类描述，提出英汉之间在形合与意合、主语突出与话题突出、树形结构与竹形结构、无灵主语与有灵主语等方面的差异是造成衔接差异的根源，翻译时要根据这些差异进行有效转换。曹军（2010）在《呼啸山庄》原著与杨苡和方平两个汉译本的 9 个对应章节中抽取 1595 个相关句子，就其结构转换情况进行对比分析，发现在这 1595 个句子中有 326 个存在有灵主语与无灵主语、肯定与否定、主动与被动等方面的结构转换可能，而杨译与方译都对其中的 81%（即 263 个句子）进

2. 英语无灵主语句研究综述（下）
English sentences with inanimate subjects

行了结构转换。刘巧民（2011）与盛莉敏（2016）分别对英语无灵主语句的汉译进行了研究，前者先将无灵主语进行分类并据此寻求汉译方法，后者以《文化分析与布迪厄遗产》的节译实践为基础探索英语无灵主语句的汉译途径。

王耀敏（2004）从文化、思维与语言三者关系的研究综述开始对英汉文化背景差异导致英汉思维方式差异与英汉语言表达差异进行了分析并以此解释英汉无灵与有灵主语使用现象的必然性。陈腊春（2006）就英汉思维差异对中学生英语写作的影响进行了调查，发现由于英汉思维差异意识缺失，中学生英语作文中经常出现主语使用不当的现象。冯捷（2008）通过定量与定性研究考察了高级阶段英语学习者对无灵主语句及弱化主体句的形式与意义的习得情况，发现语言形式与语言意义接口的割裂使得学习者在高级阶段仍很难产出真正地道的目的语。

樊亮亮（2011）与黄文静（2013）都对英语无灵主语双及物构式进行了研究。虽然前者没用"无灵主语"而用了"非意愿性论元"这个名称，但二者都是以戈德堡（Goldberg）的构式语法理论为基础展开分析，前者将非意愿性论元双及物构式的语义特征归纳为因果、条件、方式与让步四类关系，后者总结了无灵主语双及物构式的6种转喻和3种隐喻认知过程。孙敏（2016）也进行了生命度及认知视角下的隐喻性无灵主语句研究。

张杰（2012）的应用研究是"基于语料库的学术论文结论部分的情态序列研究"，通过对比母语为英语学者的学术论文与中国学者的英语学术论文，发现后者倾向于使用"情态动词+静态动词"和"无灵主语+情态动词"这样的情态序列来表达认知型情态。

如上文所述，23篇硕士翻译实践报告都是近6年提交的,其中,除丘巧珍(2014)与张瑛(2018)两篇是通过翻译小说《家园》与翻译《翻译研究百科全书》部分章节来探讨英语无灵主语句汉译策略与方法外,其余都只是泛泛地涉及一点无灵主语句翻译套话而已,算不上专门研究。出现这种情况,可能有两个原因:一是因近年国内大学翻译硕士招生人数猛增,并将毕业论文写作换成翻译实践报告写作,报告格式固定、要求降低所致;二是因为无灵主语句、被动句以及各类从句与长句的翻译方法讨论较多,例句又容易寻找,所以成了翻译实践报告中个案分析部分的最佳选择。

2.4 结语

总之,就目前的情况来看,虽然英语无灵主语句研究表面上热闹,但很有可能陷入低层次重复研究的危险境地。若要开创本研究领域的真正繁荣局面,需要一支稳定的高素质研究团队通过拓展研究内容与创新研究方法来引领研究方向、做出研究示范,才能达到目标。

第二章

成因、类型与汉译研究

3. 英语无灵主语句的理解与翻译[①]

3.1　引言

本节所讨论的英语无灵主语句（English sentences with inanimate subjects）暂限于指用没有生命的事物（如实物、抽象概念和动作名词等）作主语，用表达物质过程或心理过程（Halliday, 1994）的动词作谓语的句子。这类句子在英语书面语中经常出现，是一种独具特色的典型英语句子。由于中西文化、思维方式以及英汉语言之间的差异，中国学生不易掌握这类句子，具体表现在英语作文中很少使用这种表达方式（董宏乐，2002），在英汉翻译中只能机械照搬，不能灵活变通（吴群，2002）。本节拟从修辞手段、概念隐喻和语法隐喻三个层面对这一语言现象进行分析，探索英语无灵主语句的形成原因、语用特征和汉译途径。

---

① 本节内容原载于《外语教学》2003 年第 5 期。

3. 英语无灵主语句的理解与翻译
English sentences with inanimate subjects

3.2 英语无灵主语句的形成原因与语用特征

3.2.1 从修辞手段的使用看英语无灵主语句的成因

传统修辞学所论及的修辞手段大都运用于书面语中，其目的是使语言更加生动形象。一些常用修辞格，如拟人（personification）、换喻（metonymy）和提喻（synecdoche）等，就是通过给无生命的事物赋予生命，或说甲事物指乙事物，或用部分代全体等手段使语言表达生动形象。为了配合这些修辞手段的使用，达到表达生动这一目的，大量无灵主语句就在英语书面语中应运而生了。

（1）Dusk found the child crying in the street.
（2）Beijing has witnessed many changes in the past few years.
（3）White hair is crying for help.

例（1）和例（2）中的主语 Dusk 和 Beijing 是表示时间和地点的无生命名词，逻辑上本不可充当一种心理过程的主体。然而，为了表达的生动性，说英语的人们硬是通过使用表示心理活动的动词 found 和 witnessed，即通过拟人手段，给它们赋予生命，因而形成了这种广泛使用的无灵主语句。当然，例（2）也可看作换喻，是用 Beijing 来换指 people in Beijing。例（3）常被看作提喻，是用 white hair 这个部分来指 people with white hair 这个整体。拟人也好，换喻或提喻也罢，其目的只有一个，那就是为了表达的生动性，这正是英语无灵主语句的成因和特征之一。

3.2.2 从概念隐喻理论看英语无灵主语句的缘由

随着语言学的不断发展，人们发现传统修辞学囿于其形式研究，注意力主要集中在辞格的归类划分上，偏重语言形式本身的分析，将语言、认知和社会割裂开来，因而不能真实地反应客观世界（谢之君，2000）。现代语言学研究表明，比喻不仅是有效使用语言的技巧，而且是观察和认识世界的基本方法。当代认知语言学家莱考夫（Lakoff）在其与人合著的《我们赖以生存的隐喻》（*Metaphors We Live By*）(1980) 一书中指出："隐喻普遍存在于我们的日常生活中，不但存在于语言中，而且存在于我们的思想和行为中。我们赖以思维和行动的一般概念系统，从根本上讲是隐喻式的。"莱考夫提出的"概念隐喻"（conceptual metaphor）理论，其实质就是：人们在认识世界的过程中，总是存在两个认知域（cognitive domain），其中一个认知域中的概念总是向另一个认知域映射。这也就是他著名的概念映射（cross-domain mapping）理论。莱考夫在研究中还将修辞格中的拟人、换喻和提喻等都看作是诸多概念隐喻中的一种类型。既然概念隐喻如此普遍，那么像以下这样的无灵主语句的产生和使用就非常自然了。

(4) A good idea suddenly struck me.（IDEA IS PERSON）

(5) Nowadays, scientific ideas flow rapidly.（IDEA IS LIQUID）

(6) An evil idea is growing in his mind.（IDEA IS PLANT）

(7) Good ideas nurture good deeds.（IDEA IS FOOD）
(8) His idea of a bright future collapsed all of a sudden.（IDEA IS BUILDING）

3.2.3 从语法隐喻理论看英语无灵主语句的由来

语法隐喻理论的创始人韩礼德（Halliday，1994）指出，对人类经验意义的描述在语法层面上有两种方式：一致式（congruent）和隐喻式（metaphorical）。一致式是指语义（实体、事件、性质、方式），词汇语法（名词、动词、形容词、副词）与功能（参与者、过程、属性、环境因子）之间的一致。这是我们表述经验的典型方式，最贴近我们的直觉，因而是最常见的口头表述形式，属于语言表达的感性方式。隐喻式是指语义、词汇语法与功能之间的不一致。例如，不是用名词而是用动词或形容词来表述实体，即过程与属性被体现为参与者，这就有悖于人类的直觉，更接近理性思维，因而是常见的书面表述形式，属于语言表达的理性方式。

(9a) Two months after his mother died in 1921, he and Clementine lost their daughter. She was three years old. They loved her.

(9b) In 1921, the death of his mother was followed two months later by the loss of his and Clementine's beloved three-year-old daughter.（董宏乐，2002）

例(9a)是一致式,所有的过程都是由动词来体现,所有的参与者都是由名词或代词实体来体现,因而语义直接明了,符合口头表达习惯。例(9b)是隐喻式,原来的物质过程(died 与 lost)分别被表述为实体(death 与 loss),成为参与者;原来的心理过程(loved)被编码为属性(beloved);原来的参与者变成后置修饰语;原来由 after 反映出来的逻辑关系则被体现为过程(was followed),经过这番调整之后,语义结构复杂化了(semantic complication),但语法结构却简单化了(grammatical simplification),词语密度(lexical density)明显加大了。这样一来,例(9b)就完全符合书面语深思熟虑的表达习惯。与此同时,通过调整变化,四个有灵主语句变成了一个无灵主语句。

语法隐喻的实质就是名词化(nominalization)。韩礼德(Halliday,1994:352)在其《功能语法导论》中指出,"名词化是创建语法隐喻的唯一最强大的手段"(Nominalizing is the single most powerful resource for creating grammatical metaphor.)。韩礼德推测,由名词化而产生的英语隐喻在科技类书面语体中出现的频率最高,这一推测已经得到语料分析实验的证实(李力,2001)。由于书面语体中大量动词和形容词都名词化了,这就必然导致大量无灵主语句的产生。因为只有这样,书面语篇才能克服主观武断性,增加客观公正性。

(10a) I handed my essay in late, because my kids got sick.

(10b) The reason for the late submission of my essay was the illness of my children.(Eggins,1994,转引自肖建安、王志军,2001)

3. 英语无灵主语句的理解与翻译
English sentences with inanimate subjects

（11a） We can improve its performance when we use super-heated steam.

（11b） An improvement of its performance can be effected by the use of super-heated steam.

（12a） We have noticed that the number of books in the library has been going down. Please make sure to obey the rules for borrowing and returning books. Don't forget that the library is for everyone's convenience. So from now on, we're going to enforce the rules strictly. You have been warned!

（12b） It has been noted with concern that the stock of books in the library has been declining alarmingly. The rules for the borrowing and returning of books are to be strictly obeyed and the needs of others duly met. Penalties for overdue books will be further enforced.

仔细比较以上三对例子，我们可以总结出英语无灵主语句的如下基本特征：

第一，英语无灵主语句常常伴随语法隐喻（名词化）的出现而产生；

第二，英语无灵主语句的语法结构紧凑，词语密度大，语义关系隐蔽，因而更适用于正式书面语体中；

第三，英语无灵主语句的组句方式有利于摆脱行为主体的主观性，因而更具客观公正性和权威性；

第四，英语无灵主语句的名词化结构有助于主题的突显（thematization），因而也有利于语篇的衔接与连贯，使语言表达自然流畅。

3.3　英语无灵主语句的汉译

上文提到，英语无灵主语句是一种独特的语言现象。说其独特，那是因为在汉语中很少有这种语言形式。英汉对比研究表明：英美人具有发达的抽象思维能力，而中国人则善于形象思维（张海涛，1999）。所谓抽象思维，是指习惯于逻辑分析，习惯于运用概念、判断、推理来认识事物，重理性；所谓形象思维，是指善于整体观察，善于运用直觉、意象、想象、灵感来认识事物，重情感。英美人的抽象思维习惯正好与英语无灵主语句的理性表达方式相吻合，而中国人的形象思维爱好则排斥这种理性表达方式，这就是无灵主语句在英语书面语体中广泛运用，而在汉语中却难觅踪迹的原因。面对由中西不同思维方式导致的英汉语言形式特征的巨大差异，翻译只能处于尴尬的境地。刘传珠（2000）从语言功能出发对可译性问题进行了研究。他认为语言的三大功能（认知表意功能、文化功能和美学功能）与可译性的三个层次（可译、相对不可译和绝对不可译）相对应。"原语特有的形式特征是不可能移植到译语中的。这种语言形式特征的不可译性主要表现在三个方面。一是语音特征的不可译。二是文字特征的不可译。三是语言单位的组合规则和特点的不可译。……因此，译者在翻译中遇到原文以原语的形式特点为修辞手段表达某种美学效果时，便只能用某种译语的形式特征来替代，以取得相类似的美学效果。这恰是创造性翻译的一种表现。"根据这一观点，英语无灵主语句的汉译属于不可译范畴，如果要译，只能进行创造性翻译。所谓创造性翻译就是不机械地照搬规则，而是根据具体情况，权衡利弊，做出取舍。前面3.2节的分析表明，从修辞格和概念隐

3. 英语无灵主语句的理解与翻译
English sentences with inanimate subjects

喻的角度来看，英语无灵主语句是以其形式特征作为修辞手段，以获得表达生动、形象的美学效果，但从语法隐喻的角度来看，英语无灵主语句突出的是表意功能，不属修辞手段，目的不在于产生美学效果。两者有区别，就要区别对待，下面分别讨论这两类英语无灵主语句的汉译途径。

3.3.1 伴随语法隐喻形成的英语无灵主语句的汉译

3.3.1.1 找准语结（nexus），厘清逻辑关系，还原词性，大胆拆译。

找准语结，是指由名词化而产生的动作名词或抽象名词，常与其前后的修饰语构成逻辑上的主谓或动宾关系，这种主谓或动宾关系就叫语结，可以译成汉语的独立小句。如：

（13）The execution of the prisoner preceded the president's arrival.
总统尚未到达，囚犯已被处死。

（14）His acceptance of bribes led to his arrest.
他因受贿而被捕。

（15）His help will ensure my success.
他肯帮忙，我就一定会成功。

（16）His words and deeds showed his honesty.
他的言行说明他是诚实的。

例（13）的 The execution of the prisoner 和 the president's arrival，例（14）的 His acceptance of bribes 和 his arrest，例（15）的 His help 和 my success，以及例（16）的 his honesty

都是语结，都可独立译成汉语小句。

厘清逻辑关系，是指要特别注意每个语结中的中心词与修饰词之间到底是主谓关系，还是动宾关系（或到底是主动关系还是被动关系），一旦忽视这一点，就会产生误译。如前面例（13）中的 The execution of the prisoner 是动宾关系（被动关系），而 the president's arrival 则是主谓关系（主动关系）；例（14）中的 His acceptance of bribes 是一个主谓宾齐全的主谓关系（主动关系），而 his arrest 则是动宾关系（被动关系）。此外，还要厘清语结与语结之间隐蔽的时间、因果或条件等逻辑关系。

还原词性，是指将英语中充当参与者的名词化成分还原成汉语译文中相应的动词或形容词。只有这样，译文才能顺应汉语的表达习惯。例如，以上四例中的 execution, arrival, acceptance, arrest, help 和 success 都在译文中还原成了动词，而例（16）中的 honesty 则在译文中还原成了形容词。只要按以上三点去做，英语无灵主语句就能自然地译成两个或多个汉语小句。

3.3.1.2 巧用汉语"四字结构"，确保译文的语气正式、严肃，用词精练、严密，行文客观、公正。

巧用汉语"四字结构"是为了保证汉语译文在语气、用词和行文等方面与英语无灵主语句一致。例如：

（17）The cast's brilliant acting drew stormy and lengthy applause from the audience.
台上演员演技高超，台下观众掌声雷动，经久不息。

（18）The increase of interests rate owed something to

the serious consideration of the present situation.
上调利率,是出于对当前形势的认真考虑。

3.3.2 伴随概念隐喻产生,以其形式特征作为修辞手段的英语无灵主语句的汉译

3.3.2.1 如何确立汉语译文的主语

由于汉语的表达习惯要求句子的主语是人或有生命的行为主体,因此英语无灵主语句的主语不能充当汉语译文的主语。确立汉语译文的主语,常见的方法有三:一是寻找句中充当宾语或定语的相关人称代词或名词,只要句中有这样相关的人称代词或名词,大都可以作汉语译文的主语,不管其形式是宾格还是所有格;二是如果英语无灵主语句是一种普遍性陈述,句中没有任何相关的人称代词或名词,那就可以用"人们""我们""大家""你"等泛指词做汉语译文的主语;三是将英语无灵主语句译成汉语的无主语句。

(19) Pork has priced itself out of his dish.
猪肉太贵,他吃不起。
(20) Space does not allow us to further analyze this problem here.
限于篇幅,我们不能在此对这个问题做进一步分析。
(21) By now optimism had given way to doubt.
至此,人们不再盲目乐观,而是疑惑重重。
(22) When something a little out of the ordinary takes place in the bar, the sense of it spreads quickly.
酒吧里稍有异常情况,大家很快就能感觉到。
(23) The exigency of the case admitted of no alterna-

tive.
情况紧急，别无选择。

(24) Pit closure sees violent scenes.
关闭矿井，抗议强烈。

当然，在少数情况下，也有可能保存原主语。

(25) Adversity and struggle lie at the root of evolutionary progress.
逆境和奋斗是进化与发展的根源。

3.3.2.2 如何处理英语无灵主语

由于汉语译文寻找了新的有灵主语，英语无灵主语就该另做处理。通常有两种办法：一是将英语无灵主语的词性还原，让其在汉语译文中充当谓语；二是将英语无灵主语译成汉语的状语或定语。

(26) A careful comparison of the two will show you the difference.
你仔细比较二者，就会知道其间的差别。

(27) Bitterness fed on the man who had made the world laugh.
这位曾使世人欢笑的人自己却饱尝辛酸。

(28) Autumn finds a beautiful sunny Beijing.
秋天里，北京阳光灿烂，景色优美。

(29) History knows only two kinds of war, just and unjust.
历史上的战争，只有正义的和非正义的两类。

当然，有时也可将英语无灵主语译成汉语宾语。

（30）That word always slips my mind.
我总记不住<u>那个词</u>。

3.3.2.3　如何处理英语无灵主语句中的谓语动词

一般说来，英语无灵主语句中的谓语动词有两大功能：一是体现逻辑关系，常见的有 owe to, ensure, contribute to, lead to, bring about, result in, draw, bring, precede, follow, require 等，这类词比较客观；二是制造修辞效果，常见的有 find, see, witness, know, show, offer, tell, determine, decide 等，这类词比较主观。

英语无灵主语句中体现逻辑关系的客观性谓语，通常转换成表示逻辑关系的汉语连词或助词，将隐含的逻辑关系明显化，如例（13）中的"尚未""已"，例（14）中的"因"，例（15）中的"就"等；而目的在于制造修辞效果的主观性谓语，则通常在译文中省去，它们与无灵主语共同制造的修辞效果要用译语的其他方式给予补偿。

王宗炎先生（1985：219）指出，"学一种语言，在某种程度上得把这种语言所体现的观念、态度、信仰吸收过来。例如说英语的人常常把抽象事物和具体事物当作同类东西，所以英语中有许多人格化和比喻说法，如'a flight of fancy'，'the grip of fear'等。这些并不是什么特殊的修辞手法，而是常用的词句"。英语无灵主语句也属于这种情况。

3.4　结语

本节探讨了英语无灵主语句的形成原因、语用特征和基本汉译方法，认为英语无灵主语句的产生机制，一是概念隐喻，二是语法隐喻。伴随概念隐喻形成的无灵主语句是拟人、换喻、提喻等修辞手段的体现，目的在于使语言生动形象，增强表现力；伴随语法隐喻形成的英语无灵主语句，则具有正式书面语体的各种特征：语气严肃、庄重，用词精练、严密，行文客观、公正。英语无灵主语句的汉译方法包括：灵活调整词语在句中的语法功能，理清逻辑关系，找准语结，大胆拆译；根据实际情况，合理选择译文的主语，灵活处理原语中的主语和谓语，确保译文符合汉语表达习惯；巧用汉语"四字结构"，努力再现原文凝练、正式和客观等特色。

4. 英语无灵主语句与英汉思维特征对比[①]

4.1 引言

语言与思维密不可分。(潘文国,1991)近年来,国内学者(刘宓庆,1992;胡曙中,1993;贾玉新,1997;张海涛,1999;毛忠明,2002)对英汉思维特征进行了大量对比研究。这些研究成果或宏篇巨著,或短小精悍,但很少就某一具体语言形式或语言现象做个案研究。本节试图通过对比英汉思维的某些主要特征来探讨英语无灵主语与汉语有灵主语普遍存在的原因。

4.2 理性思维与感性思维

不同的历史背景与哲学渊源导致不同的思维方式。古希腊哲学家亚里士多德所开创的形式逻辑和盛行于16至18世纪欧洲的理性主义对说英语的人们产生了深远的影响。(毛忠明,2002)首先,形式逻辑对英美人思维的影响直接体现

[①] 本节内容原载于《株洲师范高等专科学校学报》2003年第4期。

在英语的形态严格性上。例如，充当英语主语的唯一前提就是词的名词性特征。也就是说，任何词，只要是以名词的形式出现，或任何具有名词特征的词，都可以充当英语句子的主语。由于英语词汇屈折变化频繁，几乎所有的英语动词、形容词和副词都可以通过词形变化而具备名词形式，因此英语中存在大量无灵主语句就不足为怪。其次，理性主义者认为，理性思维是获取知识的唯一重要手段。（连淑能，2002）由于理性主义对整个西方世界具有及其深远的影响，因此说英语的人们一直崇尚科学，独具逻辑思维和分析思维的习惯。这种思维习惯在语言上的反映就是英语的形合性。在形合语言中存在大量无灵主语句是很自然的事。

此外，与英美人理性思维习惯密切相关的是他们的客体意识。自古以来，在西方哲学传统里，人们一直认为自然是认知的主要目标。只有理解自然，才能控制和征服自然。在探索自然的过程中，包括英美人在内的西方人认识到自然客体与人类主体是同等重要的。英美人很强的客体意识沉淀在他们的思维习惯里，也反映在他们语言表达的方式中，那就是表达的客观性。英语无灵主语句正好能充分体现英语表达的客观性。

恰恰相反，说汉语的中国人由于长期受儒、道、佛三大哲学思想的熏陶，形成了与英美人完全不同的思维模式。

首先，儒家思想集政治、伦理与哲学等于一体，主要宗旨是教育人们忠孝谦恭，精忠报国。（连淑能，2002）自古以来，中国人讲究的就是礼义谦让，含蓄委婉。这种价值观与思维习惯反映在汉语表达方式上就是语义隐晦。例如，在古汉语中根本不存在标点符号。同一段文字，经不同解读，可以获得不同的理解。由于这一语言传统，中国人一般只关注语言的内在含义，很少考虑语言的形态与句法结构。即使

4. 英语无灵主语句与英汉思维特征对比
English sentences with inanimate subjects

在现代和当代汉语中，句子的主语和谓语也没有形态限制。也就是说，主语不一定硬要名词来充当，谓语也不一定硬要动词来承担。

中国先哲有一个重要哲学概念，那就是"天人合一"的整体思想。他们认为："人和自然是一气相通、一理相连的整体。在这个整体结构中，身心合一，形神合一，精神与物质、思维与存在、主体与客体合一。'道''气''太极''理'是整体的基本范畴，阴阳、五行、八卦是整体的基本要素。"（连淑能，2002）中国式思维是先从"阴阳"对称中衍生出中庸、兼顾和联系等二元结构，后又从二元结构发展到"五行"之类的多元结构，最后才形成独具特色的整体性思维的。中国人因而提倡"中庸"，注重适中与适度，反对过分与不足，主张调和对立，实现中道。与逻辑思维和分析思维截然相反的整体思维在语言形式上的直接反映就是汉语的意合性。在汉语这样的意合语言中，无灵主语显得很不自然，甚至难以接受。

中国先哲的另一个哲学传统就是提倡直觉体悟。道家认为"自然是一个整体，不可分析，只可感觉、体验与领悟"。佛教也主张"顿悟"，力求排除语言文字对思维的束缚，在超时空、非逻辑的精神状态下实现绝对超越，进入佛性本体境界。（连淑能，2002）此外，感性思维与主体意识密不可分。很强的主体意识必然导致汉语的主观性突显。这正好说明为什么非生命实体或无灵事物不可充当汉语主语，为什么汉语主语大都由有生命的人来承担。在英汉互译过程中，我们务必牢记这一点。例如：

（1）The remembrance of this incident will add zest to his life.

他一想起这件事，就会更加感受到生活的乐趣。
（2）Astonishment, apprehension and even horror oppressed her.
她感到惊讶和忧虑，甚至有些恐惧不安。
（3）他开车时心不在焉，几乎出了车祸。
His absence of mind during the driving nearly caused an accident.
（4）她疾病缠身，丧失了完成这项任务的信心。
Illness robbed her of the confidence in accomplishing the task.

4.3　抽象思维与形象思维

语言是人类认知活动的产物。（毛忠明，2002）由于人们常常以不同的方式来认知和反映客观现实，因此不同的语言体现出不同民族的独特思维方式。英语是一种拼音文字，用来拼写的字母体系不能提供对自然现象的直接摹拟。字母是一种人造符号系统。由于字母符号只能提供声音，不能提供图像，因此很难直接在人脑中产生形象。同理，单词的拼写形式与单词的意义之间没有直接的联系。因此，为了通过单词的拼写形式来传递单词的意义，就必须要有一套固定的抽象概念系统来连接特定的语言形式与特定的语言意义。此外，要确定某个词语的特定概念意义，就不得不依赖分析和推理能力。这样一来，使用拼音文字的人们，包括说英语的人们，自然要具备发达的理性思维能力。如上所述，英语是一维的表音文字，其词义只能通过概念作为中介来予以理解。这就必然使得英美人习惯于通过分析来进行抽象思维。

4. 英语无灵主语句与英汉思维特征对比
English sentences with inanimate subjects

英美人的这种抽象思维习惯又反过来体现在英语句子的主语选择上。表达抽象概念的英语名词毫无例外地可以充当句子主语。这就是英语无灵主语句广泛存在于英语中的一个内在原因。例如：

(5) Loneliness held the immigrants together and poverty kept them down.
移民因孤独而聚居一处，因贫困而一筹莫展。

(6) Absence and distance make the overseas Chinese increasingly fond of the mainland.
华侨离乡背井，远居国外，所以越来越向往大陆。

汉语是象形文字。每个古汉字都逼真地摹拟一种自然现象或人文情景，因而能在人脑中直接产生图像或意象。象形文字诚然也是一种人造符号系统，但这些符号可以在人脑中直接产生形象，符号形式与文字意义之间存在一种直接的联想关系。由于存在这种形式与意义之间的直接联系，因此使用象形文字的人们就没有必要像使用表音文字的人们那样依赖抽象概念作为中介来进行沟通。此外，象形文字的确同时也是一种表音文字，但中国哲人认为，在传递意义的过程中，视觉是第一位的，听觉则是第二位的。由此看来，是形式与意义之间的直接联系妨碍了使用象形文字的人们，包括中国人，通过抽象概念来进行思维。相反，他们更习惯于通过具体形象进行思维。以上分析表明：中国人的思维过程可以概括为"意象——联想——想象"的过程，而英美人的思维过程则可总结为"概念——判断——推理"的过程。根据这一思维模式，中国人善于类比而不习惯分析。由于有了这种思维习惯，汉语句子很少以抽象概念开始。换句话说，汉语句子总是需要一个具体的有生命的实体作主语。例如：

(7) 她焦虑不安，心如刀绞。
Anxiety tore her into pieces.
(8) 他连日辛劳，已经瘦下好几磅了。
Successive exertion has already chipped a few pounds off him.

4.4 结语

语言与思维密不可分，不同的语言形式反映出不同的思维方式。本节仅就英汉两种语言体现出来的主要思维特征进行了简要的对比。对比结果表明：英美人善于理性思维和抽象思维，重视逻辑分析，强调语言表达的客观性；中国人则善于感性思维，重视类比和整体感知，强调语言表达的主观性。这些截然相反的思维特征能有效地解释英语无灵主语和汉语有灵主语普遍存在的原因。

5. 英语无灵主语句的隐含逻辑语义关系分析[①]

5.1 引言

语言、思维与逻辑密不可分。语言是思维的工具和产物，思维的过程同时也是使用语言的过程，二者都离不开逻辑。虽然语言规律通常由语法来反映，思维的规律一般由逻辑来体现，语法不等于逻辑，逻辑也不是语法，但是语言既然是人类进行思维和表达思维成果的工具，就必然要受到体现思维规律的逻辑制约。因此，我们在进行语句分析和语义理解的时候，既要借助语法，又要依靠逻辑。语法意义和逻辑关系相辅相成。在缺乏关联词语的语句中，找出隐含的逻辑语义关系对于正确理解语义尤为重要。

由于英语复合句是把两个或多个命题按照一定的逻辑语义关系通过关联词语组织在一个句子里，其最基本的逻辑语义关系就凝固在关联词语之中，因而其逻辑语义关系一般是外显的。（程晓堂等，2004）例如：

[①] 本节部分内容原载于《湖南工业大学学报（社会科学版）》2009年第3期。

(1) a. I'll get tired if I run.（条件关系）
b. I got tired because I ran.（因果关系）
c. I got tired after running.（时间关系）
d. I got tired by running.（方式关系）
e. I got tired running.（缺乏语境和关联词语，逻辑语义关系隐晦）

上例表明：在语境等其他因素不变的情况下，小句复合体（复合句）所表达的逻辑语义最为清晰，小句（简单句）次之，非限定小句（非谓语动词短语）又次之。（杨炳钧等，2007）

英语无灵主语句是一种独具特色的典型英语句子，一般都以小句（简单句）形式出现，具有句型多样、结构严谨、词汇密度大以及表达客观、生动形象等特点，加上句中缺乏标示逻辑关系的连接词语，其逻辑语义关系十分隐晦，常常给英语学习者带来理解和使用困难。为了揭示英语无灵主语句的隐含逻辑语义关系，本节拟在叶斯柏森（Jespersen）的语结（nexus）理论和奈达（Nida）的语义范畴（Semantic category）思想指导下，以七种常见逻辑语义关系和六种英语常用句型为线索，通过大量实例分析，探索英语无灵主语句中隐含逻辑语义关系的形成机制和体现方式。

5.2 语结理论与语义范畴思想概述

叶斯柏森（Jespersen，1960）的语结（nexus）这个术语，也有人译为"连接式"，与另一术语"组合式"（junction）相对应。所谓语结就是指一个词或一个词组具有一个句子的意义。例如，a furiously barking dog 含有 A dog barks furiously 之意；the doctor's arrival 含有 The doctor arrived 的逻辑语义。语结有两个特征：一是语结里并不要求出现限定动词；二是语结可以表达完整句子的意思。如果修饰语和被修饰语共同指称一个事物，构成一个本来就可以用一个独立单词表达的事物名称时，这样的词组就不是语结，如：a newborn dog 就是 a puppy；a silly person 就是 a fool；a female horse 就是 a mare。它们都无法表达一个意义完整的句子的意思。总之，语结必须包含两个各自独立和分离的概念，第二个用语必须为已经提及的名称增加新的内容。语结比较柔韧，隐含生命，而且结构严紧。

除名词性语结之外，叶斯柏森还列举了如下不同形式的语结：不定式语结（infinitival nexus）、语结宾语（nexus object）、无动词语结（nexus without a verb）、语结次添加语（nexus subjunct）和贬抑语结（nexus of deprecation）等等。更为重要的是，叶氏还区分了两类语结名词：动词性语结名词（如 arrival）和表语性语结名词（如 cleverness）。这与韩礼德（Halliday, 1994）的语法隐喻（grammatical metaphor）或名词化（nominalizarion）概念具有异曲同工之妙，对我们分析英语无灵主语句的隐含逻辑语义关系具有很大的指导意义。

奈达（Nida，1968，1986）在其交际理论中创造性地提出了英语的四个语义范畴（semantic category）概念，认为词语可依据其上下文逻辑语义关系，分别归属于不同的语义范畴：一是物体词（objects）；二是活动词（events）；三是抽象词（abstracts）；四是关系词（relations）。这是一种以语义分析为目的的词类划分，四个语义范畴所反映的是词与词、词组与词组之间的逻辑语义。（阎佩衡等，2001）具体说来，物体词不仅仅是"名词"的概念，它们还常常透露出一个动作所涉及的方方面面信息，如动作的主体（主语）或动作的受事（宾语）等；活动词是逻辑上的动词，但所表达的不仅仅是动词概念，通过它可以透视出一个逻辑上的句子来，因为其逻辑上的主体（主语）和受事（宾语）等有助于补充和完整其自身的逻辑语义；关系词也不仅仅是"介词"和"系词"的概念，因为它们能反映出其前后词项的逻辑关系，从而折射出一个或多个逻辑语句来；抽象词相当于传统语法中的形容词和副词，一般处在定语和状语的位置，但又不能直接与形容词和副词划等号，因为它们反映的是逻辑句式中的某些成分。由此可见，从理论上说，英语的短语或词组，甚至一个内涵丰富的单词，都可以在理解时看作一个逻辑语义完整的句子。这一思想对我们分析英语无灵主语句的逻辑语义关系具有直接的指导意义。

5.3 英语无灵主语句中七种逻辑语义关系的形成机制和体现方式

如上文所述，语结是一种浓缩了的语言形式，表面上，它只是一个单词或词组，但就语义而言，它能表达一个句子所表达的概念。换句话说，一个语结表达一个命题，语结与语结之间的逻辑语义关系实际上就是命题与命题之间的逻辑语义关系，只不过没有用显性的逻辑连接词语体现出来而已。逻辑语义关系种类繁多，限于篇幅，本节仅举例分析常见的因果、条件、方式、让步、时空、程度和对比等七种逻辑语义关系的形成机制和体现方式。

为了方便理解和分析，有必要根据奈达的语义范畴思想，对语结的逻辑意义理解途径之一"逆转换"作一简述。奈达认为，语义并非诸词项意义的总和。语义既与作者意图

5. 英语无灵主语句的隐含逻辑语义关系分析
English sentences with inanimate subjects

有关，又与语言功能相连，涉及的因素很多。要准确理解语义，特别是逻辑语义，"逆转换"是一条有效的途径，因为它有助于揭示语义结构中隐含的逻辑语义关系。例如，就名词语结的理解而言，我们可以进行这样的逆转换：his car → he owns a car; her failure → she failed; his arrest → he was arrested; your honesty → you are honest; our beloved ruler → we love the one who rules over us; the creation of the world → (God) creates the world. 以上例子表明，掌握这种"逆转换"理解方式对正确分析逻辑语义很有帮助。

5.3.1 因果关系

认知语义观认为，语义是语法结构的中心，语义分析离不开语义结构分析。因果语义结构是一个意义整体，在这个整体中，必须存在两个或两个以上独立的概念单位，它们之间的逻辑关系是原因和结果的关系。在英语无灵主语句中，这种因果语义关系常由谓语动词连接起来。因果语义结构是英语无灵主语句中最常见的语义结构，也就是说，因果关系是此类句子中最常见的逻辑语义关系。例如：

（2） Short hair made you look younger.

句中的无灵主语 short hair 是一个名词语结，可逆转换为 you wore short hair；宾语 you 和宾补 look younger 组成一个不定式语结，可逆转换为 you looked younger。这两个语结代表了两个独立的概念单位，它们之间存在着因果逻辑关系：Because you wore short hair, you looked younger. 句中的谓语动词 made 起连接作用，体现这两个独立概念之间的因果关系。再如：

(3) His honesty brought him many friends.

句中两个语结所表达的概念意义分别是：He was honest. He had many friends. 它们之间一因一果，形成因果语义结构，相当于 Because he was honest, he had many friends.

例（2）和例（3）都是先因后果，即无灵主语表因，宾语和/或补语表果。连接此类因果语义结构的动词常有：lead to, result in, give rise to, cause, allow, permit, enable, bring, make, give, keep 等。当然也有不少先果后因的语义结构，即无灵主语表果，宾语和/或补语表因，连接此类因果语义结构的动词常用：represent, justify, show, indicate, imply, result from, betray 等。例如：

(4) This glorious achievement represents the principle of self-reliance.
（They have made this glorious achievement because they adhere to the principle of self-reliance.）
(5) Her trembling hands betrayed her nervousness.
（As she was very nervous, her hands trembled.）

5.3.2 条件关系

一般说来，条件与结果的关系和原因与结果的关系不易区分，因而有人将前者纳入后者的范畴，并称之为准因果关系（张梅岗等，1994，2008）。然而，从准确理解语义关系的角度出发，还是有必要将其区分开来，尽管差别非常细微。

(6) The application of computers will make a tremendous rise in labour productivity.
(If we use computers, there will be a tremendous rise in labour productivity.)
(7) A little flattery would draw him out.
(If you flattered him a little, he would pour himself out.)

以上两例表明：在条件语义结构中，也要存在两个独立的概念单位，它们一个为条件，一个为结果，仍由谓语动词将其连接起来。虽然此类句子中的动词与含因果逻辑语义关系句子中的动词在语义上难以区分，但在时态上却有个明显的倾向，那就是多用将来时态。值得注意的是，在条件语义结构中，条件与结果概念的融合性更大，逻辑语义关系更加隐蔽。在这种情况下，动词一般用现在时，表示客观事实。例如：

(8) The wheel of the car obeys the slightest touch.
(Even if you touch the wheel very slightly, the car will react immediately.)
(9) The hill commands a fine prospect.
(If you stand on top of the hill, you can get a fine prospect.)

5.3.3 方式关系

英语无灵主语句中的方式语义结构有显性和隐性两种。显性的方式逻辑语义一般由充当状语的介词词组来体现。

(10) a. Darkness fell <u>like a grey blanket</u> over the sea.
　　 b. The happy news came <u>to the satisfaction of all</u>.
　　 c. Life is measured <u>by thought and action, not by time</u>.

隐性的方式逻辑语义常常体现在无灵主语中。

(11) a. Her frown gave him a speechless message.
　　　 (She gave him a frown and the frown acted as a speechless message. → She gave him a speechless message by showing him a frown.)
　　 b. Her glamour throws other ladies into shade.
　　　 (She is glamourous and this throws other ladies into shade. → Other ladies are thrown into shade by her being glamourous.)
　　 c. A few steps across the lawn brought me to a large splendid hotel.
　　　 (I took a few steps across the lawn and I reached a large splendid hotel. → I reached a large splendid hotel by taking a few steps across the lawn.)

5.3.4　让步关系

与方式逻辑语义结构一样，英语无灵主语句中的让步语义结构也有显性和隐性之分。显性的让步逻辑语义一般存在于句子的插入成分和形容词或副词的最高级形式中。

5. 英语无灵主语句的隐含逻辑语义关系分析

(12) a. The sight of the light, <u>even in the distance</u>, brings warmth from the window all the way to the heart.
  b. Sound reasoning and logic, <u>present in all good writings</u>, are essential to a causal analysis.
(13) a. Her words wring tears from <u>the hardest heart</u>.
  b. The wheel of the car obeys <u>the slightest touch</u>.

隐性的让步逻辑语义常常存在于无灵主语及其夸张表达方式中。

(14) a. Love will go through stone walls.
  (So long as love exists, no stone wall can stop it.)
  b. Words failed to convey my gratitude to you.
  (No matter what I might say, I could not convey my gratitude to you.)

5.3.5 时间与空间关系

英语无灵主语句中的隐含时间逻辑语义关系有两种体现方式：一是由表达时间意义的无灵主语与拟人化转义谓语动词体现；二是由起连接作用的时间语义动词体现。

(15) a. Dusk found the child crying in the street.
  (When dusk came, the child was crying in the street.)
  b. Every day sees our motherland flourishing.

(As the day goes by, our motherland flourishes.)
(16) a. The execution of the prisoner preceded the president's arrival.
(The prisoner was executed before the president arrived.)
b. The death of his mother was followed two months later by the loss of his three-year-old daughter.
(After his mother died, he lost his three-year-old daughter two months later.)

本节所指的空间概念是指处所、方向与方位等意义范畴。英语无灵主语句中隐含的空间语义关系一般由表达处所、方向及方位等空间概念的无灵主语及其拟人化转义谓语动词体现,或由此类无灵主语本身的隐喻意义体现出来。

(17) a. Beijing first saw the start of the movement.
b. The work site bustled with activity.
(18) a. The path to glory is always rugged.
b. Thailand is a smugglers' delight.

5.3.6 程度关系

程度包括极限程度和渐变程度。在英语无灵主语句中,极限程度逻辑语义一般体现在否定的谓语部分里;而渐变程度逻辑语义则常常由谓语与状语共同体现。

(19) a. His presence of mind <u>never deserted him</u>.
　　 b. This medicine <u>knows no bounds of effectiveness</u>.
(20) a. The visibility of his impatience <u>increased second by second</u>.
　　 b. The reefs <u>loomed</u> in front of them <u>with startling clarity</u>.

5.3.7 对比关系

当英语无灵主语句通过陈述成对概念来阐释"哲理"或"常识"时,对比或比较的逻辑语义关系就常常隐含其中。

(21) a. Fire is the test of gold and adversity of strong men.
　　 b. Education is not the filling of a pail but the lighting of a fire.
　　 c. A bad compromise is better than a fair lawsuit.

这种含有对比逻辑语义关系的英语无灵主语句在英语谚语、成语或俗语中尤为常见。

(22) a. Excess of sorrow laughs and excess of joy weeps.
　　 b. Two is company; three is a crowd.
　　 c. Genius is one percent of inspiration and ninety-nine percent of perspiration.

5.4 六种句型英语无灵主语句中的逻辑语义关系分析

如上文所述,英语无灵主语句所隐含的逻辑语义关系就是语结与语结之间的逻辑关系。在语结与语结之间作为连接纽带的谓语动词扮演着非常重要的角色。因为谓语动词在英语句子结构中作用巨大,所以体现句子逻辑语义关系的连接图式也与充当连接纽带的谓语动词密不可分。(熊力游,2007)因此,分析谓语动词在句子结构中的意义与作用,也可以揭示句子中隐含逻辑语义关系的体现方式。

5.4.1 SVA 句型中的逻辑语义关系

在英语的实际运用中,SV 句型单独出现的情况较少,它一般要与表达地点、时间、方式等概念的状语(以介词短语最常见)相结合,形成 SVA 句型,才容易广泛使用。在 SVA 句型中,谓语动词主要起连接语结的纽带作用,其次也与其他成分相结合产生附加意义,语结(S 或 SV)与语结(VA 或 A)之间可以存在因果、条件和方式等各种逻辑语义关系。

(23) a. The case snowballed into one of the most famous trials in U. S. history.
　　b. His diligence resulted in his success.
(24) a. The heart would break without hope.
　　b. His eloquent description can arise only out of his deep love for his motherland.
(25) a. Her voice tailed off into silence.
　　b. The happy news came to the satisfaction of all.

5.4.2 SVC 句型中的逻辑语义关系

在 SVC 句型中，S 与 C 一般都是独立语结，在语义上相当一个意思完整的句子，谓语动词只起连接纽带作用，不产生附加意义。上文提到，这种结构常常用来阐述"哲理"或"常识"，可隐含因果、条件和对比等逻辑语义关系。

(26) a. Arrogance and complacence turned out to be his ruin.
(Because he was arrogant and complacent, he ruined himself.)
b. This novel was the beginning of his fame.
(As he wrote this novel, he began to be famous.)

(27) a. Good company on the road is the shortest cut.
(If you have a good company on the road, you will find yourself on the shortest cut.)
b. Unpleasant advice is good medicine.
(If the advice is unpleasant, it may act as good medicine.)

(28) a. The weight lost by the anode is exactly equal to the gain in the weight by the cathode.
b. Prosperity is not without many fears and disasters, and adversity is not without comforts and hopes.

5.4.3 SVO 句型中的逻辑语义关系

英语无灵主语句最常用的是 SVO 句型，其中的主语

（S）与宾语（O）都是独立语结，在逻辑上相当于意思完整的句子，因而谓语动词有时没有具体意义，只起语法和逻辑纽带作用；有时虽具有一定意义，但总要受其所连接的前后两部分语义的影响与制约。SVO句型隐含的逻辑语义关系以因果关系最常见，有时也隐含方式等其它逻辑语义关系。

(29) a. The appearance of a distant sail kindled his hope of rescue.
b. The knowledge of cellular structure and organization has permitted a better understanding of cell division.
c. Her trained ear detected the weaknesses and exaggeration of the story.

(30) a. Only a very light and scattering ripple of half-hearted handclapping greeted her.
b. A thick coat of gloom enveloped the valley.
c. A faint smile lights up the woman's face.

5.4.4　SVOA句型中的逻辑语义关系

在SVOA句型中，A表面上是地点或方位状语，但从深层语义去分析，OA或VOA常常形成一个独立语结，表示结果。以SVOA句型出现的英语无灵主语句都是隐喻句。句中的谓语动词大都是使役动词（causational verb），具有"传递"作用。这种英语无灵主语句常常隐含因果逻辑语义关系，有时也暗存方式、让步等逻辑语义关系。

(31) a. Business took him to the town.
   b. Fear rooted her to the ground.
   c. Their charity accepted me in the orphanage.
(32) a. The downpour plastered his shirt to his body.
   b. Her glamour throws other ladies into the shade.
(33) a. Her words wring tears from the hardest heart.
   b. Words can't convey my gratitude to you.

5.4.5 SVOO 句型中的逻辑语义关系

在以 SVOO 句型出现的英语无灵主语句中，无灵主语（S）总是隐含原因，具有传递意义的谓语动词一般都失去其本来的词汇意义，只起因果连接作用，双宾语（OO）隐含结果逻辑语义。在这一结构中，既有"传递"又有"接受"的概念，这里的因果关系就是通过"传递"和"接受"来实现的。值得注意的是，在这个隐含因果关系的隐喻结构中，直接宾语一定是由抽象或泛指名词来充当。

(34) a. The use of dialect lent the work great charm.
   b. The news gave me quite a start.
   c. His slip of the tongue almost cost him a good friend.

5.4.6 SVOC 句型中的逻辑语义关系

以 SVOC 句型出现的英语无灵主语句，总是隐含一种因果和条件逻辑语义关系。无灵主语（S）总是隐含"原因"或"条件"，宾语和补语（OC）共同形成"结果"逻辑语义，谓语动词（V）多为使役动词，以 make 为其典型代表。值得注意的是，隐喻性 SVOC 结构呈现十分复杂的多义现象，如因果行为、因果状态或属性、因果运动等。也就是说，随着补语（C）的词义和语法形式的变化，句子可隐含各种各样的因果逻辑语义关系。

（35）a. Einstein's theory of relativity and his other discoveries make him world-famous.
　　　b. Absence makes the heart grow fonder.
　　　c. The noise outside made it impossible for me to go on with my work.
　　　d. My shyness prevented me from speaking first.
（36）a. Short hair will make you look younger.
　　　b. Benefits often make a man a slave.
　　　c. A little flattery would draw him out.

5.5　结语

　　正确理解英语无灵主语句中的隐含逻辑语义关系是正确使用和翻译这类句子的前提。本节从语结理论和语义范畴思想出发，对英语无灵主语句的隐含逻辑语义关系的形成机制与体现方式进行了尝试性分析。分析表明：英语无灵主语句中隐含的逻辑语义关系种类繁多，包括因果、条件、方式、让步、时间、空间、程度、以及对比等，其中以因果关系最为常见，最为复杂。不同句型中英语无灵主语句所隐含的逻辑语义关系主要由谓语动词的意义与功能来体现，谓语动词的使役意义和转递意义（包括显性和隐性两种）以及谓语动

5. 英语无灵主语句的隐含逻辑语义关系分析
English sentences with inanimate subjects

词的连接功能是英语无灵主语句隐含逻辑语义关系的发源地，不同的谓语动词和不同的句子结构体现不同的逻辑语义关系。

6. 英语无灵主语句的认知突显分析[①]

6.1 引言

　　主语研究是认知语法的核心内容之一。根据 Langacker (1991:308) 的典型主语定义，无灵主语只是一种非典型主语，是主语范畴中的边缘成分，但从其广泛存在性这一语言事实来看，却很有必要从不同角度对其进行全面探讨。本节拟在认知突显观的指导下，通过不同认知突显方式的分析，对英语无灵主语句的存在理据和生成机制进行探讨。文中讨论的英语无灵主语句仅指那些用不具备生命意义的实体（如实物、抽象概念和动作名词等）作主语，用表达物质过程或心理过程的动词作谓语的句子。

6.2 认知突显概念与小句主语选择

　　Ungerer & Schmid (1996:37-39) 认为：目前，认知语言学主要体现为三种研究路向（approach）：经验观（experiential view）、突显观（prominence view）和注意观（attention view）。认知突显观超越了逻辑推理和客观主义的约束，强

[①] 本节内容原载于《外语教学》2009 年第 5 期。

6. 英语无灵主语句的认知突显分析
English sentences with inanimate subjects

调人类主观认知过程，为小句如何选取和安排信息提供了解释。认知语言学中的突显概念常用"prominence"或"salience"来表达，但与这一概念相关的术语还有图形与背景（figure vs ground）、侧面与基体（profile vs base）以及射体与界标（trajector vs landmark）等。这些不同的术语与概念同时又体现为不同的突显方式。

图形与背景（figure vs ground）的划分充分体现了认知语言学的突显观（prominence view）。丹麦心理学家 Rubin 在研究视觉感知时最早采用脸与花瓶幻觉图（face-vase illusion）来说明图像感知与背景的关系，如图 6-1 所示。

图 6-1　脸与花瓶幻觉图

Talmy（1983：232）首先将图形与背景理论运用于认知语言学研究中。他认为："图形是一个运动的或概念上可动的物体，其场所、路径或方向可被视为一个变量，其特别的价值是突显。背景是一个参照体，它在参照框架中是固定的。相对于背景这个参照体，图形的场所、路径或方向可得到特定描写。"认知语言学还认为，同样的原则还反映在句法结构的层面上。传统的主、谓、宾结构也可体现图形与背景的区分这一认知原则。一般情况下，主语对应于图形，宾语对应于背景，动词则显示主语与宾语的关系。选择不同的

部分作为图形,就会得出不同的句法构造。例如:

(1) a. Children fear darkness.
   b. Darkness frightens children.
(2) a. Bees swarmed in the garden.
   b. The garden was swarming with bees.

以上例句表明:客观情景中的任何成分都具有作为图形充当主语而获得突显的"权利"。小句成分的选择是由说话人的认知视点决定的。认知主体的识解方式不同,视角也会不同,表达方式当然也不同。这种认知突显方式可以视为英语无灵主语句的存在理据之一。

与图形—背景理论近似的,还有射体—界标理论。两者的区别在于,前者一般指静态结构关系,后者阐述的是动态结构关系。如飞机飞过地面时,飞机是射体,地面是界标;子弹出膛时,子弹是射体,枪管和周边的环境是界标。上面的例句也可以近似地用射体—界标理论来分析。在这两种理论中,图形和射体是当前结构体(configuration)中的突显侧面(profile),射体和界标是作为背景或参照物的基体(base)。在侧面与基体的对立中,我们可以理解无灵主语的生成机制。

6.3 主语语义角色的不同突显方式与英语无灵主语句的生成机制

Langacker(1991:308)指出:"总之,典型主语同时具备以下四大主题性语义因素:施事性、人类性、确定性以及过程侧面关系中的图形特征。这种高度主题性暗含认知突显

6. 英语无灵主语句的认知突显分析
English sentences with inanimate subjects

性,所以主语极易成为语法结构中的参与者。"(To summarize, a prototypical subject ranks highly with respect to all four topicality factors: it is agentive, human, definite, and the figure within the profiled relationship. The cognitive salience implied by this high degree of topicality makes a subject easily accessible for participation in grammatical constructions.) 也就是说,只有以上四大语义因素齐全的主语才是最理想和最典型的主语。例如:Henry hit the ball at the goal with a club. 例中 Henry 这个人物是击球过程中的施事,是行为链的启动者,是整个动态事件中最醒目的图形,也是该情景中的焦点突显实体,集上述四大语义因素于一身,是及物主动小句中的典型主语。然而,在实际语言应用中,并非所有描述常态认知过程的主语都同时具备上述四大语义因素。也就是说,非典型主语也广泛存在于语言之中,而英语无灵主语就是其中之一。以下将通过分析主语语义角色的不同突显方式,探讨英语无灵主语句的生成机制。

6.3.1 无灵主语句生成于过程侧面突显焦点的移动

认知注意观告诉我们,语言所表达的内容常常只反映经验过程中能引起人们注意的部分。一个完整的行为过程一般都有不止一个侧面,而根据语言运用中的经济原则,并非一个完整过程中的每个侧面都要同时突显。因此,当突显焦点随着观察者的注意力在行为链上来回移动时,参与者身份就会发生变化,工具和受事都有可能作为施事而成为小句主语,如此便可生成大量无灵主语句。如上述表达击球全部过程并包含典型主语的句子,就很有可能因此而生成至少两个无灵主语句。

(3) a. Henry hit the ball at the goal with a club.
    b. The club hit the ball.
    c. The ball hit the goal.

类似的例子俯拾皆是:

(4) a. A car knocked them down.
    b. The computer has solved the problem.
    c. My axe has felled that tree.
    d. The magic spades of archaeology have given us the whole lost world of Egypt.

其实,这种以工具主语句出现的无灵主语句,广泛存在于英语语言中。

6.3.2 无灵主语句生成于环境成分的突显

环境成分包括事件、地点、空间、因果关系、客观事物、自然景象等多种语义成分。在认知舞台模式中,这些成分作为固定场景,通常不是过程参与者。在认知过程中,一般重点突显的是场景中的图形,而不是场景本身。然而,认知者有时为了获得某种特殊的认知效果,有意调整观察视角,选择特别视点来突显环境成分,于是就有了各种环境成分充当小句主语,并因而生成许多无灵主语句。

6.3.2.1 时间语义成分的突显

时间作为一种环境成分,不具备实体特征,因而不能作为经验过程的参与者,成为小句主语。然而,认知者有时由于特殊原因,或为了创造特殊效果,在认知过程中利用反常规的焦点突显手段,也可能使其成为小句主语。这在传统修

6. 英语无灵主语句的认知突显分析
English sentences with inanimate subjects

辞学里叫拟人手段。例如:

(5) a. A great man was born on that day.
　　 b. That day witnessed the birth of a great man.
(6) a. The child was crying in the street at dusk.
　　 b. Dusk found the child crying in the street.

6.3.2.2　地点与空间语义成分的突显

地点与空间可统称为处所。最近张法科和仇伟(2006)对处所主语句进行了认知研究。研究表明:处所主语是主语范畴的边缘成分,与对应的常规句子相比,处所主语句标示了不同的识解方式并突显了处所成分。处所词要经过主语化转换才能成为表层结构里的主语,从而形成处所主语句。例如:

(7) a. Five adults can sleep in this cottage.
　　 b. This cottage sleeps five adults.
(8) a. Music echoed in the hall.
　　 b. The hall echoed with music.

6.3.2.3　因果关系和自然情景等语义成分的突显

客观事件间的各种因果关系,常常通过人们在认知活动过程中产生的意象图式,投射到语言表达形式中。因果关系反映说话人对事件间逻辑关系的认识,是认知主体同认知对象相互"协商"的结果,是主客观互动的产物,徐盛桓和李淑静(2005)对各种复杂的因果关系进行了主客观分类研究。这里涉及的因果关系英语无灵主语句,是指由谓语动词连接起来的两个含有隐性因果关系概念的语言表达方式。

63

例如:

(9) a. Short hair makes you look younger.
    b. This medicine will ensure you a good sleep.
(10) a. This glorious achievement represents the principle of self-reliance.
     b. The present stable political situation justifies the drastic measures.

例(9)中的主语为"因",宾语部分为"果";而例(10)中的主语为"果",宾语则为"因"。

这类因果无灵主语句的存在理据,还可用Lakoff(1987)意象图式理论中的连接图式来解释。连接图式的生理基础是人的第一连接物:脐带。它由两个实体和一个连接物构成。在脐带连接母体和婴儿构成的连接图式里,母体和婴儿都是实体,都有自己的内部结构。同理,一个独立的实体应该有其内部结构,一个概念单位也应有其内部结构,甚至由一个词表达的概念,也有其内部结构。在上述小句中,动词连接的主、宾两个语言实体,也必然具有自己的内部结构,才能构成一个连接图式。因此,意象中的因果图式在语言表达中就是通过谓语动词将"因"与"果"连接起来而形成的因果小句。

客观现象与自然情景等语义成分作小句主语,与其他环境成分一样,也是主语范畴的边缘成分,其认知突显方式和生产机制与时间和处所主语相似。例如:

(11) a. Thus, I often hasten home in a hurrying crowd when it's getting dark.

6. 英语无灵主语句的认知突显分析
English sentences with inanimate subjects

b. Thus, the gathering dark often finds me hastening home in a hurrying crowd.

（12）a. He decided to sit down in the first convenient shade as he felt weary and it was getting hot.

b. The increasing heat and his weariness determined him to sit down in the first convenient shade.

6.3.3 无灵主语句生成于过程侧面的突显

与上文6.3.1所讨论的过程侧面突显焦点的移动不同，这里是指整个过程侧面的突显。根据Halliday（1994）系统功能语言学原理，过程由动词来体现。过程的作用在于维系事件参与者之间的关系。过程本身不是事件的参与者，不具备实体特征，因而在自然和常规状况下，不可成为小句主语。然而，在对客观世界进行认知的过程中，如果认知者选取特殊视角，将整个过程作为突显焦点，把过程突显为实体，那就是将过程概念实体化，相当于系统功能语言学中的名词化（nominalization）或语法隐喻（grammatical metaphor）。对此，笔者（何明珠，2003，2005，2007）已有详细论述。伴随过程侧面的认知突显，必然产生小句语义成分的重新组合，将一个小句浓缩为一个名词短语，充当另一个小句的主语。由此而生成的抽象名词，虽不再拥有动词特性，但仍然暗含特定的行为特征，仍可体现其固有的主、被动关系。例如：

（13）a. If he helps me, I will surely succeed.

b. His help will ensure my success.

(14) a. Napoleon was defeated and it changed the history of Europe.
b. Napoleon's defeat changed the history of Europe.

6.4 结语

本节在认知语言学的突显理论指导下，通过分析不同认知突显方式，初步解释了英语无灵主语句的存在理据与生成机制。研究发现：①与 Langacker 的典型主语相比较，无灵主语只能归入非典型主语之列，是主语范畴的边缘成分，然而，英语无灵主语句却是一种广泛存在的英语语言现象，因而有必要从不同视角对其进行全面探讨；②认知突显存在多种方式或途径，如图形、侧面和射体等，每一种突显方式都有可能生成无灵主语句；③无灵主语与典型主语一样，都是认知过程中的突显焦点，但不是真正意义上的典型图形、侧面或射体；④无灵主语的生成都源自认知过程中非常规突显，例如过程侧面突显焦点的移动、非参与者环境成分的突显以及过程侧面本身的突显等。本节分析表明：认知突显观是分析和解释英语无灵主语句和生成机制的重要理论依据，运用这一理论对英语无灵主语句进行认知研究，有助于揭示语言结构的认知本质。

7. 英语无灵主语句的隐喻性与生命性认知探源[①]

7.1 引言

由无灵主语和有灵谓语构成的英语无灵主语句广泛存在于当代英语中，而汉语中却少有这种语言现象。许多英汉对比研究者从不同角度探讨了英汉语言之间存在这一差异的原因。潘文国（1997：363-367）从英汉思维模式差异的角度进行了研究，认为重悟性的中国哲学强调主体的参与意识，而重理性的西方哲学强调客体的距离意识。习惯于主体意识的汉语爱用有灵主语造句，因而很少使用无灵主语句；相反，习惯于客体意识的英语除常用有灵主语造句外，还偏爱使用无灵主语句。喻家楼和胡开宝（1997：52-54）从英汉动词与名词的搭配和表达习惯的差异角度进行了分析，认为"汉语和英语其所以在有灵与无灵倾向上存在明显差别，主要原因在于：英语中有灵动词和无灵动词之间的区分不严格和动词的被动结构出现率高，而汉语中的情况正好相反"。他们举英语动词 bear 为例，指出"动词 bear 可以和有灵主语搭配，也可以和无灵主语搭配，有时用于主动结构，有时

[①] 本节内容原载于《外国语文》2011 年第 5 期。

用于被动结构，非常自由灵活"。邵志洪和邵惟韺（2007：1-5）在英汉拟人法使用对比研究中区分了词汇化拟人和修辞性拟人，并探讨了英语无灵主语句广泛存在的原因。他们认为拟人可分成隐性和显性两类。前者是词汇化拟人（lexicalized personification），后者是修辞性拟人（rhetorical personification）；前者属 dead metaphor（死的隐喻），后者属 live metaphor（活的隐喻）。由于英汉语在语法特征和语言心理等方面存在较大差异，两种语言在拟人法的使用上也很不相同：英语动词系统中有十分丰富的词汇化拟人表达法，而汉语指称系统中有十分丰富的词汇化拟人表达法。由于英语无灵主语句通常为词汇化拟人，而汉语无灵主语句通常为修辞性拟人，词汇化拟人又大大多于修辞性拟人，因此英语中的拟人远比汉语多，英语无灵主语句也就必然很常见。笔者（2003：51-55；2005a：1-14；2005b：87-90）发现每个客观精练、生动形象的英语无灵主语句都是隐喻句，并以认知语言学的概念隐喻（conceptual metaphor）理论与系统功能语言学的语法隐喻（grammatical metaphor）理论为依据，分析了英语无灵主语句的生成机制，从而解释了英语无灵主语句广泛存在的原因。本节试图在已有研究的基础上，根据认知语言学的隐喻工作机制之一，概念跨域映射（conceptual cross-domain mapping）原理，探索英语无灵主语句的隐喻性根源；并在认知隐喻的经验基础（experiential basis of metaphor）上，探索英语无灵主语句的生命性始源，从而进一步解释英语无灵主语句的普遍性和生动性原因。

7.2 概念跨域映射与英语无灵主语句的隐喻性

认知语言学家 Lakoff 与 Johnson（1980：3-6）认为隐喻

7. 英语无灵主语句的隐喻性与生命性认知探源
English sentences with inanimate subjects

不仅是一种语言现象,更是一种认知方式,这个观点已成为人们的共识。他们的这种认知论概念隐喻的工作机制是:每一个隐喻包含始源域和目标域两个部分,隐喻的认知力量就在于将始源域的图式结构映射到目标域之上。这种映射发生在概念层次,且是系统性的,两个域的结构之间存在固定的配对。(蓝纯,2005:116)后来,Lakoff 与 Turner(1989:63)认为隐喻具有内部结构。每一个隐喻映射都包括以下过程:①始源域图式中的空缺(slots)被映射到目标域的空缺上;②始源域中的关系被映射到目标域的关系上;③始源域的特征被映射到目标域的特征上;④始源域中的知识被映射到目标域中的知识上。(束定芳,2000:170-171)隐喻的这种概念跨域映射工作机制能合理解释英语无灵主语句的隐喻性特征。

如上所述,本节讨论的英语无灵主语句是指由无灵主语和有灵谓语构成的句子。有灵就是具有生命特征,无灵就是不具有生命特征。很明显,每一个英语无灵主语句都存在两个概念域:具有生命特征的概念域(谓语)和不具有生命特征的概念域(主语),且在这两个不同概念域之间"生命性"这个上义层次的概念可以进行跨域映射。此外,英语无灵主语句中的生命性概念跨域映射可满足"系统性"和"方向性"两个要求。

一方面,生命性概念普遍存在于人类自然语言或话语之中,以致人们习焉不察。较早涉及生命性范畴的语言学研究是基于词汇的语义成分分析。词汇意义由系列语义特征结合体构成,如构成 father 的意义包括[+ANIMATE],[+ADULT],[+MALE],[+PARENT]等语义特征。Comrie(1981)将生命性视为与语言结构有关的语言外特征,表征为一个语义成分等级:[HUMAN] > [ANIMATE] > [INANI-

MATE]。(刘礼进,2003:111-119)由此可见,生命性概念映射存在系统性。

另一方面,如果我们把世界上的事物按照下面的方法进行分类:

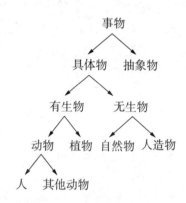

那么,事物的生命性等级或生命度应该是:人 > 其他动物 > 植物 > 无生物 > 抽象物。由于隐喻涉及跨域映射,所以生命性概念的跨域映射只有一个方向,并且是固定的。那就是从有生命的概念域向无生命的概念域映射,或从生命度高的概念域向生命度低的概念域映射。反之,则行不通。

让我们用一个实例来检验一下英语无灵主语句中的概念跨域映射是否存在隐喻映射的四个过程:His words hurt me.

Source domain   Target domain
(People hurt people) by hand   → (Words hurt people) by mouth
with something visible and hard   → with something invisible and soft
to cause pain to the body   → to cause pain to the feeling
…   …

如此可见，正是始源域和目标域中各要素之间的一系列对应关系为跨域映射提供了可能，才把始源域中的某一特征赋予了目标域，从而形成隐喻。第一，具有生命性特征的概念域（始源域）图式中的空缺（slots）可以映射到不具生命性特征的概念域（目标域）的空缺上。将始源域中的行为或动作的主体"人"这个空缺映射到无生物或抽象物这一目标域，就意味着把无生物或抽象物理解为"人"。第二，始源域中"人"与行为或动作的关系被映射到目标域后，就成了无生物或抽象物与"行为或动作"之间的关系。第三，始源域的"生命性"特征被映射到目标域后，无生物或抽象物就被赋予了"生命性"特征，因而能实施行为或执行动作。第四，始源域中的行为或动作需要"人"来实施或执行的知识被映射到目标域后，赋予了"生命性"特征的无生物或抽象物因而也就有能力实施行为或执行动作。

以上分析表明：英语无灵主语句就是一种概念隐喻，其工作机制与隐喻的工作机制完全一样。也就是说，生命性概念的跨域映射直接体现了英语无灵主语句的隐喻性。

7.3 人的动作或行为与英语无灵主语句的生命性

经验现实主义哲学观认为：人类的认知蕴涵于身体，我们现在拥有的这些概念隐喻是由我们的身体经验和物理经验（bodily and physical experience）决定的。（蓝纯，2005：119）许多认知语言学家，如 Lakoff and Johnson（1980），Foley（1997）等，用大量的事实论证了"隐喻不是任意的，而是以身体的经历为基础的"，"人类任何对目标域的理解首先及最早的是使用人体及其对物体世界的相互作用。人体是隐喻最杰出的始源域"等结论。国内也有许多研究者(王文斌,2001:57-60;卢卫中,2004:470-485;覃修桂,2008:37-43)利用汉语或汉英语料论证或对比了英汉人体隐喻的普遍性。这些研究主要涉及人体或人体部位的形状、功能、特征等作为概念始源域的隐喻,较少涉及人的行为或动作作为始源域的隐喻。钟小佩(2004:487-499)在研究汉英"世界是人"的隐喻概念时也涉及人的行为或动作,例如:

(1) 地貌风景的行为就是人的行为:
The stream had thinned down to a mere trickle.
The hole yawned open in front of them.
(2) 植物的动作就是人的动作:
The trees here did not bear fruit this year.
Orchids grow very slowly here.
(3) 机器的动作就是人的动作:
The steamer nosed its way along the winding creek.
My computer is thinking about the problem.
(4) 语言有人的动作:
The gossip will soon die down.
The rumor has gradually stretched away.
(5) 社会、国家的行为就是人的行为:
Our society is making great strides.
The nation finally stood up.
(6) 经济有人的动作:
Petrol price jumped.
Recently the economy has been straddling between a recession and an anemic growth.

7. 英语无灵主语句的隐喻性与生命性认知探源

但因研究视角的不同，该文未能将所有这类无灵主语句归纳为一种概念隐喻来研究。本节将在已有研究的基础上进一步讨论英语无灵主语句的生命性源泉。

语言为人类所独有，人又为世界上万物之灵并拥有最高生命度，因此语言中的任何生命性特征都离不开人。由于生命在于运动，人的动作与行为因而就是生命性特征的最佳体现形式。英语无灵主语句的生命性特征就体现在人的动作或行为中。以下仅从人的手脚动作、视觉行为、听觉行为、言语行为、心理行为等方面举例展示英语无灵主语句的生命性始源。

7.3.1 手脚动作与英语无灵主语句

人的手和脚是人类获取经验、体验外界事物和改造世界最直接和最重要的工具。由手脚发出的动作是人类最主要的活动，最能体现人的运动和生命特征。手脚动作在语言中主要表现为动词，手的动作多为及物动词，脚的动作多为不及物动词。所有展现手脚动作的动词当然都是有灵动词，其生命度很高，因而隐喻性很强。英语中这类动词都是常见动词，也是最主要的有灵动词，数多量大，因此普遍存在于英语中的隐喻性无灵主语句就是由这类动词充当谓语成分的。这里稍作归纳并略举数例如下：beat, break, bring, catch, capture, create, deprive, draw, drive, embrace, enjoy, feed, fill, gather, give, hit, hurt, hold, have, keep, kill, knock, lay, lock, make, mend, open, overthrow, place, put, raise, rob, seize, strike, show, take, throw, tie, wrench; arrive, come, enter, escape, fall, follow, go, kick, leave, lead to, move, precede, rise, reach, slip, stand, travel, wander, 等。

(7) Peace brings prosperity.
　　（先有和平环境，才会有繁荣昌盛。）
(8) The Globe brings you the world in a single copy.
　　（一册《环球》在手，纵览世界风云。）
(9) His enthusiasm struck his teacher favorably.
　　（他很热情，老师对他的印象不错。）
(10) The thick carpet killed the sound of his footsteps.
　　（走在厚厚的地毯上，他没有发出一点脚步声。）
(11) Talking mends no holes.
　　（空谈无济于事。）
(12) Last year, the company's total assets reached 3 billion yuan and its business revenues hit 1.8 billion yuan.
　　（去年该公司的总资产达到30亿元，其营业收入突破18亿元。）
(13) When poverty comes in at the door, love flies out of the window.
　　（家境穷，恩爱终。）
(14) His reputation still stands on slippery grounds.
　　（他的声誉还不牢靠。）
(15) Her name obstinately escapes me.
　　（我总想不起她的名字。）
(16) The 11th National Games kicked off in Jinan last week.
　　（第十一届全运会上周在济南开幕。）

　　上列有些动词，如 have, hold, keep, possess, enjoy 等，虽动作性不很明显，但意志力很强，生命度很高，并离不开

双手,因而也常见于隐喻性英语无灵主语句中。例如:

(17) Honesty keeps the crown of the causeway.
(诚实人行得正立得稳,不怕明枪与暗箭。)
(18) China has enjoyed rapid economic growth all these years.
(中国近年来经济发展迅速。)

7.3.2 视觉行为与英语无灵主语句

睁开的眼睛既是生命的象征又是心灵的窗户,人类通过自己的眼睛体验和认识世界,世界万物也要通过眼睛才能刺激大脑。这种双向互动就是一种生命性始源,因此表现视觉行为的英语动词自然常常用来构建隐喻性英语无灵主语句:discover, find, notice, observe, see, witness, 等。其实,人类自诞生以来就一直主动用眼睛观察事物,获取事物的表面或内在特征,然而,随着人类认知能力的发展,许多事物或现象的特征也自然而然地直接向人们昭示。因此,像 disclose, expose, reveal 等英语动词表现的就是反向视觉行为,由其构成的英语无灵主语句非常自然,其隐喻性常常习而不察。例如:

(19) The video camera observed the whole scene.
(摄影机将整个场景都录下来了。)
(20) The fifth day saw them at the summit.
(他们在第五天爬上了山顶。)
(21) Nanjing has witnessed great changes in recent years.

（南京近年发生了巨大变化。）
(22) Love always finds its way.
（爱情无法阻拦。）
(23) Investigation has revealed him as a confirmed criminal.
（侦查表明他是惯犯。）

7.3.3　听觉行为与英语无灵主语句

与视觉行为一样，听觉行为也是人类体验和认识世界的重要途径。人类既借助声音通过耳朵体验和认识世界，世界万物同样也借助声音通过人耳刺激人脑，这种双向互动直接体现出生命性特征。虽然人的听觉行为与言语行为紧密相连、难以切分，但是为了方便分析，这里可从两个方面对其加以区别：听觉行为是指人与世界万物之间的直接互动，而言语行为是指人与人之间的直接互动；听觉行为强调声音的传递和行为过程，而言语行为则重视信息的传递和行为结果。英语中表达听觉行为的动词也常用在隐喻性无灵主语句中：call, echo, hear, murmur, ring, sound, whisper, whistle, 等。例如：

(24) Saturday called Mr. Collins away from his amiable Charlotte.
（一到星期六，柯林斯先生就要从温柔可爱的夏绿蒂身边走开。）
(25) Moscow won't hear such excuses.
（这样的借口在莫斯科无人会接受。）
(26) The bell sounded dismissal earlier today.

（今天的放学铃响得早些。）
(27) The leaves whispered in the breeze.
（树叶在微风中沙沙作响。）
(28) Bullets and shells were whistling overhead.
（子弹与炮弹在头顶上呼啸而过。）

7.3.4　言语行为与英语无灵主语句

言语是生命的象征，语言是人类的标志。语言是人类赖以生存和发展的必不可少的认知和交流工具。语言行为虽不是人的全部生存状态，却是人的基本生存状态。（钱冠连，2005）离开言语行为，经验和知识就难以转播，思想和情感就难以交流，人类的生存和发展就会面临危险，生命性也就难以彰显。因此，表达言语行为的动词生命度极高，构建英语无灵主语句的言语行为动词非常丰富：admit, acclaim, allow, ask, blame, boast, confirm, convince, declare, demand, define, explain, express, flatter, forbid, greet, inform, inquire, invite, notify, offer, permit, promise, question, read, repeat, report, require, say, speak, state, talk, tell, warn, 等。例如：

(29) Facts speak louder than eloquence.
（事实胜于雄辩。）
(30) Her blush told the whole story.
（她脸红了，让人不言自明。）
(31) The time limit admits of no delay.
（时间有限，不容拖延。）
(32) The dress flattered her figure.
（这件衣服使她尽显窈窕。）

(33) Examination confirmed the quality of the product.
   (经检查,产品质量合格。)

7.3.5　心理行为与英语无灵主语句

这里所说的心理行为包括感觉、知觉、思维和情感等行为。感觉是客观事物的个别特性在人脑中的反应,是最简单的心理过程,是形成各种复杂心理过程的基础。知觉是反映客观事物整体形象和表面联系的心理过程,是在感觉基础上形成的更为复杂和完整的心理过程。思维是在表象和概念基础上进行的分析、综合、判断、推理等认知活动,是人类特有的精神活动。情感是人类从事各种活动时产生的某种心理状态。(王珏,2004:245-246)心理行为和言语行为是人类区别于其他动物的特有行为。心理行为的生命性主要体现在人的意志力和自主度上。英语中表达心理行为的动词非常丰富,因而由心理行为动词构成的英语无灵主语句也很普遍:affect, attract, feel, impress, induce, smell, taste; accept, believe, desert, enjoy, find, ignore, know, obey, refuse; cause, create, decide, determine, encourage, make, prevent, reflect, remind; amaze, astonish, delight, disappoint, frighten, inspire, offend, oppress, please, puzzle, satisfy, suffer, threaten, upset, worry, 等。例如:

(34) Everything feels nice on a warm bright day.
   (温暖明媚的日子里一切都感觉舒畅。)
(35) Ambition knows no father.
   (野心勃勃的人六亲不认。)
(36) His presence of mind never deserted him.

7. 英语无灵主语句的隐喻性与生命性认知探源
English sentences with inanimate subjects

（他时刻保持着清醒的头脑。）

(37) His weariness and the increasing heat determined him to sit down in the first shade.
（他疲乏不堪，天气又越来越热，他于是决定一遇荫凉就坐下来休息。）

(38) The sight of the toy train delighted the child.
（那孩子一看到玩具火车，就兴高采烈起来了。）

以上分析表明：体现人的动作或行为的有灵谓语动词，一旦与无灵主语结合，其生命性特征就会向句子主语进行跨域映射，使其临时获得不同程度的生命性，从而产生大量生动形象的隐喻性英语无灵主语句。

此外，如果人的动作或行为不是由动词充当谓语来体现，而是由名词充当主语来体现，即通过名物化（nominalization）或语法隐喻（grammatical metaphor）手段来体现，其生命性特征仍在，同样可以产生隐喻性无灵主语句。请比较：

(39) a. The sun shines overhead at noon.
（正午太阳当头照。）
b. Happiness shone on every face.
（每个人的脸上都洋溢着幸福的表情。）
c. * Children shine on their faces.①

(40) a. Cooking smells wafted up from downstairs.
（烧菜的香味从楼下飘了上来。）
b. Worry and anxiety wafted in Southeast Asia about the earthquake and tsunami.

---

① 带 * 号的句子为不合表达习惯，难以接受的句子。

（东南亚各地的人们对这次地震和海啸都满怀担心和忧虑。）
c. * People wafted in Southeast Asia about the earthquake and tsunami.

以上（39a）和（40a）是非隐喻性无灵句。（39b）和（40b）是隐喻性无灵主语句。这里之所以将 Happiness 和 Worry and anxiety 仍视为无灵主语，是因为它们的生命性特征不是存在于作为体词的指称（designation）意义上，而是仍然存在于作为谓词的陈述（assertion）意义上。它们在句中虽然充当了主语，但在指称意义上没有生命性特征。这种通过名物化或语法隐喻手段生成的英语无灵主语句，其生命性概念的跨域映射机制更为复杂。（39c）和（40c）之所以难以接受或不能存在，是因为存在于体词的指称意义上的生命性概念难以或不能进行跨域映射，无法形成概念隐喻。

7.4 结语

每一个客观精练、生动形象的英语无灵主语句都是隐喻句。本节在此结论的基础上，根据概念跨域映射原理，探讨了英语无灵主语句的隐喻性根源，并在认知隐喻的经验基础上，探索了英语无灵主语句的生命性始源。研究发现：①英语无灵主语句的隐喻性直接来源于生命性概念的跨域映射；②英语无灵主语句的生命性概念存在于人的动作或行为中；③只有当生命性概念体现在谓词的陈述意义上，而不是存在于体词的指称意义里，才能进行跨域映射，形成概念隐喻。以上三点，对于解释英语无灵主语句的普遍性和生动性，应该更为清晰、更为合理。

8. 英语无灵主语句的生成机制与表现形式再探[①]

8.1 引言

英语无灵主语句是英语书面语中的常见句型和独特语言现象。何明珠（2003）曾根据"概念隐喻"（conceptual metaphor）和"语法隐喻"（grammatical metaphor）理论对英语无灵主语句的形成原因、语用特征和汉译途径进行过探讨（见第 3 节）。该节虽然解释了英语无灵主语句广泛存在于英语书面语中的原因，但研究的对象仅限于"用没有生命的事物（如实物、抽象概念和动作名词等）作主语，用表达物质过程或心理过程的动词作谓语的句子"。本节试图在此基础上根据系统功能语言学家韩礼德的及物性过程理论，继续对各种英语无灵主语句的生成机制及其表现形式的多样性进行探讨。

[①] 本节部分内容原载于《外语与外语教学》2005 年第 7 期。

8.2 功能、小句与及物性过程理论概述

韩礼德（Halliday, 1994）在《功能语法导论》的引言中指出："功能语法是以功能概念为框架，而不是以形式为框架建立起来的。其功能具有三种既紧密联系又存在区别的意义：语篇解释意义、系统解释意义和语言结构成分解释意义。"所有语言都由三大意义组成，即概念意义、人际意义和语篇意义，这些意义成分统称为三大纯理功能。韩礼德把纯理功能也相应地分为：概念功能、人际功能和语篇功能，其中概念功能又分为经验功能和逻辑功能。

在功能语法中，级阶由四个级组成：小句、词组、单词和词素。小句以上的单位是小句复合体，指两个或多个小句通过并列或从属关系联结起来而构成的一个更大结构单位。小句由词组组成，词组由词组成，词由词素组成。词组包括名词词组、动词词组和副词词组三大类，此外还有小量介词词组和连词词组。小句是个统一体，它的构建不是一种单一结构，而是主语、主位和动作者三种不同功能的多元结构，每种结构解释一种不同的意义，即小句的信息功能、交换功能和表述功能。汤普森（Thompson, 1996：16）认为：小句是指以动词词组为中心延伸出来的语言单位。一个小句必须具有一个含有限定成分的动词词组。

语言的三大纯理功能都分别包括各自的三个系统：概念功能包括及物性、语态和归一性三个系统；人际功能包括语气、情态和语调三个系统；语篇功能包括主位结构、信息结构和衔接三个系统。在及物性系统中，韩礼德分别阐释了六种过程类型：物质过程、心理过程、关系过程、言语过程、

行为过程和存在过程。在系统功能语法中,小句体现上述各个系统的意义。及物性系统中的过程与其参与者和环境成分紧密配合、相互作用。参与者的角色、环境成分的意义类别,以其说明不同的过程而具有不同的意义。不同的过程与其参与者的角色也不同。

8.3 功能语法小句与传统语法句子的区别

如上所述,功能语法中的小句(clause)是一个统一体,它体现主语(subject)、主位(theme)和动作者(actor)三种不同功能所产生的三种不同结构。例如:

结构 功能\小句	The monitor	has cleaned		the room	today
概念 (表述)	动作者 Actor	过程 Process		目标 Goal	环境 Circumstance
人际 (交换)	主语 S(Subject)	限定 F(Finite)	谓体 P(Predicator)	补语 C(Complement)	状语 A(Adjunct)
语篇 (信息)	主位 Theme	述位 Rheme			

首先,从上表可以看出,一个功能语法小句具有三种语法结构,体现三种不同意义和功能,而传统语法句子则只能解释命题意义,只具有一种句法结构。此外,传统语法只注重词、短语和句子的研究,只注重句法功能和句法结构,只看重命题意义,常常忽略功能意义。

其次，一个功能语法小句一般含有三种成分：过程、过程的参与者和与过程相关的环境。这三种成分一般分别由词汇语法中的动词词组、名词词组和副词词组（介词短语）来体现。三者中以过程为核心，它是体现概念（经验）意义的主体。及物性分析也就是小句成分分析，主要分析三种成分之间的关系。不同的过程类型决定不同的参与者角色，而传统语法中的英语句子则固定为 7 种基本句型：SV、SVO、SVC、SVA、SVOO、SVOC 和 SVOA（Quirk, 1992），句子成分之间的关系趋于单一。

再次，功能语法小句是语法的基本单位，两个或多个小句之间若存在逻辑依赖或逻辑语义关系，则可结合起来构成小句复合体，而小句复合体则相当于传统语法中的复合句。韩礼德认为，传统语法中的句子不能从语法特征上区分简单句和复合句，只是一个书写单位，而功能语法中的小句则是实实在在的语法单位。

最后，传统语法句子中的"主语"概念是心理主语（psychological subject）、语法主语（grammatical subject）和逻辑主语（logical subject）的统一体。然而，在实际语篇中，情况并非总是如此。因此，在功能语法小句中，上述三个概念获得三个不同的功能标记名称：主位（theme）、主语（subject）和动作者（actor）。这就给小句的功能和语法分析带来了极大的方便。

以上分析表明：一方面，正是由于传统语法句子和功能语法小句之间存在上述区别，我们才有可能运用功能语法及物性系统中的过程类型理论来解释多种形式的无灵主语句广泛存在的原因。另一方面，虽然传统语法句子与功能语法小句存在上述区别，但从根本上说，它们都是语言的基本应用单位，是不同语法系统用来分析和解释相同语言现象的中介，总体说来，同大于异。以下提到的无灵小句或小句复合体与无灵主语句指同一语言现象。

8.4 及物性过程类型与英语无灵主语句的生成机制和表现形式

如上文所述，韩礼德将及物性系统中的过程区分为六种类型：物质过程、心理过程、关系过程、行为过程、言语过程和存在过程。为了便于解释英语无灵主语句的成因与多样性特征，特对各种类型的过程举例进行分析。

8.4.1 物质过程

物质过程就是"动作"过程。动作可以涉及一个实体（entity），也可以涉及两个实体，也就是说，物质过程可以有一个参与者，也可以有两个参与者。如果只有一个参与者，这个参与者肯定就是动作者（actor）。体现该物质过程的动词词组在传统语法中叫不及物动词。由于动作者大都是生命体或有灵实体，即人或动物，所以在这种情况下一般不会有无灵小句出现。如果有，那只能通过概念隐喻（conceptual metaphor）来实现。（何明珠，2003）例如：

Nowadays	scientific ideas	flow	rapidly
	Actor	Process: material	
A	S	FP	A

（1）His idea of a bright future collapsed all of a sudden.

（2）Silence reigns everywhere.

（3）News arrived too late.

85

如果某个物质过程具有两个参与者,动作者和目标(goal),那么,将它们分别安排在过程的前后位置上,便是对主动语态与被动语态的选择。若选择主动语态,无灵小句的产生也要借助概念隐喻手段。如:

Presently	something	hit	the door
	Actor	Process	Goal
A	S	FP	C

(Bloor and Bloor, 2001: 112)

(4) Anxiety tore her into pieces.
(5) Successive exertion has already chipped a few pounds off him.
(6) Their brilliant acting drew stormy and lengthy applause from the audience.

相反,若选择被动语态,则会自然产生无灵小句。但这种无灵小句一般不难理解,也很难产生生动形象的表现效果。如:

Presently	the door	was opened	by something
	The door	was opened	by Jerry
	Goal	Process	Actor
A	S	FP	A

(Bloor and Bloor, 2001: 112)

语态的选择在传统语法的句法分析中很重要,因为主动语态句中作宾语的成分到了被动语态句中就充当主语了,但在功能语法中无论语态如何,参与者(动作者与目标)角色

保持不变。(Bloor & Bloor, 2001: 112)

8.4.2 心理过程

心理过程描述心理状态或心理活动,常用 think, know, feel, smell, hear, see, want, like, hate, admire, enjoy, fear 等动词来实现。心理过程有两个参与者:感觉者(senser)和现象(phenomenon)。感觉者一定能感觉,必须由人或动物等有灵生物来充当,而现象则既可以是有灵生物也可以是无灵事物。虽然主动语态的心理过程小句通常都是有灵小句,但通过如下途径生成的心理过程无灵小句或无灵小句复合体也很常见。

8.4.2.1 隐喻化

上文提到,物质过程无灵小句的生成主要借助隐喻化途径。同样,心理过程隐喻化现象也很普遍。最常见的隐喻化心理动词包括:see, witness, know, find, believe, determine, decide 等。在这种情况下,过程参与者之一的感觉者被拟人化了。如:

Beijing	has witnessed	many changes	in the past few years
Senser	Process	Phenomenon	
S	FP	C	A

(7) Dusk found the child crying in the street.

(8) Her excitement knows no bounds.

(9) His weariness and the increasing heat determined him to sit down in the first convenient shade.

8.4.2.2 双向成对心理动词

英语中有一种双向成对的心理动词，或称 like-please 类成对心理动词，可以直接生成无灵小句。like 类动词要求充当主语的感觉者是生命体（animate entity），因为感觉者应该具有感知力；而充当 please 类动词主语的现象可以是无生命体（inanimate entity），因为现象不需要感知力，可用无生命代词 it 来指代。如：

Children	fear	darkness
Senser	Process	Phenomenon
S	FP	C

Darkness	frightens	children
Phenomenon	Process	Senser
S	FP	C

这种双向成对的心理动词韩礼德（1994：117）列出了 10 对：like, please; fear, frighten; wonder at, amaze; not understand, puzzle; enjoy, delight; forget, escape; notice, strike; believe, convince; admire, impress; mind, upset。卓勇光（2004）在此基础上增补了三对：fancy, attract; worry about, worry; know, be familiar to。

"虽然 like 类心理动词并非都有一个在语义上完全相等的 please 类心理动词来对应，但这类动词的双向性，即感觉者和被感觉的现象都可以充当主语，且无需改变语态，则是此类心理动词的普遍特征"（Halliday, 1994：116）。唐青叶（2004）归纳了 27 个 like 类和 34 个 please 类心理动词，当然这类动词还远远不止这些。使用 please 类心理动词直接生

8. 英语无灵主语句的生成机制与表现形式再探
English sentences with inanimate subjects

成的无灵主语句在英语中广泛存在，且表现力极强。例如：

(10) A good idea suddenly struck me.
(11) But the quiet puzzles me all the same.
(12) The answer surprised me all the more.

8.4.2.3 被动语态

很明显，上述双向成对心理动词中只有 like 类动词的被动式才能生成无灵小句或无灵小句复合体。例如：

(13) His impudence is known to all.
(14) Kindness is more easily forgotten than rudeness.
(15) It is firmly believed that communism will triumph throughout the world.
(16) It has been strongly desired that the dry weather could soon be over.

例（15）和（16）中由无生命代词 it（在功能语法中叫 dummy subject 或 empty subject；在传统语法中叫 formal subject）引导的无灵小句复合体，因其具有委婉、含蓄和客观等特点，而在英语正式书面语中特别常见。此外，这种无灵小句复合体如能与语法隐喻表达式并用，其客观性可以达到极致。卓勇光（2004）通过如下例句展示了语义客观性的渐变过程：

A. I like what he said on that matter. （明确主观）
B. What he said on that matter pleases me. （非明确主观）

C. The agreement of our opinions on that matter is a delight.（非明确客观）
D. It is a delight that there is an agreement of opinions on that matter.（明确客观）

8.4.3 关系过程

关系过程有多个次类，分别拥有不同的参与者。其中有些次类可以直接生成无灵小句。

8.4.3.1 描述性关系过程

此类关系过程的参与者，载体（carrier）与属性（attribute）既不能直接换位也不能通过语态换位。体现此类关系过程的动词除了 be 以外，还有 look, sound, smell, feel, taste; seem, appear, turn out; remain, stay, keep; become, turn, grow, get; 等等。借助这些动词，可直接生成关系过程无灵小句。不过，这类句子很普遍，没有特殊的修辞效果。若能借助无生命代词 it 生成关系过程无灵小句复合体，则修辞效果大不一样。例如：

(17) Your story sounds complete nonsense.
(18) The weather has become warm today.
(19) A lot of work remains unfinished.
(20) It seems to be a great pity that he can't join us.

8.4.3.2 识别性关系过程与其他

此类关系过程的参与者——被识别者（identified）与识别者（identifier）或标记（token）与价值（value）——之间可直接双向换位，但换位后由于视角发生变化，语义也会

8. 英语无灵主语句的生成机制与表现形式再探
English sentences with inanimate subjects

变化。体现此类关系过程的动词除了 be 以外，还有 play, act as, serve as; mean, indicate, imply, suggest, reflect; equal, add up to, make; comprise, include; represent, stand for; exemplify, illustrate; express, signify; 等等。

此类关系过程无灵小句不受语态限制。但随着语态的改变，参与者角色也会改变，因而意义也可能发生某些变化。例如：

(21) This offer represents your best chance to win a prize.
(22) One criterion is represented by genetic diversity.
(23) My story concerns a terrible traffic accident.
(24) a. The fair takes up the whole day.
　　 b. The whole day is taken up by the fair.
(25) a. Music accompanied her dance.
　　 b. Her dance was accompanied by music.
(26) a. The piano is Peter's.
　　 b. The piano belongs to Peter.
　　 c. The piano is owned by Peter.

例（21）和（22）中体现关系过程的动词（represent）无论主动式还是被动式都相当于 be；但两者的参与者位置正好相反。例（23）（24）和（25）中的动词相当于 be 加上一个相关的介词（is about, is for 与 was with），这种过程因而也叫环境性关系过程，这些动词就叫环境性动词（circumstantial verb）。例（26）反映的是一种属有关系，此类过程与其参与者角色也很不相同，因而又叫属有性关系过程。

8.4.4 行为过程

行为过程是指人的生理和心理行为,因其兼有物质过程、心理过程以及言语过程的特征而成为六类过程中最难区分的一类。行为过程的参与者只有一个,那就是行为者(behaver)。行为者通常是人,所以行为过程无灵小句的形成只能借助拟人等隐喻化手段。例如:

(27) Fortune is smiling on us now.
(28) The machines are chattering and clattering all the while.

有人把"The car slid away."也看作行为过程小句(Bloor and Bloor, 2001:126),但从时态特征来看,更应属物质过程小句。

8.4.5 言语过程

言语过程的主要参与者,言语者(sayer),可以是生命体,也可以是非生命体。韩礼德(1994:140)指出:"言语者可以是发出信号的任何事物。"(The sayer can be anything that puts out a signal.) 言语过程的这一特征是言语过程无灵小句和小句复合体广泛存在的主要原因。例如:

(29) The red light says stop.
(30) The notice tells you to be quiet.
(31) My watch says it is half past ten.
(32) The guidebook tells you where everything is.

8. 英语无灵主语句的生成机制与表现形式再探
English sentences with inanimate subjects

言语过程的参与者除言语者外，还有言语接受者（receiver）、言语内容（verbiage）和言语目标（target）。三者中，言语内容往往是无生命体，因此让言语内容充当被动式小句的主语，或选用无生命代词 it 充当形式主语，动词用被动式，是生成言语过程无灵小句和小句复合体的主要途径。例如：

(33) The mystery has never been explained.
(34) A story is being told about the hero's adventure.
(35) It is said that the new government will carry out a series of reforms.
(36) It has been suggested that a subway should be built between Changsha and Zhuzhou as soon as possible.

很明显，例（35）和（36）与例（15）和（16）有很大的相似性，这是因为言语过程兼有心理过程和关系过程的特征，处于二者的中间状态，需要细心分辨。其实，及物性系统中六大过程类型之间的关系组成了一个圆周形连续统（Halliday, 1994: 108）。韩礼德（1994: 141）以动词 imply 为例说明了从言语过程到关系过程的渐进历程：

A. Responding, the minister implied that the policy had been changed.
B. Responding, the minister implied a change of policy.
C. The minister's response implied that the policy had been changed.
D. The minister's response implied a change of policy.

以上例子还告诉我们,在过程类型的渐变进程中,借助语法隐喻手段,进行形式糅合,使意义潜势的客观化与隐喻化同现,是生成英语无灵主语句的重要机制和主要目的。

8.4.6 存在过程

在功能语法中,存在过程小句中的"there"没有表意功能,但需要它充当主语,称为 empty subject 或 dummy subject,与其他过程小句中作状语的副词"there"在功能上有明显区别。体现存在过程的典型动词是 be,但其他常见的存在动词 exist, remain, arise, occur, happen; follow, precede, ensue; stand, lie, stretch; erupt, flourish, prevail; 等等,更能展示存在过程小句的生动形象性。存在过程的主要参与者被称为存在者(existent),既可以是人或实物,也可以是抽象概念、行为或事件等。因此,英语的存在过程小句是英语中最常见和最具特色的无灵主语句之一。例如:

(37) There seems to be a serious problem here.

(38) Has there been a phone call for me?

(39) a. There prevailed a vigorous revolutionary atmosphere throughout the country in the 1960's.

b. A vigorous revolutionary atmosphere prevailed throughout the country in the 1960's.

(40) a. There took place a robbery in the street last night.

b. A robbery took place in the street last night.

例(39)a 和(39)b 与例(40)a 和(40)b 这两对小

8. 英语无灵主语句的生成机制与表现形式再探
English sentences with inanimate subjects

句所表述的意义差别不大,但它们各自属于不同的过程类型[①]:前者为存在过程,后者为物质过程。不同的过程类型具有不同的主位(信息)结构和不同的语篇功能。因此,在选用哪种过程类型来表述某一意义时,应视具体语境而定。

8.5 结语

根据功能语法及物性系统过程类型理论,对英语无灵小句和小句复合体(即英语无灵主语句)的生成机制和表现形式进行的分析表明:经验功能及物性系统六种过程(物质过程、心理过程、关系过程、行为过程、言语过程和存在过程)都适合无灵小句和小句复合体的产生,但生成机制和表现形式各不相同,能产性也不一样。无灵小句在物质过程和行为过程中能产性不高,必须借助拟人等隐喻化手段方可生成;无灵小句在心理过程、关系过程和言语过程中的能产性较高,生成机制也各不相同:有的可以自然生成,有的则需要借助语态转换、使用无生命代词 it、或使用双向成对心理动词等途径来实现;无灵小句在存在过程中的能产性很高,因为在此过程中,无灵小句能自然生成,无需借助其他任何手段。文中例句已将英语无灵主语句的各种形式基本列出,虽然未能穷尽,也已举其大端。从无灵主语句这个侧面,体察一种形式蕴涵多种意义,相似语义依存多种形式这一语言事实,对提高语言理解和表达能力具有一定的理论和实践意义。

---

① 有关不同过程类型的区分,请参见 Halliday (1994: 106 – 175)。

9. 生命性与英语无灵主语句的类型分析[①]

9.1 引言

无灵主语又叫非人称主语或物称主语,钱歌川先生(1981)曾称之为无生物主语。无灵(inanimate)指无生命,有灵(animate)指有生命。本节讨论的英语无灵主语句(English Sentences with Inanimate Subjects, ESWIS)包括英语中所有用无生命特征的词、短语或从句充当主语的句子。为了更好地分析与理解广泛存在于英语中的无灵主语句这一独特语言现象,本节拟从主谓语生命性搭配关系,主语类型和语义特征三个角度,对英语无灵主语句进行尝试性分类研究。

[①] 本节内容原载于《湘潭师范学院学报(社会科学版)》2005年第4期。

9. 生命性与英语无灵主语句的类型分析
English sentences with inanimate subjects

9.2 英汉主谓搭配关系与生命性体现的差异

9.3.1 英汉主谓搭配关系差异

英汉对比研究表明：英语重形合，汉语重意合。著名语言学家王力先生（1985）曾指出："就句子结构而论，西洋语言是法治的，中国语言是人治的。"当代学者徐通锵先生（1993）也指出：英语是一种"语法型语言"，汉语是一种"语义型语言"。作为形合、法治和语法型的英语，其句子都必须具有主语，并且以动词为核心，在主语和谓语之间存在许多相互制约的语法关系。由于这种语法形式上的制约关系，英语里只有名词才能作主语，其他任何词要想作主语，必须使其具有名词的性质，做一些形式上的改变。（马秉义，1995）相反，作为意合、人治和语义型的汉语，其句子中的主语，一是可以在意义清晰的情况下省略，二是几乎可以让任何词性的词直接作主语，主语与谓语之间没有语法形式上的严格限制。然而，英语句子中主语与谓语之间语义和逻辑搭配关系却由于词义的引申幅度大等原因而没有严格限制；相反，汉语句子中的主语和谓语之间在语义与逻辑搭配关系上一般都有严格的制约。英汉主谓之间的生命性搭配关系就是一个很好的例子。这也是本节将要探讨的主要内容之一。例如：

（1）a. The man killed the fish in the river.
（主语是施事）
b. 那人杀死了河里的鱼。

(2) a. Poison killed the fish in the river.
   （主语是工具）
   b. 毒药把河里的鱼毒死了。
   （比较：毒药杀死了河里的鱼*。）①
(3) a. Pollution killed the fish in the river.
   （主语是原因）
   b. 污染把河里的鱼弄死了。
   （比较：污染杀死了河里的鱼*。）

例（1）a 和 b 中的主语"the man"和"那人"都是生命体，具有施发动作和行为的能力，谓语"killed"和"杀死"都是有意识的行为和动作。主谓在生命性这一意义域中的搭配是一致的，因而英汉句子都是正常的表达方式。例（2）a 和 b 与例（3）a 和 b 却不同：在英语中，主语与谓语在生命性这个意义域里没有严格的一致性限制，（2）a 和（3）a 是正常的表达式；而在汉语中，表示工具和原因的无灵主语没有实施动作和行为的能力，主谓在生命性这一意义域中的搭配不一致，因而很难成为可接受的表达方式，必须调整主谓搭配。

9.3.2　生命性在英汉主谓搭配之间体现的差异

"生命性（animacy），即对生命体与非生命体之间的区分，在人类语言的语法中普遍存在。对生命性的语言表征及心理现实性探索已成为语言研究的热点之一"（张京鱼等，2004）。生命性不仅体现在充当句子主语的名词这种客观实体上，而且还反映在充当句子谓语的动词这种动作、过程或

---

① 带＊号的句子为不可接受或很难接受的句子。

9. 生命性与英语无灵主语句的类型分析
English sentences with inanimate subjects

状态中。在现代汉语中,不仅有灵名词和无灵名词区分严格,而且还有有灵动词和无灵动词的明确区别:"有灵动词表示人和人类社会组织才有的行为或动作,如:看、讲、说、写、杀、送、切、拿、提、取、爱、恨、哭、笑等。无灵动词表示无生命事物的一些无意志的运动、作用或变化,如:倒、变、吸引、排斥等。"(张今,1981)由于汉语思维往往以"人"这个主体为中心,认为只有"人"才能执行有意识的动作或行为,因此有灵动词作谓语必须与有灵主语密切配合,无灵动词作谓语,只能与无灵主语相搭配。由此可见,生命性限制了汉语句子主语与谓语的选择与搭配。

然而,在英语中,一方面由于有灵动词与无灵动词界限划分并不十分清楚(喻家楼等,1977),同一动词,由于词义的引申幅度大等原因,有时用作有灵动词,有时又用作无灵动词,全凭该动词在具体语境中的特定意义来决定。例如:

(4) a. He has escaped punishment.
    b. His name escaped me.(刘树阁,1995)
(5) a. I slipped a note into his hand under the table.
    b. Sorry, your birthday slipped my mind.

另一方面,由于英语思维强调客观,注重客体对主体的作用和影响,因而在英语句子中无灵主语得到广泛使用。这样一来,生命性无法限制英语句子主语与谓语的搭配,也就是说,无灵主语不一定硬要与无灵谓语搭配。此外,在很多情况下,为了达到表达的生动性、客观性、权威性或委婉性等目的,说英语的人们还常常通过隐喻化手段故意打破主语与谓语之间生命性搭配一致的关系。无灵主语句由此而普遍存在于英语语言中,这给中国英语学习者带来了不少理解和使用上的困难,因而有必要对其进行系统分析和分类研究。

9.3 英语无灵主语句的分类依据:生命性、主语类型与语义特征

9.3.1 生命性作为分类依据:结构性无灵主语句与隐喻性无灵主语句

如上文所述,生命性在人类语言的语法中普遍存在,不仅体现在名词上,而且还反映在动词里。虽然,英语动词的生命性常常随词义与语境的改变而变化,但这并不意味生命性不在英语动词上体现。恰恰相反,在特定的英语句子中,充当谓语的动词其生命性是很明显的。例如,在系表结构句和 there be 存在句中,若将静态动词 be 换成其他动态连系动词,其生命性便跃然纸上:

(6) Your idea sounds reasonable.
(7) There stands a new house on the roadside.

因此,我们可以依据英语主语与谓语的生命性搭配关系,将英语无灵主语句划分为两大类:结构性无灵主语句与隐喻性无灵主语句。所谓结构性无灵主语句,是指由无灵主语与无灵谓语搭配而成的句子。这类英语无灵主语句中的主语与谓语在生命性这一语义特征上的搭配关系与汉语句子相同,因此一般不会引起理解和使用上的困难,容易被中国英语学习者掌握(次类分析见 9.3.2 节)。例如:

(8) The accident happened last night.

9. 生命性与英语无灵主语句的类型分析
English sentences with inanimate subjects

(9) The work has been finished. ①

(10) It is easy to finish the work. ②

(11) There is no time to finish the work.

所谓隐喻性无灵主语句是指由无灵主语与有灵谓语组合生成的句子，或由无灵主语与无灵谓语组合而成，但其生命性语义特征隐含在主语与其修饰语之间的句子，前者为概念隐喻句，后者为语法隐喻句。这类英语无灵主语句中的主语与谓语在生命性这一语义特征上的搭配或体现与汉语句子相反或相异，常常难以被中国英语学习者理解与掌握。例如：

(12) Excitement knew no bounds at the party.

(13) His acceptance of bribes led to his arrest.

例（12）为概念隐喻句，例（13）为语法隐喻句。有关英语无灵主语句的隐喻性特征，下文（9.3.3）将举例作进一步分析。

9.3.2 主语类型作为分类依据：结构性无灵主语句的三种次类

关于主语的类型，不同的语言学家，从不同的分析角度出发，得出不同的分类结果，少的有三种，多的有十多种。这里综合两家之说，作为我们分析英语结构性无灵主语句的依据。黄伯荣等（1983）在其所著的《现代汉语》中指出："从主语与谓语的意义关系上看，主语有三种：①施事主语，

---

① 英语有灵动词的被动式相当于无灵动词。
② 动词 be 是典型的无灵动词。

即表示动作发出者；②受事主语，即表示动作承受者；③中性主语，即主语不是施事，也不是受事，而是谓语描写、判断、说明的对象。"潘文国（1997：212）在其《汉英语对比纲要》中把英语主语分为四种，即施事主语、受事主语、形式主语、主题主语。从书中所给的例句（The book is very interesting.）与解释看来，潘氏的"主题主语"与黄氏的"中性主语"基本相同，指的是同一概念。由此我们得知：英语与汉语的主语类型基本相似，只有"形式主语"是英语的"特产"。

很明显，结构性无灵主语句中没有施事主语，因为无灵主语不可能实施动作或行为。这样，结构性无灵主语句又可以分为三种次类：无灵中性主语句、无灵受事主语句和无灵形式主语句。

9.3.2.1 无灵中性主语句

无灵中性主语句是指无灵主语在句中充当谓语描写、判断、说明的对象。这类句子根据其谓语动词的类别和语义特征，可表现为如下四种类型：

第一，S + link V + C。例如：

(14) A spade and a rake are necessary tools for this work.
(15) Your ideal is unrealistic.

这一句型中的连系动词只能是 be, seem, appear 等少数几个，如果使用 sound, look, feel, smell, taste, lie, stand 等其他连系动词，就应算作隐喻性无灵主语句，因为那样句子就会具有隐喻意义。

第二，S + Vi。例如：

(16) The rain stopped but the snow continued.
(17) Traffic accidents happen frequently on this road.

这一句型中的不及物动词一般反映自然现象或事件的发生、延续或终止，常见的有：start, begin, rise, fall, occur, approach, coincide, suffice, elapse, collapse, 等等。

第三，S + Vt + O。例如：

(18) The appointment slipped my memory.
(19) Tractors facilitate farming.

这一句型中的及物动词一般陈述事实，含有使役意义，必须与无灵主语搭配使用，常见的有：cost, elude, embody, exemplify, defy, symbolize, suffice, 等等。

第四，S + Vt + O (sb.)。例如：

(20) Darkness frightens children.
(21) His answer puzzled me.

这一句型中的及物动词一般表现一种心理状态或感受，由于句子的无灵主语代表一种现象，而宾语则是这种现象的感受者，因而又叫宾语经验者动词。常用的此类动词包括：amaze, amuse, delight, dismay, horrify, perplex, surprise, thrill, upset, vex, frustrate, irritate, remind, convince, 等等。

9.3.2.2 无灵受事主语句

无灵受事主语句一般通过有灵及物动词的被动语态来生成。这种句子容易理解与掌握。例如：

(22) The plan will soon be examined.//
(23) The yellow leaves were scattered everywhere in the autumn wind.

需要说明的是,并非所有有灵及物动词的被动语态都能生成无灵主语句。例如,上述宾语经验者动词或双宾语及物动词等的被动语态则很少生成无灵主语句。

9.3.2.3 无灵形式主语句

如上所述,形式主语是英语的"特产",汉语中无此概念。其实,形式主语都是无灵主语。因此,无灵形式主语句的说法有语义重复之嫌,但为了将其与其他两种无灵主语句区分开来的分类目的,这里只好不得已而称之。无灵形式主语句还可分为两类,其表现形式复杂,下面分别举例说明。

9.3.2.3.1 由 It 引导的无灵形式主语句

由 It 引导的无灵形式主语句有如下五种情况:

第一,It 作主语,泛指时间、距离、天气和自然环境等抽象概念,或复指上下文提及的事物或概念,句中没有其他真正主语。例如:

(24) It is six o'clock now, it is clearing up and it is quiet everywhere.//
(25) It is going to be an increased satisfaction to our customers if we are happy. (赵桂华,2002)

第二,It 作形式主语,不定式短语作句子的真正主语。例如:

(26) It does my heart good and it gives me pleasure to

9. 生命性与英语无灵主语句的类型分析
English sentences with inanimate subjects

confide a little in you.
(27) It is his fate to leave here in the evening.

第三，It 作形式主语，动名词短语作句子的真正主语。例如：

(28) It's no use crying over spilt milk.
(29) It does not make any difference my beingthere.

第四，It 作形式主语，主语从句作句子的真正主语。例如：

(30) It is reported that the president will visit China in June.
(31) It does not matter whether he attends the meeting or not.

（当然，上述不定式短语、动名词短语或主语从句也可以不用形式主语 It 指代，而分别直接作主语，生成无灵主语句，在此不详述。）

第五，It 作形式主语，构成强调句型。例如：

(32) It was John who met your sister in the zoo yesterday.
(33) It was in the zoo that John met your sister yesterday.

9.3.2.3.2 由 There 引导的无灵形式主语句

人们对 There + be 句型有不同解释。传统语法将 be 后面的无定名词或名词短语当作主语，把 there 看作引导词。在韩礼德的系统功能语法中，there 被看作空主语（empty subject），或形式主语（dummy subject），动词 be 体现存在过程。

(34) There were staring eyes and dropping jaws all around us.
(35) There was a moment of throbbing suspense.

9.3.3 语义特征作为分类依据：隐喻性无灵主语句的两种次类

上文（9.3.1）提到，根据生命性语义特征的体现形式，隐喻性无灵主语句可分为概念隐喻无灵主语句（ESWIS from conceptual metaphor）与语法隐喻无灵主语句（ESWIS from grammatical metaphor）两种次类。这里将根据两类无灵主语的语义特征，分别举例简述各自不同的组句方式。

9.3.3.1 概念隐喻无灵主语句

如上文所述，这类句子由无灵主语与有灵谓语搭配生成，其新颖、生动的表达效果是通过概念隐喻产生的。莱考夫（Lakoff）概念隐喻理论中的核心内容就是概念映射（cross-domain mapping）原理，即人们在认识世界的过程中，总是存在两个认知域（cognitive domain），其中一个认知域中的概念总是向另一个认知域映射。就我们正在讨论的这类无灵主语句而言，概念隐喻产生的过程就是：通过将（谓语的）生命性认知域中的概念映射到（主语的）非生命性认知域中，使无生命的事物或概念获得生命性语义特征。这也就是传统修辞学中的拟人修辞格。充当这类无灵主语的可以是具体事物也可以是抽象概念，如时间、地点等。例如：

(36) A good idea suddenly struck me.
(37) Dusk found the child crying in the street.
(38) Beijing has witnessed many changes in the past few years.
(39) His presence of mind never deserted him.

9.3.3.2 语法隐喻无灵主语句

从某种意义上说，这类句子应该归纳在结构性无灵主语句一类中，因为它实际上体现的是英语"化零为整"（许嘉庆，2001）的组句方式。然而，由于这类句子的生成完全依赖于韩礼德所阐述的语法隐喻，因此我们将由此生成的无灵主语句归纳在隐喻性无灵主语句一类中。上文提到，这类句子表面上由无灵主语与无灵谓语搭配而成，但实际上句中的生命性语义特征体现得淋漓尽致，这本身就是一种"隐喻"。另外，语法隐喻的核心是名词化（nominalization），名词化就是将动词或形容词转换成名词，即不用名词而用动词或形容词来表述实体，将过程或属性体现为参与者。很明显，充当这类无灵主语的名词都是由名词化生成的名词，他们表面上是抽象的无灵名词，但在语义上仍保留了相关动词或形容词的某些生命性语义特征，加上与其搭配的修饰语之间的相互映射，生命性语义特征尽显无遗。例如：

(40) The execution of the prisoner preceded the president's arrival.
(41) The discovery of a gun in his possession leads to the suspicion of his being the murderer.
(42) The visibility of his impatience was very great.

9.4 结语

本节从英汉主谓搭配关系的差异分析着手,解释了生命性对英汉两种语言主谓搭配关系的制约力大小不同的原因。然后,以生命性为主要分类依据,将英语无灵主语句分为两大类:结构性无灵主语句与隐喻性无灵主语句。在此基础上,又以主语类型和语义特征作为分类依据,将英语无灵主语句分为五种次类:在结构性无灵主语句中分出无灵中性主语句、无灵受事主语句和无灵形式主语句三类;在隐喻性无灵主语句中分出概念隐喻无灵主语句与语法隐喻无灵主语句两类。最后,在五种次类的基础上,条分缕析,举例分析了13种类型的英语无灵主语句,图示如下:

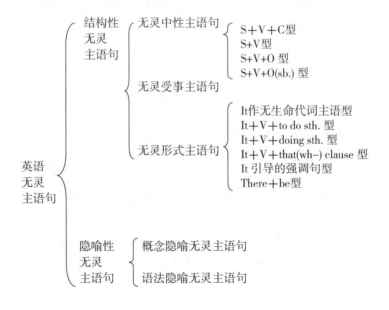

9. 生命性与英语无灵主语句的类型分析
English sentences with inanimate subjects

本节对英语无灵主语句所做的分类研究仅为一种尝试。虽然分类依据的合理性、解释的精确性以及分析的全面性和系统性都还有待进一步论证，但分类探讨英语无灵主语句有利于更加全面、深刻地理解这一语言现象，更加正确、灵活地运用这一独特而又常见的句型，这一点是毋庸置疑的。

10. 英语无灵主语句的汉译策略与方法探讨[①]

10.1 引言

由于英语无灵主语句是一种有别于汉语表达方式的独特语言现象,对中国英语学习者来说不易理解和掌握,因而不少学者对其进行了大量研究。尤其对这种常见而又特殊句型的汉译研究更是不在少数:钱歌川(1981)、陈文伯(1990)、连淑能(1993)、刘树阁(1995)、潘文国(1997)、喻家楼和胡开全(1997)、吴显友(1998)、席建国和马苏勇(2002)、赵桂华(2002)、吴群(2002)、何明珠(2003a)等。这些研究大都从英汉思维特征对比等角度出发,选择归化策略,通过更换主语或改变句型结构的意译途径,探讨将这种独具特色的典型英语句子译成地道规范汉语句子的有效方法。然而,魏志成(2003:335)在其近著《英汉语比较导论》中,通过对英汉5个基本句型的常式和变式逐一进行比较,得出英汉句型大同小异,"汉语句型的使用范围至今仍然处于一种动态的演化过程之中"的结论,

---

[①] 本节部分内容原载于《中南大学学报(社会科学版)》2005年第3期。

并提出"译文在可以被接受的情况下,没有必要任意变动原文形式(如主语或句型),因为形式就是意义的体现",并以英汉无灵主语句的互译为例对其结论进行了论述。本节试图在已有研究的基础上,通过问卷调查和译例分析,对英语无灵主语句的汉译策略与方法作进一步探索。

10.2 理论概述与研究思路

讨论翻译策略与方法离不开两对概念:归化与异化和意译与直译。近期,我国译界对这两对概念的讨论非常热烈,发表了不少真知灼见,明确了各自的定义,辨别了二者的异同。"在合乎译文语言的全民规范的情况下,译文刻意求真,通过保留原作形貌(表达方式)来保持原作的内容和风格,这种翻译方法叫直译。使用译文语言中功用与原文相同或相似的表达方式,以代替原作中因两种语言不同而无法保留的内容与形式之间的相互关系。力求做到虽失原作形貌,但从不同范围的上下文看,仍不失原作的内容而且与原作的风格相适应。这种翻译方法叫意译。"(乔曾锐,2000:244 – 291)归化指"在翻译中采用透明、流畅的风格,最大限度地淡化原文陌生感的翻译策略",而异化指"在一定程度上保留原文的异域性,故意打破目标语言常规的翻译"(转引自王仁强,2004)。直译与意译的区别是在原文内容与风格得以较好传达的前提下,看是否保留了原作的句子形式特点,主要体现在表达形式这一层面上。而归化与异化不仅表现在语言形式层面上,而且也表现在对文化因素的处理上。总之,直译与意译是翻译方法,而归化与异化是翻译策略,二者不在一个层次上,后者指导前者。(刘艳丽和杨自俭,2002)

英语无灵主语句这种独特句型的汉译，主要涉及具体的翻译方法，但翻译方法的选择需要翻译策略的指导，所以本文对策略与方法都有所论及，但主要集中讨论在异化策略指导下，直译这类句子的可行性和局限性。孙致礼（2003）指出，文学翻译中运用异化策略有两个制约因素，"一是译入语语言文化规范的限度，二是译入语读者接受能力的限度"。本节试图通过问卷调查和译例分析证明：在英语无灵主语句的汉译过程中运用异化策略进行直译也要受上述两个因素的制约。问卷调查将有助于我们了解不同汉语读者对异化策略指导下直译英语无灵主语句的接受限度；译例分析，即分析不同译者对同一英语无灵主语句的汉译结果，将帮助我们认识汉语语言文化规范对译者进行直译的局限性。

10.3 直译英语无灵主语句的接受度问卷调查

10.3.1 调查设计

本调查所使用的调查工具是由笔者从不同出处选取的25个英语无灵主语句的"直译"汉语句子组合而成。这里所说的直译，是指在汉译句子中既保留英语句子的无灵主语，又保持句型结构不变。所选英语句子的无灵主语和句型结构，种类齐全、涉及面广、具有代表性（参见附件1）。为了不给懂英语的受试带来选择干扰，以保证他们仅凭汉语语感做出判断，问卷上未附对应英语句子和"意译"汉语句子。但为了对比和讨论的方便，特在此将二者列出。

（1）The pain in his arms made it difficult to undo his

10. 英语无灵主语句的汉译策略与方法探讨
English sentences with inanimate subjects

  clothes.

  他手臂疼痛，脱衣服不方便。

（2）His presence of mind never deserted him.

  他向来都能遇事保持镇定自若。

（3）The introduction of the new equipment in the factory has led to a steady increase in production.

  该厂引进了新设备，生产稳步增长。

（4）Presence is often made known to the occupants by a knock on the door.

  来人常常先敲门，以便房间里的人知道有人来了。

（5）Computerization of the office has greatly facilitated management.

  办公室实现了电脑化，这给管理工作带来了很大方便。

（6）His impatience to get started was written on his face.

  一看他脸上的神色，就知道他迫不及待地想要行动起来。

（7）My suggestion is a ban of smoking in the meeting room.

  我建议会议室里禁烟。

（8）The past five centuries witnessed great development in Chinese drama.

  五百年来，中国戏剧有了很大发展。

（9）Shouts of protest sprang up from the angry crowd.

  愤怒的人群发出了抗议的呼声。

（10）The discovery of a knife in his possession lends to all a suspicion of his being the murderer.

大家发现他拥有一把刀，因而怀疑他就是凶手。

(11) Like good looks and money, quick-mindedness passed her by.
她模样不好，手里没钱，脑子也不灵光了。

(12) A new thought had struck him.
他有了一个新想法（念头）。

(13) Life had never brought them a gloomier hour.
他们一生中从未经历过比这更阴郁的时刻。

(14) Between six and seven will suit me.
对我来说，在6点至7点之间比较适合。

(15) This medicine knows no bounds of effectiveness.
这种药的效力无限。

(16) Sickness robbed her of the confidence in accomplishing the task.
她疾病缠身，丧失了完成这项任务的信心。

(17) Successive exertion has already chipped a few pounds off him.
他连日辛劳，已经瘦下好几磅了。

(18) His acceptance of bribes led to his arrest.
他因受贿而被捕。

(19) His help will ensure my success.
他肯帮忙，我一定会成功。

(20) Pork has priced itself out of his dish.
猪肉太贵，他吃不起。

(21) Poison killed the fish in the river.
毒药把河里的鱼毒死了。

(22) Pollution killed the fish in the river.
污染把河里的鱼弄死了。

(23) His wealth enables him to do anything.
他有钱,什么都可以做。
(24) Bad weather prevented us from starting.
天气太坏,我们无法动身。
(25) A few steps across the lawn brought me to a large, splendid hotel.
我横过草坪只走几步,就来到了一座华丽的大旅馆。

本调查的调查对象分4组共80人。他们是随机抽取的湖南工业大学师专校区20名40岁以上中文专业教师、20名40岁以下英语专业教师、20名中文专业二年级学生和20名英语专业三年级学生。(80名受试所作选择的详细情况见附件2)

10.3.2 调查和统计方法与调查结果

本调查于2004年12月完成。学生受试分组在6分钟内独立完成选择任务,教师受试随机在5分钟内做出选择。所有调查和统计工作全部由笔者完成,80份问卷全部有效。问卷给每个汉译句子提供5个选项:a 完全可接受;b 基本可接受;c 不能确定;d 基本不可接受;e 完全不可接受。统计时,为了计算方便,视选择a或b两项者均为接受该直译译文,选择其他三项者皆为不接受。统计结果见表10-1。

10.3.3 调查结果分析

4组受试中,中文专业师生两组对直译句子的接受度明显大于英语专业师生两组。接受度最大的是中文专业教师组(63%),接受度最小的是英语专业学生组(47%)。出现这

表 10-1 4组（80名）受试对25个直译句子的接受程度调查统计

接受度 句序	20名中文教师 选a, b项（人）	比例（%）	20名英语教师 选a, b项（人）	比例（%）	20名中文系学生 选a, b项（人）	比例（%）	20名英语系学生 选a, b项（人）	比例（%）	合计 选a, b项（人）	平均比例（%）
1	5+13	90	3+13	80	7+9	80	2+15	85	17+50	84
2	1+5	30	0+6	30	5+6	55	4+0	20	10+17	34
3	8+7	75	8+8	80	6+7	65	2+10	60	24+32	73
4	0+1	5	0+1	5	1+7	40	2+4	30	3+13	20
5	9+8	85	11+5	80	7+7	70	9+4	65	36+34	75
6	4+3	35	2+5	35	2+8	50	1+3	20	9+19	35
7	7+8	75	9+10	95	7+8	75	2+8	50	25+34	74
8	7+7	70	17+2	95	8+8	80	8+7	75	40+24	80
9	12+6	90	11+9	100	16+1	85	8+7	75	47+23	88
10	0+5	25	0+4	20	2+3	25	0+0	0	2+12	18
11	9+8	85	7+9	80	12+2	70	5+6	55	33+25	73
12	12+8	100	7+9	80	8+6	70	5+2	35	32+25	71
13	3+10	65	2+10	60	6+8	70	2+8	50	13+36	61

10. 英语无灵主语句的汉译策略与方法探讨

续表 10-1

接受度句序	20名中文教师 选a,b项(人)	20名中文教师 比例(%)	20名英语教师 选a,b项(人)	20名英语教师 比例(%)	20名中文系学生 选a,b项(人)	20名中文系学生 比例(%)	20名英语系学生 选a,b项(人)	20名英语系学生 比例(%)	合计 选a,b项(人)	合计 平均比例(%)
14	2+5	35	0+4	20	4+1	25	1+4	25	7+14	26
15	0+2	10	0+2	10	0+4	20	0+1	5	0+9	11
16	4+5	45	3+6	45	7+6	65	2+6	40	16+23	49
17	2+9	55	3+3	30	5+6	55	2+2	20	12+20	40
18	11+9	100	9+9	90	8+9	85	2+14	80	30+41	89
19	8+10	90	9+9	90	6+9	75	4+12	80	27+40	84
20	3+4	35	0+2	10	3+4	35	1+2	15	7+12	24
21	9+9	90	11+8	95	12+5	85	6+6	60	38+28	83
22	1+11	60	8+8	80	7+6	65	3+8	55	19+33	64
23	5+11	80	1+14	75	5+10	75	4+9	65	15+44	74
24	9+10	95	4+12	80	10+5	75	7+8	75	30+35	81
25	0+8	40	0+1	5	2+4	30	4+2	30	6+15	25
平均		63		59		61		47		58

种情况的原因有二：一是中文专业师生阅读翻译文学作品的量大于英语专业师生，因而前者受欧化汉语的影响大于后者。相反，借助专业优势，英语专业师生大都愿意直接阅读英美文学作品，因而所受欧化汉语影响反而较小。二是英语专业师生大都能自觉进行英汉语言特征对比，对地道英语与地道汉语之间的差别的敏感性较中文专业师生强。

如果我们把60%以上受试认为可接受的直译句子定为可接受的译文，把接受比例在50%以下的句子定为不可接受的译文，那么，本调查所涉及的25个直译句子的分界是比较明确的。可接受的译句15个，不可接受的译句10个，前者占60%，后者占40%。这表明英语无灵主语句这种独特的语言表达方式已基本上为汉语读者所熟悉，直译这类句子，在意义清晰的情况下，是可以接受的。

仔细分析问卷表上那10个被认为不可接受的译句，有助于我们探索英语无灵主语句的汉译方法。笔者（2003a）发现英语无灵主语句本质上都是隐喻句，必须从隐喻的角度进行探讨。因此，笔者曾将英语无灵主语句分为修辞型（rhetorical）和句法型（syntactical）两类（见本书第9节）。修辞型无灵主语句在传统修辞学里体现为拟人、提喻或转喻等修辞格，在莱考夫（Lakoff）的认知语言学里则与概念隐喻（conceptual metaphor）密不可分。这类句子的最大特点是生动、形象，表现力强。句法型无灵主语句在韩礼德（Halliday）的系统功能语言学里表现为语法隐喻（grammatical metaphor），其主要特征是句子结构紧凑，词汇密度大，语义关系隐蔽、复杂。上述问卷表上那10个被认为不可接受的汉译句子，其英语原句也正好分属这两类：第2，15，16，17和20句，生动形象，拟人手段很明显，属修辞型无灵主语句；第4，6，10，14和25句，结构紧凑，语义内

10. 英语无灵主语句的汉译策略与方法探讨
English sentences with inanimate subjects

隐,修辞效果不明显,属句法型无灵主语句。仔细比较可以发现,那5个修辞型英语无灵主语句的汉译句子平均接受度(32%)比另5个(25%)稍高。其不被接受的原因也不相同:前者是因缺乏上下文语境,拟人等比喻手法的使用显得突兀,加上英汉思维习惯与文化传统的差异,而未被完全接受,但若仔细推敲,句子的意思还是比较清晰的,随着时间的推移,也许会慢慢地被汉语读者所接受;后者却因语义含混、概念矛盾、信息缺失而无法理解,难以接受。例如,第4句中缺失了谁"到场"这种必要的信息;第6句中的"要开始的不耐烦"属语义矛盾,正常的说法应该是"等得不耐烦"或"迫不及待要开始";其余三句也都因缺失"谁"或"什么"之类必要信息而无法理解和接受。直译句法型英语无灵主语句常常导致信息缺失,这与语法隐喻的形成密切相关。因为语法隐喻最常见的形成方式是名词化(nominalization),而名词化可通过删除动词的情态成分,模糊动作的时间概念,以及掩盖过程参与者等手段,创造一种非人格化(impersonal)效果,即遮掩动作实施者的效果。(王晋军,2003)

以上分析表明:翻译修辞型英语无灵主语句,必须预测目的语读者对由英语思维习惯与英语文化积淀所形成的概念隐喻的接受能力。当然,随着全球化进程的不断推进以及跨文化交际的全面深入,英语中越来越多的概念隐喻将被目的语读者所接受,但只要有翻译的存在,译者就必须考虑目的语读者对异质文化积淀和不同思维习惯的接受能力。翻译句法型英语无灵主语句,则必须化隐为显,将语法隐喻中因名词化而删除、模糊或掩盖了的信息,在译文中加以补充或明显化。要做到这一点,也有赖于译者对目的语读者的语言接受能力作出正确估价。其实,显性化存在于一切翻译之中,翻译中的显性化是一种普遍趋势。双语转换中，不管两种语言系统的特点如何，不管原文属于何种语篇体裁，也不管翻译的目的如何不同，从原文到译文总是由隐到显，而不是相反。(申连云，2003) 由此看来，本次调查中那10个不能接受的汉译句子的产生，完全是因译者没有预测目的语读者的接受能力所致，属于异化过度。

10.4 直译英语无灵主语句的译例分析

10.4.1 分析设计与数据统计

为了分析不同译者对同一英语无灵主语句的汉译策略，以便了解汉语规范对译者进行汉语表达时的限制程度，笔者从《傲慢与偏见》《飘》《葛底斯堡演说词》《谈读书》《红字》以及《德伯家的苔丝》等名著中选取了15个英语无灵主语句，并对比分析了不同译者对这15个英语句子的汉译情况。之所以从这些名著中选取英语无灵主语句，是因为这些名著已有多种汉语译本出版；也正是因为一个英语无灵主语句有多种公认的汉语译文，我们才有可能进行对比分析。为了节省篇幅，笔者在此仅将15个英语句子列出，各句的不同汉语译文请参见冯庆华（2002：226—405）和魏志成（2003：345—378）。

（1）This was invitation enough. (Jane Austen: *Pride and Prejudice*)

（2）"How so? How can it affect them?" (ibid.)

（3）"Is this his design in settling here?" (ibid.)

10. 英语无灵主语句的汉译策略与方法探讨
English sentences with inanimate subjects

(4) The disagreement subsisting between yourself and my late honoured father always gave me much uneasiness. (ibid.)

(5) Her new green flowered-muslin dress spread its twelve yards of billowing material over her hoops and exactly matched the flat-heeled green morocco slippers her father had recently brought her from Atlanta. (Margaret Mitchell: *Gone with the Wind*)

(6) The dress set off to perfection the seventeen-inch waist, the smallest in three counties, and tightly fitting basque showed breasts well matured for her sixteen years. (ibid.)

(7) The habit of command sat upon him now, a quiet air of self-reliance and authority, and grim lines were beginning to emerge about his mouth. (ibid.)

(8) There was something new and strange about the square set of his shoulders and the cool bright gleam of his eyes. (ibid.)

(9) The world will little note nor long remember what we say here, but it can never forget what they did here. (Abraham Lincoln: *The Gettysburg Address*)

(10) Reading maketh a full man; conference a ready man; and writing an exact man. (Francis Bacon: *Of Studies*)

(11) A new thought had struck him. (Nathaniel Hawthorne: *The Scarlet Letter*)

(12) Life had never brought them a gloomier hour. (ibid.)

（13）The accumulating days and added years would pile up their misery upon the heap of shame. (ibid.)
（14）Morning would break, and find him there. (ibid.)
（15）A gaunt four-post bedstead which stood in the room afforded sitting-space for several persons gathered round three of its sides. (Thomas Hardy: *Tess of the D'urbervilles*)

为了便于对比分析，我们仍只把既保留了英语无灵主语作汉译句子的主语，又保持了英语句型结构不变的汉译句子视作直译；否则看作意译。不同译者翻译以上15个英语无灵主语句的有关情况列表统计如表10-2所示：

表10-2 不同译者翻译15个英语无灵主语句的有关情况统计

英语句子序号	汉译句子（个）	译者人数（人）	保留无灵主语（句）	保留句型结构（句）	直译（句）	意译（句）
1	7	7	4	0	0	7
2	7	译者同上	4	0	0	7
3	7	译者同上	1	7	1	6
4	5	译者同上	3	0	0	5
5	6	6	1	0	0	6
6	6	译者同上	3	1	1	5
7	6	译者同上	0	0	0	6
8	6	译者同上	3	2	2	4
9	7	7	4	7	4	3
10	11	11	11	0	0	11
11	6	6	5	2	2	4
12	6	译者同上	4	5	4	2

续表 10-2

英语句子序号	汉译句子（个）	译者人数（人）	保留无灵主语（句）	保留句型结构（句）	直译（句）	意译（句）
13	4	译者同上	1	4	1	3
14	4	译者同上	2	1	1	3
15	6	6	3	2	2	4
合计	94	43	49	31	18	76
百分比			52%	32%	20%	80%

10.4.2 统计结果分析

10.4.2.1 数据分析

如上所述，所选 15 个英语无灵主语句取自 6 部作品。这 6 部作品中最多的有 11 种译本，最少的也有 4 种译文。这样总共得到 94 个对应的汉译句子作为分析对象，这 94 个汉译句子分别由 43 位译者提供。在这 94 个汉语句子中，保留了英语无灵主语作译句主语的句子 49 个，占总数的 52%；保持了英语句型结构不变的译句则只有 31 个，占 32%。而这两种情况同时出现在同一译句上的，即直译的句子，仅有 18 个，约占 20%；其余的 76 个译句均应视为意译，占 80%。

10.4.2.2 原因分析

如果将 10.3 的调查结果与本节的统计结果联系起来思考，我们不禁要问：为什么人们对英语无灵主语句直译的接受度与人们实际直译这类句子的比例存在如此之大的反差呢？这个问题可从两方面来考虑：一方面，这种反差是可以理解的正常情况，因为理解和接受与表达和运用之间存在很大区别，能理解和接受的不一定能表达和运用，这是很明显的道理。另一方面，译者在英译汉的过程中更受汉语语言文化的制约。文化规范的制约在此主要体现在中国人重主体的思维习惯上,而思维习惯对语言表达方式有重大影响。(何明珠,2003b)因此,译者将英语无灵主语转换成汉语有灵主语,完全是思维定势使然。语言规范的制约在此则主要表现在汉语的意合特征上。关于汉语意合特征对直译英语无灵主语句的制约性,笔者将从信息量与信息结构两方面通过实例加以阐述。

语句中的信息量与语义清晰度密不可分。信息的缺失必然导致语义含糊,而语义含糊的句子则必然丧失汉语的意合特征,当然就会受到汉语语言规范的制约。上文提到,句法型英语无灵主语句是通过(语法隐喻)名词化途径产生的。名词化主要是将动词或形容词转化为名词。使用名词化的动词,就是用过程来充当实体的。凡是过程一定要涉及相关的参与者,即传统语法中的逻辑主语和/或逻辑宾语。这些信息在重形合的英语句子中可以被掩盖或省略,而在重意合的汉语句子中则绝不可少,一旦缺失就要受汉语语言规范的制约。例如,在本节所选的第 1 个英语无灵主语句中,由于 invitation 是一个名词化的动词,与 invite 这一过程相关的参与者信息全部被掩盖了,这在英语中属正常现象。但在汉语中却因信息量不足而不合语言规范,因此汉译这个句子时必须补足所缺信息。然而,一旦补足信息,就要增加词语,而一旦增加词语,就势必要更换英语无灵主语或改变英语句型结构,故 7 位译者都无法将这个简单的英语句子"直译"为汉语。使用名词化的形容词,就是用属性来充当实体。凡是属性一定要涉及相关的情感和时空等概念,而这些信息在名词化的形容词中常被"淘砺"出去,从而使概念抽象化。因此,把含有名词化形容词的英语无灵主语句译成汉语时,若要保持其无灵主语和句型结构不变(即若要直译),则必须

10. 英语无灵主语句的汉译策略与方法探讨
English sentences with inanimate subjects

增加相关必要信息,使抽象概念具体化,否则译文无法让人理解和接受。例如,若将"Absence and distance make the overseas Chinese heart increasingly fond of the mainland."译成"缺席与距离使华侨们的心越来越向往大陆",则无法让人理解。但若将其译为"离乡背井和远居国外使华侨们的心越来越向往大陆",则能让人欣然接受。

句子的信息结构与语义连贯密切相关,因为语义或语篇的连贯性主要通过信息结构或主位结构的合理构建来实现。所以,翻译单个句子时,则不必考虑语义和语篇的连贯性,也无需调整主位或信息结构,而是更多地保留英语原句的主语和句型结构,即更多地"直译"。然而,在具体的语篇翻译过程中,译者必须考虑语义与语篇的连贯,必须对原文中的某些信息结构或主位结构进行调整,否则就会不合译入语的语言规范。例如,在本节所选的第 7 个英语无灵主语句中,"The habit of command sat upon him now."的表达形式非常生动形象,翻译时本应保留这种特色鲜明的语言形式。但是,为了使这个句子与其前面的句子在视角上保持一致,在语义上保持连贯,6 位译者都只好忍痛割爱,在译文中改变此句的主位和信息结构,将汉译句子的主语换成"他",从而舍"直译"为"意译"。再如,本节所选的第 10 句,如果脱离语篇,不顾上下文,将"Reading maketh a full man."译成"读书(能)创造一个充实的人",也未尝不可。但原文此句后面隔一句,就有"Histories make men wise."的句式。为了上下文的贯通,语义的连贯与一致,11 位译者无一例外地改变了英语句子的句型结构,将其译为"读书(能)使人充实"。以上译例足以说明:汉语的意合特征对直译英语无灵主语句具有很强的制约性。

10.5 结语

关于翻译方法与策略,译界对直译与意译、异化与归化的争论由来已久,针锋相对的观点时有交锋。这种争论与交锋无疑有利于加深人们对这个哲理深邃的论题的理解与认识。笔者无意奢谈广义的翻译策略选择,只想专心探索英语无灵主语句这种独特句型的汉译方法与策略,以求管中窥豹,可见一斑。本节通过问卷调查与译例分析得出如下结论:在英语无灵主语句的汉译过程中若选择异化策略和直译方法,译者必须预测汉语读者的接受能力限度并接受汉语语言文化规范的制约。否则,不仅会使译文诘屈聱牙,破坏原文的形式美,而且还会歪曲原文意义,混淆译文是非。

附件1:问卷调查表

感谢您参与本项调查!以下是25个翻译句子,请您仔细阅读后凭语感判断一下它们的可接受度。您只需在每个句子前的括号里填上a,b,c,d,e中的任何一个:a表示完全可接受,b表示基本可接受,c表示不能确定,d表示基本不可接受,e表示完全不可接受。

( ) 1. 他手臂上的疼痛使得脱衣服很困难。
( ) 2. 他的镇定从未抛弃过他。
( ) 3. 工厂里新设备的引进带来了生产的稳步提高。
( ) 4. 到场常常通过敲门而让房子里面的人知道。
( ) 5. 办公室的电脑化大大方便了管理。
( ) 6. 他那要开始的不耐烦写在脸上。

10. 英语无灵主语句的汉译策略与方法探讨
English sentences with inanimate subjects

( ) 7. 我的建议是在会议室里禁烟。
( ) 8. 过去的五百年见证了（目睹了）中国戏剧的巨大发展。
( ) 9. 抗议的呼声从愤怒的人群中爆发出来。
( ) 10. 发现一把他拥有的刀给大家提供了他就是凶手的怀疑。
( ) 11. 就像美貌和金钱一样，敏慧也离她而去。
( ) 12. 一种新的思想打动了他。
( ) 13. 生命从未带给他们一个比这更阴郁的时刻。
( ) 14. 在6点至7点之间将适合我。
( ) 15. 这种药不知道效力的限制。
( ) 16. 疾病抢走了她完成这项任务的信心。
( ) 17. 连续辛劳已经从他身上削去了几磅。
( ) 18. 他的受贿导致他的被捕。
( ) 19. 他的帮助会确保我的成功。
( ) 20. 猪肉把价定到他的菜碗外了。
( ) 21. 毒药杀死了河里的鱼。
( ) 22. 污染杀死了河里的鱼。
( ) 23. 他的财富使他什么都可以做。
( ) 24. 坏天气阻止了我们出发。
( ) 25. 横过草坪的几步带我到了一座华丽的大旅馆。

附件2：问卷调查详细情况统计

句序\选择	20名中文教师					20名英语教师					20名中文专业学生					20名英语专业学生				
	a	b	c	d	e	a	b	c	d	e	a	b	c	d	e	a	b	c	d	e
1	5	13	0	2	0	3	13	0	4	0	7	9	0	4	0	2	15	0	1	2
2	1	5	0	8	6	0	6	2	6	6	5	6	2	3	4	4	0	4	4	8
3	8	7	0	5	0	8	8	0	4	0	6	7	2	3	2	2	10	1	6	1
4	0	1	2	7	10	0	1	2	7	10	1	7	4	2	9	2	4	3	3	8
5	9	8	0	2	1	11	5	1	1	2	7	7	4	1	1	9	4	1	6	0
6	4	3	2	7	4	2	5	1	10	2	2	8	4	3	3	1	3	2	6	8
7	7	8	1	1	3	9	10	1	0	0	7	8	1	3	1	2	8	1	7	2
8	7	7	0	5	1	17	2	1	0	0	8	8	2	4	0	8	7	1	2	2
9	12	6	0	1	1	11	9	0	0	0	16	1	2	0	1	8	7	1	4	0
10	0	5	0	5	10	0	4	3	5	8	2	3	5	7	3	0	0	5	7	8
11	9	8	1	2	0	7	9	2	1	1	12	2	2	1	3	5	6	4	5	0
12	12	8	0	0	0	7	9	2	1	1	8	6	2	4	0	5	2	5	5	3

10. 英语无灵主语句的汉译策略与方法探讨
English sentences with inanimate subjects

续表附件 2

选择/句序	20名中文教师 a	b	c	d	e	20名英语教师 a	b	c	d	e	20名中文专业学生 a	b	c	d	e	20名英语专业学生 a	b	c	d	e
13	3	10	4	2	1	2	10	6	2	0	6	8	4	2	0	2	8	2	6	2
14	2	5	2	6	5	0	4	5	7	4	4	1	5	7	3	1	4	3	6	6
15	0	2	2	6	10	0	2	2	5	11	0	4	3	9	4	0	1	0	5	14
16	4	5	2	8	1	3	6	2	6	3	7	6	3	3	1	2	6	2	5	5
17	2	9	3	3	3	3	3	6	4	4	5	6	4	4	1	2	2	5	6	5
18	11	9	0	0	0	9	9	1	1	0	8	9	3	0	0	2	14	1	1	2
19	8	10	1	1	0	9	9	1	1	0	6	9	3	1	1	4	12	2	2	0
20	3	4	0	6	7	0	2	2	4	12	3	4	5	5	3	1	2	2	0	15
21	9	9	2	0	0	11	8	1	0	0	12	5	2	0	1	6	6	5	1	2
22	1	11	1	5	1	8	8	3	2	0	7	6	4	2	1	3	8	3	2	4
23	5	11	0	2	1	1	14	3	2	0	5	10	2	3	0	4	5	4	5	2
24	9	10	0	1	0	4	12	1	3	0	10	5	3	2	0	7	8	1	3	1
25	0	8	3	6	3	0	1	3	10	6	2	4	4	9	1	4	2	5	3	6

第三章

应用研究

11. 英语无灵主语句与汉式英语[①]
——从英语书面语与口头语的差异谈起

11.1 引言

汉式英语（Chinglish，又称中式英语或中国式英语）是中国英语学习者提高英语写作水平的重大障碍之一。毛荣贵（1998）曾在其《英语写作纵横谈》一书中指出，"谁早一日注意提防 Chinglish，谁就会在英语学习和英语写作中多一分进步"。国内对汉式英语的研究不少（Pinkham，2000；He，2000；蔡基刚，2001；毛荣贵，1998；李文中，1993；贾德霖，1990；等），但绝大多数研究都是围绕母语的负面影响这一因素去探索汉式英语的形成原因和表现形式。本节拟从语言特征对比的角度，分析英语无灵主语句（ESWIS）与汉式英语（Chinglish）的优缺点，阐明恰当、正确地使用英语无灵主语句有助于克服汉式英语的观点。

[①] 本节内容原载于《西安外国语大学学报》2007 年第 4 期。

11.2　汉式英语的口语化缺陷与英语无灵主语句的书面语特色

大量英语写作研究（马广惠，2002；文秋芳，2003；简庆闽等，2003；王立非等，2004；蔡金亭，1998；朱中都，1999；等）表明：中国学生的英语作文口语化倾向严重。写作的口语化与汉式英语的产生关系密切。蔡基刚（1995）分析指出："比较一下英语口语和英语书面语的特点，不难发现英语口语更接近汉语的表达方式和习惯。经常使用口语，导致的往往不仅是学生作文的口语化，而且是作文的汉语化。"也就是说，中国学生在英语口语训练和汉语表达习惯的双重影响下，写出来的作文常常充满汉式英语。

另外，英语研究者发现：英语无灵主语句是英语书面语中的常见句型和独特语言现象，具有句型多样，结构简练，词汇密度大，表达客观公正和生动活泼等特征（何明珠，2003a；范武邱，2004；董宏乐，2002；吴群，2002；王竹，1997；王桂珍，1996；等）。也就是说，在文体正式的英语书面语中，英语无灵主语句是一种常用而又独特的表达方式，中国学生应该学会正确使用这一表达方式。

那么，英语口头语与书面语到底存在哪些特征差异呢？黄国文（2005）在分析电子语篇的特点时，从表达方式、语境特征和语言特征三个方面，对此进行了详细区分。限于篇幅，本节仅从语言特征对比着手，分析口语化英语（即汉式英语）与书面体英语（即英语无灵主语句）在结构的松散与紧凑、句式的繁杂与简洁、表达的主观与客观、语义的显露与隐含等四个方面的差异及其相应的优缺点，以期帮助中国英语学习者正确使用英语无灵主语句，克服汉式英语。

11. 英语无灵主语句与汉式英语
English sentences with inanimate subjects

11.2.1 结构的松散与紧凑

如上文所述，口语化英语十分接近汉语的表达方式与习惯。因此，本节在以下的语言特征对比和分析中，将借用英汉语言特征对比的研究成果作为论述依据。英汉对比研究表明：英语重形合，汉语重意合。表现在句子结构上，那就是汉语句子像竹竿，英语句子呈树形。（潘文国，1997：198）还有学者称汉语句子为波浪式流水句，其结构之松散，不言而喻。例如：

(1) 有些人成功，有些人失败，根本区别不在机会的多少，而在于能否抓住机会。
   a. Some people succeed. Some people fail. The essential difference is not the number of opportunities. It is whether they can take advantage of opportunities.
   b. One essential difference between those who succeed and those who fail lies in the way they can take advantage of opportunities rather than their numbers.

例（1）a 是典型的竹竿状汉语式英语句，其松散的结构导致主次不分，意义晦涩。如果说这样的表达，因其句界分明，符合语法规则，而勉强可以在英语口头语中接受的话，那么若再往汉语靠近一步，用逗号连接各分句，则就成了完全不可接受的汉式英语。例如：

(2) 火车开始移动，我也开始流泪。

a. * The train began to move, I also began to cry.①
b. Tears came to my eyes as the train began to move.

11.2.2 句式的繁杂与简洁

在语言研究中,对于同一个概念或意义,如果用一个短语来表达,就叫分析型表达法(analytic expression);如果只用一个词来表达,则称综合型表达法(synthetic expression)。汉语倾向于分析型表达,而英语则趋向于综合型表达。就使役意义的表达而言,英语既可用分析型表达法(如使用 make + O + C 句型来表达),又可在更多的情况下用综合型表达法(如通过增加词的前后缀来表达),而汉语则只能用繁杂的分析型表达法。由于中国学生已经习惯了汉语的分析型表达法,却未掌握英语简洁的综合型表达法,因而在其英语作文中必然充满汉式英语。例如:

(3) 他有犯罪史,不能上大学。
    a. * He had committed crimes in the past and this made him unable to go to college.②
    b. His criminal record disqualified him from being admitted to college.

王寅(1992)也曾指出,"表达一个同样的意思,汉语

---

① 例句前有 * 号,表明这句话是不可接受的汉式英语句。
② 带 * 号的不可接受的句子中,底线表明语病之所在。

11. 英语无灵主语句与汉式英语
English sentences with inanimate subjects

往往取较高级阶的句法单位,而英语则取较低级阶的句法单位"。换言之,英语的词汇化程度高于汉语。有时,英语用一个单词表达的意思,汉语要用一个短语或一个句子才能表达。若能注意英汉表达的这一差别,就可写出简洁地道的英语,克服汉式英语。例如:

(4) 孩子们看到那道菜就喜形于色,这说明那是他们很难吃到的一道菜。
   a. The children were delighted when they saw the dish. This showed that it was a rare dish.
   b. The delight of the children at the sight of the dish showed that it was a rarity.

综上所述,在英语写作中,化繁为简,可避免汉式英语。具体而言,有如下三方面的工作可做:
第一,简化复合句。

(5) 早点出发就能在中午到达。
   a. If you start early, you will get there at noon.
   b. An early start will get you there at noon.
(6) 我对橱窗里琳琅满目的商品着了迷,忍不住要注目而视。
   a. I was so fascinated by the splendid display in the shop window that I could not resist the temptation.
   b. The splendid display in the shop window had an irresistible fascination on me.

第二，简化主语或语态不一致的并列句和复合句。

（7）我能吃苦，开始没被解雇。
   a. I could work very hard and so the boss did not dismiss me in the beginning.
   b. My capacity for hard work saved me from an early dismissal.
（8）教授上完课就马上离开了教室。
   a. The professor left the classroom immediately after the lecture was over.
   b. A prompt close of his lecture brought the professor out of the classroom.

第三，简化流水式长串短句。

（9）人们看到的是一栋破旧房子，位于一条人去楼空的小巷，景象很凄凉。
   a. People see an old and dilapidated house. It is situated in a deserted lane. It looks dismal.
   b. The old and dilapidated house in a deserted lane makes a dismal picture.

11.2.3　表达的主观与客观

表达方式的差异源自思维方式的不同。英汉思维特征对比研究表明（何明珠，2003b）：英美人善于理性思维和抽象思维，重逻辑分析，强调语言表达的客观性；中国人则善于感性思维

11. 英语无灵主语句与汉式英语
English sentences with inanimate subjects

和形象思维，重视类比和整体感知，强调语言表达的主观性。这些截然不同的思维特征能有效解释英语无灵主语和汉语有灵主语普遍存在各自语言中的原因。此外，汉语倾向于使用主观性的有灵主语，同汉语属于重主题的语言有关。主题结构反映这样一种思维过程：讲话人首先想到的是一个具体的主体——人，然后再提及主体的行为或语言，因此，出现在主语位置上的以人为多。英语是重主语的语言，首先考虑的是句子结构的完整性。如果句子结构需要，随时可用无灵主语。因此，在英语中，同一意思可有主观和客观两种不同的表达方式。若用有灵主语，则为主观的口头表达方式，与汉语表达方式基本相同；若用无灵主语，则为客观的书面表达方式，与汉语截然不同，却是独特而地道的英语表达方式。如此可见，在英语写作中，重视客观表达方式，善于使用无灵主语，无疑有助于克服汉式英语。这种例子，俯拾皆是。例如：

(10) 不同的人对退休持不同的态度。

    a. Different people have different attitudes towards retirement.

    b. Attitudes towards retirement vary from person to person.

(11) 我永远忘不了这个教训。

    a. I will never forget this lesson.

    b. This lesson will take root in my mind.

(12) 由于计划不周，我浪费了所有金钱和时间。

    a. Because of poor planning, I wasted all my money as well as my time.

    b. Poor planning wasted all my money as well as my time.

11.2.4 语义的显露与隐含

语义的显与隐和表达的露与含，密不可分。口头表达的实时性使讲话人无法拥有充足的时间去从容选择词语或句子结构，因而浅显的词语和松散的句子结构能保证语义表达的直接明了和信息传递的快速直达。相反，书面表达因不受时间和空间限制，作者拥有充足的时间去深思熟虑和锤词炼句，因而深邃的词语和紧凑的句子结构可使语言含而不露，隐而不显，尽其委婉与曲折之所能。例如：

（13）没有人相信他的话。
    a. Nobody believed his story.
    b. His story convinced no one.

（14）我很惊讶，说不出话来。
    a. I was unable to speak because I was so astonished.
    b. Astonishment deprived me of my power of speech.

（15）她病了，失去了完成任务的信心。
    a. She lost confidence in finishing the task because of her illness.
    b. Illness robbed her of the confidence in accomplishing the task.

（16）他长期不断地劳累，瘦了好几磅。
    a. He lost a few pounds of weight after a long period of hard work.
    b. Successive exertion chipped a few pounds

off him.

详细说来，英语无灵主语句作为一种独特的书面语表达形式，其意义的含蓄与委婉表现在如下五个方面：

第一，逻辑关系的隐含。

(17) 由于不知道什么知识将来会更有用，因此选课时很难做出正确选择。
   a. * <u>Because</u> one cannot know what kind of knowledge will be more useful in the future, <u>so</u> he cannot make a sound choice when taking a course.（因果关系外显）
   b. One's inability to predict what kind of knowledge will be more useful in the future prevents him from making a sound choice in taking courses.（无灵主语隐含因果关系）

(18) 他若能帮忙，我就肯定会成功。
   a. * <u>If</u> he helps me, <u>then</u> I will surely succeed.（条件关系外显）
   b. His help will ensure my success.（无灵主语隐含条件关系）

(19) 我一看到那条河，就想起家乡。
   a. * <u>As soon as</u> I saw the river, I <u>remembered</u> my hometown.（时间先后关系外显）
   b. The sight of the river reminded me of my hometown.（无灵主语隐含时间先后关系）

第二，行为主体的隐含。

(20) 仔细比较二者，就能看出其中的差别。
　　a. If you compare the two carefully, you will see the difference between them.
　　b. A careful comparison of the two will show the difference.
(21) 酒吧里稍有异常情况，大家马上就能注意到。
　　a. When something a little out of the ordinary takes place in the bar, all the people there immediately realize it.
　　b. With anything a little out of the ordinary in the bar, the sense of it spreads quickly.

第三，言语态度的隐含。

(22) 下令关闭矿井，招来强烈抗议。
　　a. When the authorities ordered to close the pit, the villagers and the relatives of the trapped miners protested violently outside the pit.
　　b. Pit closure saw violent scenes.

第四，幽默语气的隐含。

(23) 肉价太贵，他吃不起。
　　a. As the price of pork is too high, he cannot afford it.
　　b. Pork has priced itself out of his dish.

第五，强烈情感的隐含。

11. 英语无灵主语句与汉式英语
English sentences with inanimate subjects

(24) 老年人急需帮助。
    a. Old people are in bad need of help.
    b. White hair is crying for help.

以上分析了英语无灵主语句的几个主要书面语特征和表达优势。但需要特别注意的是，英语无灵主语句不可过度使用，滥用英语无灵主语句同样可以导致汉式英语。这一方面是由于汉语重视主题结构，英语讲究主谓结构，因而汉语的主谓搭配习惯和英语的主谓搭配习惯不尽相同：汉语中可以搭配的主谓关系，在英语中有时却行不通。赵元任（1968：69—70）曾经指出，"在汉语中，主语与谓语间的语法关系与其说是施事与动作的关系，不如说是话题与说明的关系，施事和动作可以看作是话题和说明的一个特例"。因此，如果不考虑英汉两种语言的不同表达习惯，甚至不顾基本的语法规则，直接把汉语无灵主语句译成英语无灵主语句，那就会不可避免地产生无法接受的汉式英语。例如：

(25) 我肚子饿了。他年纪很轻。
    a. * <u>My stomach</u> is hungry. * <u>His age</u> is very young.
    b. I am hungry. He is very young.
(26) 他的英语讲得好。人们的生活离不开电视了。
    a. * <u>His English</u> speaks well. * <u>People's life</u> can't leave TV.
    b. He speaks good English. People can't do without TV now.

另一方面，汉语的拟人化程度高于英语。拟人化现象在汉语中十分常见,而过度拟人在英语中常被视为语病或不正常的蠢话。因此,在英语写作中,过度拟人就会导致不可接受的汉式英语。例如:

(27) 在过去20年里,我们的航空事业取得了一个又一个胜利。
    a. * In the past 20 years, <u>our aeronautics cause</u> has won one victory after another.
    b. In the past 20 years, we have won a series of victories in aeronautics technology.

(28) 宗教绝不能干扰政治。
    a. * <u>Religion</u> must not interfere with politics.
    b. Nobody should interfere with politics in the name of religion.

11.3 结语

英语无灵主语句是英语书面语中独具特色的生动表达方式;汉式英语是中国英语学习者在使用英语过程中因受母语负迁移影响而产生的严重口语化倾向这一病态语言现象。本节通过英语口头语与书面语的特征对比,分析了英语无灵主语句与汉式英语句的主要特征和优缺点。分析表明:英语无灵主语句具有结构紧凑、句式简洁、表达客观和语义深邃等优点;汉式英语句存在结构松散、句式繁杂、表达主观和语义浅显等缺陷。因此,中国英语学习者若能恰当、正确地使用英语无灵主语句,则可有效提高英语写作表达水平。

12. 英语书面与口头语篇中的无灵主语句对比分析[①]
——以韩礼德一项相关研究中的实例为语料

12.1 引言

"近年来无灵句研究已经引起国内学者的广泛兴趣,成为近期英汉对比语言学的一个热点问题"(孙兴文,2006:125)。的确,若在中国知网上用"无灵句"和"无灵主语句"为关键词检索近5年国内发表的相关论文,仅以这两个关键词为标题的文章就有50余篇。然而,综观这些文章,会发现仍然存在不少问题,主要表现为规格不高、质量不过硬,原因在于研究内容不够丰富、研究方法不够新颖(何明珠,2011)。就研究内容而言,国内研究者都把无灵主语句作为一种笼统的语言现象来研究,不区别其所在语境,也不区分相关的话语或语篇类型。国外的同类研究则特别重视其所在话语或语篇的类型差异,例如,对于学术语篇中的无灵主语句,即 inanimate subject + active verb 句型,目前有影响的研究有 Master(1991;2001)、Low(1999)、以及 Ses-

---

[①] 本节部分内容原载于《湖南工业大学学报(社会科学版)》2012年第6期。

kauskiene(2009；2010)等。就研究方法而言，国内仍无实证研究，囿于举例与解释，缺乏数据与实验。国外则以实证研究为主，例如上述研究，几乎篇篇都有实验或统计数据。除此以外，当前国内相关研究还存在因术语不规范而引起的概念混乱现象，例如对"无灵主语""无灵句"以及"无灵主语句"等术语不加区分，造成概念混乱现象（何明珠，2012）。本节将首先明确区分这几个术语所表达的概念，然后以韩礼德一项相关研究中的实例为语料，对英语无灵主语句在书面与口头语篇中的分布状况和语用特征进行对比分析。

12.2 无灵主语、无灵句、无灵主语句及其他

这里的"灵"即"灵性"或"生命性"，"无灵"就是"不具生命性"。"无灵主语"，顾名思义，就是由不指称生命实体的代词或名词或名词短语充当的主语。"无灵主语"与"有灵主语"对应，其区别就在于所指称的对象是否是人或动物等具有生命的实体。如此可见，"无灵主语"是主语的一个类别，研究"无灵主语"就是研究主语，一般涉及主语类型、跨语言主语对比等语言类型学研究，很少研究会把无灵主语作为独立的研究对象。因此，迄今为止尚未发现单独专门研究"无灵主语"的论著。通常对"无灵主语"的研究是将其置于句子之中作为一种语言现象来研究，也就是下文要讨论的"无灵句"与"无灵主语句"研究。国内曾经使用过的指称"无灵主语"的术语还有"无生物主语""无生命主语""非人称主语"以及"物称主语"等（何明珠，2011）。

12. 英语书面与口头语篇中的无灵主语句对比分析
English sentences with inanimate subjects

"无灵句"与"无灵主语句"虽然只是"主语"两字有无之别,但所指的对象却完全不是同一个概念(何明珠,2012)。例如:

(1) a. Winter is cold.
　　b. It often rains.
　　c. Leaves have fallen.
(2) a. Here comes winter.
　　b. It often sees cold rain and fallen leaves.

例(1)是三个"无灵句",而例(2)则是两个"无灵主语句"。"无灵句"由无灵主语和无灵谓语构成,整个句子都不存在明显的生命性,既没有主语指称意义上的外显生命性(animacy in designation),也没有谓语陈述意义上的内含生命性(animacy in assertion)。"无灵主语句"则由无灵主语和有灵谓语组成,或由虽在指称意义上不具外显生命性但在陈述意义上具有内含生命性的名词化主语(subject through nominalization)构成,即整个句子通过生命性概念的跨域映射而成为一种隐喻表达方式。何明珠(2005)曾以生命性为分类依据,将英语无灵主语句分为结构性无灵主语句和隐喻性无灵主语句两类。实际上,结构性和隐喻性分类与"无灵句"和"无灵主语句"区分基本上是一回事:"结构性无灵主语句"相当于"无灵句","隐喻性无灵主语句"就是"无灵主语句",因为生命性跨域映射是其共同的分类或区分依据。总之,"无灵句"不具生命性,不存在生命性跨域映射，不是隐喻句①；"无灵主语句"具有生命性，存在生命性跨域映射，是隐喻句。

然而，生命性有强弱之分，呈梯级状分布，形成一个连续统（continuum），两极分明但中间很难找到一条清晰的分界线：Human > Animate > Inanimate。同样，隐喻性也只有程度之别。因此，我们不能说"无灵句"就根本没有隐喻性，"无灵主语句"就一定隐喻性很强。"无灵句"与"无灵主语句"虽然可以分辨，但明确的分界线则不易划定。即使在"无灵主语句"之间，也存在隐喻性强弱不同的现象。例如：

(3) a. It is already night now.
b. Night has fallen here in Boston.
c. Night has arrived at his door without being noticed.

很明显，例（3）a 是"无灵句"，例（3）c 是"无灵主语句"，而例（3）b 应该归入"无灵句"还是"无灵主语句"则必须考虑其所在上下文语境以及其所在的语篇类型。此外，何明珠（2005）曾将英语无灵主语句分为概念隐喻（conceptual metaphor）无灵主语句和语法隐喻（grammatical metaphor）无灵主语句。显然，概念隐喻无灵主语句的生命性和隐喻性要比语法隐喻无灵主语句的生命性和隐喻性更强。

---

① 这里专指由生命性概念跨域映射而产生的隐喻，是与"无灵主语句"相比较而言的。如果"无灵句"中存在其他种类的概念跨域映射，那也可以具有隐喻性。例如，"This bedroom is a dustbin"，就存在功能或用途概念的跨域映射，也具隐喻性，但这种"无灵句"仍与"无灵主语句"不同，不在本文的讨论范围之内。

12. 英语书面与口头语篇中的无灵主语句对比分析
English sentences with inanimate subjects

如上所述,无灵主语句的生命度越高,其隐喻性就越强;隐喻性越强的无灵主语句,其新颖性(originality)则越明显。隐喻性和新颖性一方面能使句子语义丰富、结构严谨、形象生动,另一方面也能使句子语义隐晦、歧义横生、增加理解难度。这大概就是人们常说无灵主语句只用于正式书面语篇和文学作品中的原因。这种概括性结论本身不无道理,但无灵主语句的分布状况并非这么简单明晰,值得深入研究。根据以上分析,本节的假设是:生命性和隐喻性强弱不同的无灵主语句分布在不同类型的语篇中,并具有不同的语用特征。下文将以实例论证这一假设。

12.3 语料介绍与研究方法

系统功能语言学的创始人韩礼德教授曾于1992年发表了一篇题为《语篇"人口零增长"的词汇语法特征分析》(*Some Lexicogrammatical Features of the Zero Population Growth Text*)的论文(该文已收入《韩礼德文集》第2卷)。这篇论文既是语篇和话语的功能语法分析典范又是书面和口头语篇对比分析的楷模。文章从主位、信息结构、语气和情态、及物性、小句复合体、词汇衔接、名词化和语法隐喻等七个方面,对一封题为"人口零增长"的公益性筹资信函(日常书面语篇)进行词汇语法特点分析。特别重要的是,在分析该语篇的名词化和语法隐喻这一特点时,作者借助自己以英语为母语的这一优越条件,为该书面语篇创造了一篇能让12岁儿童理解和接受的对等口头语篇。这是一份难得的真实对应语料,本节将借用这一语料(见文后附件)进行个案研究。

该原始信件有30个部分,其中开头和结尾的称呼、日期、地址、别言、签名、身份等 8 个部分,由于信件的格式功能,没有小句特征,因而省略不予分析。这样,原始书面语篇由 22 个部分组成。这 22 个部分实际上就是传统语法所谓的 22 个句子,因系统功能语法研究的基本语言单位是小句(clause)而非句子(sentence),故称其为部分(segment)①。系统功能语法将小句分为简单小句(clause simplex)和小句复合体(clause complex)两类。此外,还有级别式小句(ranking clause)和嵌入式小句(embedded clause)之分。这样,原始书面语篇的 22 个句子里有 36 个级别式小句和 19 个嵌入式小句,共有 55 个小句。详见 Halliday(1992)。

由于上述 55 个小句里包含了一些传统语法所谓的分词短语、不定式短语以及介词短语等语言单位,不适合本研究要进行的主语和谓语生命性判断与分析。因此,本节将根据 Master(1991)等国外同类研究的做法,按照主谓对子(subject-verb pair)来重新划分原始书面语篇中的 22 个句子和对应口头语篇中的 23 个句子进行统计和对比分析。笔者采用定量与定性相结合的研究方法:首先,将原始书面语篇中的 22 个句子和对应口头语篇中的 23 个句子分别按顺序编号;其次,手工标出所有主谓对子并进行统计;然后,仔细辨认每一个主谓对子,标出无灵句和无灵主语句并分别进行统计;最后,根据统计数据对比分析无灵主语句在书面和口头语篇中的分布状况和语用特征。

---

① 关于小句、小句复合体与句子之间的异同,请参见 Halliday,1994:215–216。

12. 英语书面与口头语篇中的无灵主语句对比分析

English sentences with inanimate subjects

12.4 无灵主语句在书面与口头语篇中的分布状况对比分析

经过编号、标注、辨认以及统计得出下列各类基本数据，分别列表并对比分析如下。

表12-1 主谓对子在原始书面语篇的22个句子中的分布状况

句子种类	22个句子的顺序编号	主谓对子数
简单句（含1个主谓对子）	1；2；3；5；9；10；11；13；14；18；19；21	12×1=12
并列句（含2个主谓对子）	12	1×2=2
复合句（含2个主谓对子）	8；16；17；22	4×2=8
复合句（含3个主谓对子）	4；6；15	3×3=9
复合句（含4个主谓对子）	7；20	2×4=8
合计		39

表12-2 主谓对子在对应口头语篇的23个句子中的分布状况

句子种类	23个句子的顺序编号	主谓对子数
简单句（含1个主谓对子）	1；3；11；13；20；22；	6×1=6
并列句（含2个主谓对子）	12	1×2=2
复合句（含2个主谓对子）	2；5；14；15	4×2=8
复合句（含3个主谓对子）	18；23	2×3=6
复合句（含4个主谓对子）	4；17；21	3×4=12
复合句（含5个主谓对子）	7；19	2×5=10
复合句（含6个主谓对子）	6；8；9；10；16	5×6=30
合计		74

上文所谓"主谓对子"指的就是只有一个主谓关系的简单句,其条件是:主语不可省略,谓语必须是具有时态和语态等语法特征的限定动词。简单说来,标注主谓对子就是寻找传统语法所谓简单句、分句和从句的起点和终点,也是研究无灵主语句分布状况的先决条件。如表12-1显示,在原始书面语篇中有独立主谓对子(即简单句)12个、并列主谓对子2个、分布在9个主从复合句中的主谓对子25个。表12-2表明,在对应口头语篇中独立主谓对子只有6个,并列主谓对子仍是2个,但在16个主从复合句中却分布着66个主谓对子。从对比分析表12-1和表12-2中的相关数据可以发现:①口头语篇中的独立主谓对子比书面语篇少一半;②口头语篇中的主谓对子总数却比书面语篇几乎多一半;③口头语篇中的复合句数量比书面语篇也几乎多一半,且复合句所含的主谓对子从最多4个增加到6个。这三点充分体现了对应口头语篇中句子结构的语法复杂性(grammatical intricacy)。

表12-3 原始书面语篇和对应口头语篇用词分布状况

	单词总数	实词数	句子数	句子平均词数	主谓对子数	主谓对子平均词数与(词汇密度)
书面语篇	456	278	22	20.7	39	11.7 (7.1)
口头语篇	609	280	23	26.5	74	8.2 (3.8)

表12-3显示了原始书面语篇和对应口头语篇的用词情况:①虽然书面语篇与口头语篇所用实词基本相当,但书面语篇的用词总量比口头语篇的用词总量几乎少四分之一;②虽然书面语篇的句子平均用词量少于口头语篇,但书面语篇中的主谓对子平均用词量则多于口头语篇;③书面语篇中主

12. 英语书面与口头语篇中的无灵主语句对比分析
English sentences with inanimate subjects

谓对子的词汇密度（即实词数与主谓对子数之商）大约是口头语篇的两倍。这三点充分表明原始书面语篇的词汇密度（lexical density）较大。

表12-4 原始书面语篇中39个主谓对子的生命性分布状况

	主谓都具生命性 （有灵句）	主谓都不具生命性 （无灵句）	主语不具但谓语 具有生命性 （无灵主语句）
主谓对子数	20	8	11
百分比	51%	21%	28%

表12-5 对应口头语篇中74个主谓对子的生命性分布状况

	主谓都具生命性 （有灵句）	主谓都不具生命性 （无灵句）	主语不具但谓语 具有生命性 （无灵主语句）
主谓对子数	54	15	5
百分比	73%	20%	7%

表12-4显示，在原始书面语篇中，生命性在39个主谓对子里的分布基本匀称，有灵句与无灵句和无灵主语句约各占一半。表12-5表明，在对应口头语篇中，生命性在74个主谓对子里的分布不均衡，有灵句占73%，而无灵句和无灵主语句共占27%。对比分析表12-4和表12-5中的数据可以发现：①无灵句在书面和口头语篇中所占比率几乎相同；②有灵句在口头语篇中所占百分比比在书面语篇中多22%；③无灵主语句在书面语篇中所占百分比比在口头语篇中多21%。这三点表明：书面语篇和口头语篇的差异与无灵句的多寡无关，与有灵句和无灵主语句的多寡却密切相关。书面语篇与无灵主语句的数量成正比，与有灵句的数量成反

比；口头语篇与有灵句的数量成正比，与无灵主语句的数量成反比。

表12-6 原始书面语篇中8个无灵句和11个无灵主语句所在基本句型的分布状况

基本句型	无灵句	无灵主语句
S + V + O	0	8
S + V	1	1
S + V + C	2	2
S + be + V – ed	5	0
合计	8	11

表12-7 对应口头语篇中15个无灵句和5个无灵主语句所在基本句型的分布状况

基本句型	无灵句	无灵主语句
S + V + O	0	2
S + V + O + C	0	1
S + V	2	2
S + V + C	9	0
There + be + S	1	0
S + be + V – ed	3	0
合计	15	5

表12-6显示，在原始书面语篇中，无灵句主要是被动语态句和主系表结构句；无灵主语句主要是主谓宾结构句。表12-7表明，在对应口头语篇中，无灵句主要是主系表结构句和被动语态句；无灵主语句主要是主谓宾或主谓宾补结构句。对比分析表12-6和表12-7中的数据可以发现：

12. 英语书面与口头语篇中的无灵主语句对比分析

English sentences with inanimate subjects

①无灵句在书面语篇中以被动语态句占绝对优势,而在口头语篇中则以主系表结构句最具代表性;②无灵主语句无论在书面还是口头语篇中都以主谓宾结构句为主。

12.5 无灵主语句在书面与口头语篇中的语用特征对比分析

首先请看原始书面语篇中 11 个和对应口头语篇中 5 个无灵主语句的主谓搭配情况(见表 12-8、表 12-9)。

表 12-8 原始书面语篇中 11 个无灵主语句的主谓搭配情况

序号	主语	谓语	宾语、表语、状语等
1	Calls	jammed	our switchboard all day.
2	Media and public reaction	has been	nothing short of incredible!
3	… the deluge of calls	came	mostly from reporters …
4	… that (problems)	threaten	public health and well-being.
5	… population-linked pressures	affect	U. S. cities.
6	It (The Urban Stress Test)	ranks	184 urban areas on 11 different criteria …
7	The Urban Stress Test	translates	complex, technical data into easy-to-use action tool …
8	Your support now	is	critical.
9	…, ZPG	can arm	our growing network of local activists with the materials …
10	… before they (population-linked stresses)	reach	the crisis stage.

续表 12-8

序号	主语	谓语	宾语、表语、状语等
11	… that (the decisions)	could drastically affect	the quality of our life.

表 12-9 对应口头语篇中 5 个无灵主语句的主谓搭配情况

序号	主语	谓语	宾语、表语、状语等
1	…, if this (overpopulation)	is making	people unhappy.
2	… (how much difference) it	makes	(having so many people around) …①
3	… whose opinions	count,	…
4	… if the population	goes on	growing without being controlled …
5	… which (decisions)	will make	a difference …

表 12-8 显示，在原始书面语篇的 11 个无灵主语句中：① 3 个是独立主谓对子或简单句（第一、第二和第八句），其余 8 个存在于复合句中；② 有 4 个代词主语句（第四、第六、第十和第十一句），其余 7 个为名词（或名词短语）主语句；③ 有 2 个连系动词谓语句（第二和第八句），有 1 个不及物动词谓语句（第三句），其余 8 个为及物动词谓语句。表 12-9 表明，在对应口头语篇的 5 个无灵主语句中：① 没有独立主谓对子或简单句；② 有 3 个代词主语句，2 个名词

---

① 这个主谓对子的正常语序是：Having so many people around makes much difference. 因造句需要，宾语前置了，并使用了 it 作形式主语。

12. 英语书面与口头语篇中的无灵主语句对比分析
English sentences with inanimate subjects

主语句；③有 2 个不及物动词谓语句，3 个由同一个动词构成的及物动词谓语句，没有连系动词谓语句。

对比以上两组无灵主语句可以发现：①以独立主谓对子或简单句出现的无灵主语句，因其结构简练、用词独特而生动形象，加上谓语动词的生命性极强而隐喻性非常明显，一般只出现在书面语篇中（如表 12 - 8 中的第 1 句）。②如果谓语为不具生命性的连系动词，主语就必须是动词的名词化（nominalization）形式，否则无法形成无灵主语句。虽然这类语法隐喻句的生命性和隐喻性不如概念隐喻句明显，但也因其结构简练、用词经济而语义深邃，一般也只用于书面语篇中①（如表 12 - 8 中的第二和第八句）。③虽然以代词为主语的无灵主语句在书面和口头语篇中都有，但在口头语篇中出现的几率更高（60% 比 36%）。④由于绝大多数无灵主语句的生命性体现在谓语动词上，而及物动词所体现的生命性比不及物动词更强，所以由及物动词构成的无灵主语句的隐喻性也更明显。书面语篇中的无灵主语句绝大多数是及物动词谓语句（约占总数的 73%）正体现了这一点。此外，动词所表达的动作或行为越具体，生命性就越强，句子的隐喻性也越明显。原始书面语篇中 8 个及物动词都较为具体而对应口头语篇中 3 个及物动词都是概括性的 "make" 也与这一规律吻合。⑤书面语篇中的无灵主语句大多是通过新颖独到的选词造句途径来达到生动形象的表达目的，而口头语篇中的无灵主语句则主要是借助习惯搭配和常规造句手段来满足通俗易懂的表达需要。

---

① 当然，在口头语篇，尤其是对话中，有时为了特殊交际效果，也可使用这种语法隐喻无灵主语句。例如：
—Thank you very much.
—The pleasure is mine.

12.6 结语

本节以一对目的相同、意义对等的书面和口头语篇为语料，对其中的无灵主语句进行了封闭式对比分析。分析表明：①无灵句与无灵主语句是两类性质不同、可以明确分辨的句子。无灵句在书面和口头语篇中分布均衡，不受语篇类型差异的影响，而无灵主语句则主要存在于书面语篇中，能体现书面语篇言简意赅、生动形象的特点。②无灵主语句是由生命性概念跨域映射而形成的隐喻句。由于生命性存在强弱之分，隐喻性也有程度之别，因此，无灵主语句既大量存在于书面语篇中，也少量出现在口头语篇里，但各自的语用特征不同。③书面语篇中的无灵主语句，因用词具体和造句新颖独到而生命性较强、隐喻性明显，具有生动形象的特征，而口头语篇中的无灵主语句，则因用词笼统和注重习惯搭配而生命性较弱、隐喻性不明显，具有通俗易懂的特征。

由于本研究所用语料规模较小，加上口头语篇是根据已有书面语篇生成，非自然交际状态下形成，因此部分结论值得进一步验证。

附件1

(The original version of a fund-raising letter with the title, date, address, valediction, signature, signatory, status and coda-signal omitted)

Zero Population Growth

[1]At 7 a.m. on October 25, our phones started to ring.

12. 英语书面与口头语篇中的无灵主语句对比分析
English sentences with inanimate subjects

²Calls jammed our switchboard all day. ³Staffers stayed late into the night, answering questions and talking with reporters from newspapers, radio stations, wire services and TV stations in every part of the country.

⁴When we released the results of ZPG's 1985 Urban Stress Test we had no idea we'd get such an overwhelming response. ⁵Media and public reaction has been nothing short of incredible!

⁶At first, the deluge of calls came mostly from reporters eager to tell the public about Urban Stress Test results and from outraged public officials who were furious that we had "blown the whistle" on conditions in their cities.

⁷Now we are hearing from concerned citizens in all parts of the country who want to know what they can do to hold local officials accountable for tackling population-related problems that threaten public health and well-being.

⁸ZPG's 1985 Urban Stress Test, created after months of persistent and exhaustive research, is the nation's first survey of how population-linked pressures affect U. S. cities. ⁹It ranks 184 urban areas on 11 different criteria ranging from crowding and birth rates to air quality and toxic wastes.

¹⁰The Urban Stress Test translates complex, technical data into easy-to-use action tool for concerned citizens, elected officials and opinion leaders. ¹¹But to use it well, we urgently need your help.

¹²Our small staff is being swamped with requests for more information and our modest resources are being stretched to the limit.

¹³Your support now is critical. ¹⁴ZPG's 1985 Urban Stress

Test may be our best opportunity ever to get the population message heard.

[15] With your contribution, ZPG can arm our growing network of local activists with the materials they need to warn community leaders about emerging population-linked stresses before they reach the crisis stage.

[16] Even though our national government continues to ignore the consequences of uncontrolled population growth, we can act to take positive action at the local level.

[17] Every day decisions are being made by local officials in our communities that could drastically affect the quality of our lives. [18] To make sound choices in planning for people, both elected officials and the American public need the population-stress data revealed by our study.

[19] Please make a special contribution to ZPG today. [20] Whatever you give— $25, $50, $100 or as much as you can—will be used immediately to put the Urban Stress Test in the hands of those who need it most.

P. S. [21] The results of ZPG's 1985 Urban Stress Test were reported as a top news story by hundreds of newspapers and TV and radio stations from coast to coast. [22] I hope you'll help us monitor this remarkable media coverage by completing the enclosed reply form.

附件2

(A corresponding oral version for a 12-year-old reworded by

12. 英语书面与口头语篇中的无灵主语句对比分析
English sentences with inanimate subjects

M. A. K. Halliday)

Keeping the Population No Bigger Than It Is Now

¹At 7 a. m. on October 25, our phones started to ring. ²So many people were telephoning us that the switchboard was jammed all day. ³Our staff stayed late into the night, answering questions and talking with reporters from newspapers, radio stations, wire services and TV stations in every part of the country.

⁴When we told everyone what we had found out by our Urban Stress Test in 1985 we'd no idea we'd have so many people taking notice. ⁵It was incredible how the TV, radio and newspapers, and also ordinary people, talked about it.

⁶At first the ones who kept telephoning us were mainly reporters, who were eager to tell people about the results of the stress test, and public officials, who were furious because we had "blown the whistle" on what it's like to live in their cities.

⁷But now we're hearing from ordinary citizens from all parts of the country who are worried and want to know what they can do to get local officials to accept that it's their job to tackle problems coming from overpopulation, if this is making people unhappy.

⁸When we were creating this Urban Stress Test we had to research persistently and very thoroughly for months; it's the first time anyone in the country has surveyed how much difference it makes having so many people around if you live in U. S. cities. ⁹We put 184 urban areas in order according to 11 different properties which we measured, including how crowded they are, how many children are being born, how good or bad the air is, and how much poisonous waste there is around.

¹⁰What we found out with this test is complicated and techni-

cal; but we've made the test easy to understand so that citizens who are concerned about these things, and elected officials, and people whose opinions count, can use it to get things done. [11]But to use it well we urgently need you to help us.

[12]We have only a small staff, and they've been swamped by being asked so many questions. [13]We haven't enough resources to deal with any more.

[14]You have to support us now so that we can survive. [15]The Urban Stress Test may be our best opportunity ever to get people to listen to what we are saying about population.

[16]We can use the money you contribute for sending out to the more and more people who are working for us in different places all the information they need in order to warn important members of the community that people are already beginning to suffer because of overpopulation, before this becomes a crisis.

[17]Even though our national government still ignores what happens if the population goes on growing without being controlled, we can try to do something about it in our own neighborhoods.

[18]Every day local officials in our communities are deciding things which will make a difference to the way we live. [19]So that they can choose properly when they plan for people, both elected officials and the American public need to know what we found out when we studied stresses coming from overpopulation.

[20]Please contribute extra money to ZPG today. [21]Whatever you give— $25, $50, $100 or as much as you can— will be used immediately to tell the results to the people who most need to know them.

12. 英语书面与口头语篇中的无灵主语句对比分析
English sentences with inanimate subjects

P. S. [22]The results of the test were reported as a top news story by hundreds of newspapers and TV and radio stations from coast to coast. [23]I hope you'll help us to keep a record of all this remarkable number of reports, by filling in the form I'm enclosing for you to reply on.

13. 英语无灵主语句谚语研究[①]

13.1 引言

自20世纪80年代我国的那场翻译、教学与研究英语谚语的热潮以来（曾东京，1998），人们对英语谚语研究的兴趣丝毫没有减弱，研究成果不断见于书刊。其实，英语谚语已成为语言学、哲学、心理学、教育学乃至其他众多学科的共有论题，甚至有人称，英语谚语研究作为一门独立学科即英谚学的时代即将来临（桂清扬，1988）。这是因为谚语不仅是民间文学的一种形式，还是民俗学的固有内容，更是语言的精华，以其简练的措辞、精辟的内容以及深邃的寓意而盛传于世。难怪英国著名作家培根关于谚语的名言"一个民族的天才、智慧和精神均体现在其谚语之中"（The genius, wit and spirit of a nation are discovered in its proverbs.）如此脍炙人口。我国的英语谚语研究在其定义与特点、民族性与人民性、思想性与艺术性以及始源探寻等方面已卓有成效。此外，在英汉谚语的对比与翻译以及英语谚语的分类等方面的研究成果也颇丰。然而，英语谚语研究的进一步深入，有待于从宏观研究转向微观研究。本节拟在英语谚语分类研究的

[①] 本节内容原载于《语言教育》2013年第2期。

基础上,就其中的一个小类,即以无灵主语句出现的英语谚语或称为"英语无灵主语句谚语",进行研究。

13.2 英语谚语分类与英语无灵主语句谚语

不同的分类标准决定不同的分类方法与结果。英语谚语的分类也因不同的研究目标而有不同的标准。最常见的分类标准是谚语的始源。例如,以生活经验和社会实践为标准,可分出衣食住行类、医药类与道德行为类等;以劳动经验和生产实践为标准,可分出农林牧渔类与航海航天类等;以具体出处为标准,可分出寓言类、神话类与名人名言名著类等;以译借语言为标准,可分出汉谚、法谚与俄谚等。但谚语的表达形式和思想内容更适合作为其分类的标准。

陈文伯(1987a)从翻译的角度将谚语的主要特点概括为:①形式基本上是句子结构;②内容既有教诲性(包括经验和真理)因素,又有习语性(包括比喻引申义和特殊用法)因素。并据此将英语谚语分为:纯教诲性、教诲性多于习语性、教诲性少于习语性以及纯习语性四类。这种分类法虽在谚语的区分上作用不大,但在英语谚语的汉译上具有指导意义。

桂清扬(1988)也从英语谚语的形式和内容出发,将其分为指令和非指令两大类。指令类均以祈使句为其形式特征,而非指令类又可分为训示类、说教类和警句类三种。训示类和说教类英语谚语大多以陈述句形式出现,而警句类英语谚语则为一种高度浓缩的平衡句式,如:"Least said, soonest mended." "Out of sight, out of mind."

本节所探讨的英语无灵主语句谚语是以句子形式为分类

标准划分出来的一种英语谚语，属于上述训示类和说教类中的一部分，即以陈述句中的无灵主语句形式出现的英语谚语。无灵主语句是由无灵主语和有灵谓语组成的，或由虽在指称意义上不具外显生命性但在陈述意义上具有内含生命性的名词化主语（subject through nominalization）构成的，即通过生命性概念跨域映射而产生的，一种隐喻表达方式（何明珠，2011）。例如，"Pride goes before a fall." 与 "Misery loves company." 是由无灵主语和有灵谓语组成的英语无灵主语句谚语；"Honesty is the best policy." 与 "There is many a slip between the cup and the lip." 是由名词化主语构成的英语无灵主语句谚语。虽然前者的生命性和隐喻性大于后者，但两者都是因生命性跨域映射而产生的隐喻表达式。然而，"Time is money." 与 "There is no fire without smoke." 则不同。它们虽然也是隐喻表达式，但其主谓之间不存在生命性概念的跨域映射。它们是无灵句谚语而非无灵主语句谚语。本节专门探讨由无灵主语和有灵谓语组成的英语无灵主语句谚语的分布状况、语用特征与汉译方法。

13.3 英语无灵主语句谚语的分布状况

在严格限定上述研究对象的基础上，本节选取 5 部在篇幅、编写目的与编写方法等方面都不同的英语谚语辞书和词典为语料进行统计与分析。其中 3 部为国内学者编著，2 部为国外专家编撰，分别是《101 对汉英常用谚语对照》（王晓均，2008）、《4500 双解英语谚语》（朱正键，2006）、《英语流行谚语》（王书亭等，2004）、《简明牛津谚语词典》（*Oxford Concise Dictionary of Proverbs*，Oxford University Press，1998）、《企鹅谚语词典》（*The Penguin Dictionary of Proverbs*，

Market House Books Ltd.，2000）。收录英语谚语最少的只有101条，最多的有6764条。经过认真标注和辨认，相关数据统计如下：

表13-1 英语无灵主语句谚语分布状况表

书名	收录英语谚语总数	无灵主语句谚语数	百分比
《101对汉英常用谚语对照》	101	13	12.9%
《4500双解英语谚语》	4500	548	12.2%
《英语流行谚语》	816	149	18.3%
《简明牛津谚语词典》	1075	152	14.1%
《企鹅谚语词典》	6764	1367	20.2%

上表显示，汉英对照或英汉双解谚语辞书收录的英语无灵主语句谚语少于英语谚语词典；国内编者出版的谚语辞书和词典比国外编撰的谚语词典收录的英语无灵主语句谚语少；英语无灵主语句谚语在英语谚语中所占比率约在12%至20%之间。这是通过数据统计得到的宏观结论。其实，英语无灵主语句谚语的分布并不均匀，其使用的频率与所谈及的主题（theme）相关。《企鹅谚语词典》收录的6764条英语谚语分别归属在188个主题之下。其中，有9个主题下的176条英语谚语里连一个无灵主语句都没有，这9个主题是Building, Choosing, Conformity, Lateness, Sacrifice, Self, Servants, Trouble-making, Use；而另外7个主题下的158条英语谚语中却有84个无灵主语句，占53%以上，这7个主题是Adversity, Envy, Nature, Necessity, News, Pride, Small things。

13.4 英语无灵主语句谚语的语用特征

吴雨田（1987）归纳英语谚语的主要特点为：英语民族约定俗成，反映人民生活、斗争；有持久的生命力、广泛的通俗性、生动的口语化；隐喻着真理，充满了智慧，冶炼出经验；语言洗练优美，教诲意义深刻，代表民族精神，体现国家文明。由此可见，绝大多数英语谚语都是口述耳闻、世代相传（handed down by word of mouth from generation to generation），具有明显的口头语特征，属于非正式文体。何明珠（2003）总结英语无灵主语句的基本特征为：伴随语法隐喻（名词化）的出现而产生；语法结构紧凑、词语密度大、语义关系隐蔽、适用于正式书面语体中；组句方式有利于摆脱行为主体的主观性，更具客观公正性和权威性；名词化结构有助于主题的突显，有利于语篇的衔接与连贯，使语言表达自然流畅。由此看来，英语无灵主语句具有明显的书面语特征，属于正式文体。

作为既是谚语又是无灵主语句的英语无灵主语句谚语，表面上看是一种不能存在的对立体，但实际上却是一种客观存在的和谐体，因为它兼备了口头和书面两种语体的优点。

13.4.1 英语无灵主语句谚语措辞简洁，结构紧凑，语句精炼，韵律优美

本研究从《简明牛津英语谚语词典》收入的1075条谚语中统计出152条无灵主语句谚语。其中，由10个及10个以上单词组成的无灵主语句谚语只有5条：

（1）The eye of a master does more work than both his

13. 英语无灵主语句谚语研究
English sentences with inanimate subjects

hands.
(2) One half of the world does not know how the other half lives.
(3) March comes in like a lion and goes out like a lamb.
(4) When poverty comes in at the door, love flies out of the window.
(5) All work and no play make Jack a dull boy.

而由两个单词构成的无灵主语句谚语却有 4 条：

(6) Extremes meet.
(7) Money talks.
(8) Power corrupts.
(9) Time flies.

由 3 个单词构成的无灵主语句谚语多达 16 条：

(10) Blood will tell.
(11) Familiarity breeds contempt.
(12) Fortune favors fools.
(13) Haste makes waste.
(14) History repeats itself.
(15) Length begets loathing.
(16) Love begets love.
(17) Misery loves company.
(18) Money makes money.
(19) Night brings counsel.

(20) Practice makes perfect.
(21) Time will tell.
(22) Time works wonders.
(23) Walls have ears.
(24) Circumstances alter cases.
(25) Every little helps.

这 152 条英语无灵主语句谚语的平均用词量只有 6.2 个。由此可见其语句之精炼。此外，这 152 个句子全都使用常用动词作谓语，其中使用次数最多的是 make，共用了 34 次，占总数的 22.4%；同样还有 come, go, have, bring, drive, tell, talk 等单音节常用动词，重复率也很高。这能说明此类谚语措辞之简洁。简短的句子加上单音节动词，必然产生明快的节律；头韵或尾韵的恰当使用，必然使此类谚语朗朗上口，便于记诵，如：

(26) Death pays all debts.
(27) Love laughs at locksmiths.
(28) An apple a day keeps the doctor away.
(29) A hedge between keeps friendship green.

13.4.2 英语无灵主语句谚语委婉客观，寓意深邃

谚语的目的主要是阐述哲理、传授经验和教训，以及诲人与劝诫。在英语谚语中，的确存在不少祈使句和 He who (that) …, One that (who) …, They (Those) who… 等固定句型。例如，在《4500 双解英语谚语》中，有祈使句谚语 510

多条，有 He who (that) …等句型的谚语 436 条，二者之和约占总数的 21%。这类谚语语气强硬、态度主观、表意直接，诲人与劝诫功能明显。然而，在阐述哲理、传授经验教训时，若语气委婉、态度客观，效果则会更好。这也许就是无灵主语句能够存在于英语谚语中的原因。例如：

(30) Absence makes the heart grow fonder.
(31) Beauty draws with a single hair.
(32) Charity covers a multitude of sins.
(33) Distance lends enchantment to the view.
(34) Empty vessels make the most sound.
(35) Fine words butter no parsnips.

上述各例就是语气委婉、态度客观的谚语，其喻理诲人的效果绝对不比祈使句差。

13.4.3 英语无灵主语句谚语形象生动，联想丰富

谚语是语言的精华；英语无灵主语句就是隐喻句。认知语言学家莱考夫（Lakoff, 1980）的概念隐喻理论将传统修辞格中的拟人、换喻、提喻等都纳入隐喻范畴之中，并将隐喻视为普遍存在于人们日常生活中的一种认知方式。所谓隐喻认知，就是指通过概念跨域映射，借助已知去了解未知，根据具体事物去认识抽象事物。所有这一切，都要通过形象和意境去制造联想和激活想象。英语无灵主语句谚语的魅力就在于借助具体形象，创造优美意境，激发丰富想象。例如：

(36) Lies have short legs.
(37) Fortune knocks once at least at every man's gate.
(38) Necessity knows no law.
(39) Every picture tells a story.
(40) A soft answer turns away wrath.
(41) Hunger drives the wolf out of the wood.

上述谚语只能通过形象与意境，借助联想和想象才能深刻理解其中的寓意，其生动性与形象性来自生命性概念的跨域映射。

13.5　英语无灵主语句谚语的汉译方法

英语谚语的汉译远非人们想象的那么简单。人们常常使用直译法来保持英语谚语的民族性；使用对译法（即套用汉语谚语去译英语谚语）来保持其谚语特色。殊不知，这两种看似有效的译法，也常常出现问题。早在20世纪80年代，许多学者（赖余，1984；陈文伯，1987b；燕南，1987）就指出了许多英语谚语辞书中的不少误译。直到现在，学者们（刘云波，1995；梁茂成，1995；宋志平，1996；曾东京，1991，2003；金其斌，2006）仍在不断地探索英语谚语的汉译问题。本节仅就英语无灵主语句谚语的汉译，略陈管窥之见。

13.5.1　直译必须体现谚语的喻理诲人功能

英语无灵主语句谚语既有委婉客观的语言特点，又有喻理诲人的谚语功能或特定的寓意。汉译此类英语谚语，决不能顾其一而忘其二。例如，很多人都将"A rolling stone gathers no moss."直译成"滚石不生苔"。这样译，其委婉客观的语言特点是保留了，但其谚语功能却没有实现，其深刻的寓意也未予揭示，译了也等于未译。正确的做法应该是直译之后，还要通过增益手段，揭示其寓意："滚石不生苔，转业不聚财。"类似的例子如下：

（42）Empty vessels make the most sound.
译文一：空桶声最响。
译文二：满瓶不响，半瓶叮当；博学者寡言，浅学者自擂。

（43）The bait hides the hook.
译文一：饵内藏钩。
译文二：饵内藏钩，笑里藏刀。

（44）The ebb will fetch off what the tide brings in.
译文一：涨潮冲来的，落潮退回去。
译文二：涨潮来，退潮去，得失紧相随。

（45）The sea complains of want of water.
译文一：大海怨水少。
译文二：大海怨水少，巨富不知足。

（46）Water never dries up in an old river.
译文一：老河之水，永不干涸。
译文二：老河水不涸，老人智不竭。

以上 5 个例子中的译文二，不仅揭示了谚语的寓意，体现了谚语的诲人功能，而且符合汉语谚语对称与平衡的表达习惯。

13.5.2 对译必须忠实谚语的原始寓意

英语无灵主语句谚语大都含蓄委婉，其形象和意境很容易使人产生联想。因此，人们常常使用汉语谚语来对译英语无灵主语句谚语。这时，译者稍不注意，译文就会背离英语谚语的原始寓意，达不到跨文化交际的目的。再拿"A rolling stone gathers no moss."为例。有人套用汉语谚语"流水不腐，户枢不蠹"来译此条英语谚语。殊不知，这两条汉语谚语与英语谚语各有不同的寓意。汉语谚语的寓意是："人要经常运动，才能强身健体。"英语谚语的寓意则是："A person who too frequently changes his occupation, or who never settles in one place, will not succeed or become rich."如此对译，岂不是南辕北辙或风牛马不相及？类似的误译例子的确不少：

(47) A closed mouth catches no flies.
    误译：人死病终。（通过"口闭"联想到"人死"；通过"苍蝇"联想到"疾病"。）
    改译：言多招祸。（以"closed mouth"喻"silence"；以"flies"喻"trouble"。）

(48) Empty bags can't stand.
    误译：空袋难立，人无真才实学难立脚。（通过"空袋"联想到"没有真才实学的人"））
    改译：空袋难立，家中无粮气不壮。（以"empty bags"喻"poor men without food"。）

(49) A golden key can open any door.
    误译：有了金钥匙，不愁锁不开。（通过"金钥匙"联想到"万能工具"。）

13. 英语无灵主语句谚语研究
English sentences with inanimate subjects

改译：有了金元宝，无事办不了。（以"golden key"喻"money"。）

(50) The worst wheel of the cart creaks most.
误译：叫得最凶、发誓最狠，人最坏。（通过"最坏的车轮"联想到"最坏的人"；通过"叫喊"联想到"哭闹、发誓"等。）
改译：破轮常吱嘎，懒汉爱叫屈。（以"worst wheel"喻"lazy worker"，以"creak"喻"complain"。）

(51) A new broom sweeps clean.
误译：新官上任三把火。（通过"新扫帚扫得干净"联想到"新官办事干脆利落"。）
改译：新官上任办事灵；新来的媳妇勤；新仆好使唤；新箍的马桶香；新的总比旧的好；等等。（以"new broom"喻"anybody in a new position or anything new"。）

更为重要的是，例（51）这两条英汉谚语不能对译，是因为汉语谚语"新官上任三把火"含贬义，而英语谚语"A new broom sweeps clean"根本不含贬义。

当然，英汉谚语在形义两方面都相近，且在联想和寓意两方面都偶合的情况，不是没有，只是数量有限。因此，英汉谚语只有在形、义、联想以及寓意等各个方面都偶合的情况下，使用对译法才是较为理想的翻译途径。例如：

(52) Bad news travels fast.
好事不出门，恶事传千里。

(53) Fine words butter no parsnips.

花言巧语不济事。
(54) Failure teaches success.
失败是成功之母。
(55) Actions speak louder than words.
说一尺不如行一寸。
(56) Money does not grow on trees.
天上不下钱,地里不生宝。

13.6 结语

本节对英语无灵主语句谚语的分布状况、语用特征与汉译方法进行了初步探讨。对 5 部英语谚语辞书和词典的调查、统计与分析发现：以英语无灵主语句出现的英语谚语约占其总数的 12% 至 20%，分布的疏密与谚语所涉及的主题有关。英语无灵主语句谚语，作为英语谚语的一个小类，具有三大特征：①简洁精练、音形优美；②委婉客观、寓意深邃；③形象生动、联想丰富。直译英语无灵主语句谚语，必须通过增益手段揭示其寓意，体现其喻理诲人的功能；对译英语无灵主语句谚语，必须忠实其原始寓意，避免因联想不当而导致原文与译文南辕北辙或风牛马不相及。

14. 中美大学生英语作文中无灵主语句使用情况对比分析[①]

14.1 引言

将相同题材的中国大学生英语作文与英美大学生英语作文进行对比,一定能够发现许多具有启发性的差异现象。马广惠(2001,2002)就曾借用Biber(1988)的对比修辞研究模式并利用对应语料就中美大学生英语作文的修辞特点和语言特征进行了对比分析。研究发现:中国学生英语作文的主体句型是简单句,美国学生作文的主体句型是复合句;中国学生使用定语从句和宾语从句的数量低于美国学生,使用连接词语的数量高于美国学生。此外,中国学生的英语作文较短,使用的第二人称代词、语篇虚词、连词和形容词较多;美国学生的作文较长,使用较多because引导的状语从句、that引导的宾语从句、that引导的定语从句和说服动词。中国大学生的英语作文反映了应试之作的书面语特点,信息性和正式性明显;美国大学生的英语作文则表现出很强的口语体特征,个性化和先主后补的特点明显。这些发现对中国学生的英语写作无疑具有较全面的宏观指导意义,但涉及面

[①] 本节内容原载于《当代外语研究》2013年第4期。

太广，需要微观研究加以验证与补充。

英语无灵主语句由无灵主语和有灵谓语构成，具有生动形象、简洁精练、信息量大等书面语特征，是一种独特的英语表达方式（何明珠，2003）。若以英语无灵主语句作为参照项，对比分析中美大学生的英语作文，则肯定能够发现一些更为具体的差异现象。本节拟对英语无灵主语句的分布状况和使用特点进行封闭式微观对比研究，并对相关差异进行解释。

14.2 语料来源及处理方法

本研究所使用的对应语料为 98 篇中美大学生英语作文。其中，美国大学生作文 49 篇，取自《美国大学生作文选》（王秋海，1999）；中国大学生作文 49 篇，选自《中国大学生英语作文评改》（毛荣贵 & Houston，1997）。后者共收英语作文 100 篇，为《科技英语学习》期刊（1996）征集的参赛作文，题材和内容与前者基本相同，都是大学生活的真实反映，都是大学生的所见所闻、所思所想。为了方便对比，本研究从这 100 篇作文中依序隔一篇选一篇，取单数的前 49 篇。这 98 篇英语作文来自中美两国不同大学的 98 名学生，应该具有一定的代表性。此外，这 98 篇英语作文在题材、内容、作者年龄、写作年代等方面基本相同。因而具有较强的可比性。

根据系统功能语言学理论，小句（clause）具有相对完整的表意功能，是最具意义的语法单位（刘礼进，2003），所以本研究的有效统计都以小句为单位。此外，传统语法所谓的分词短语、不定式短语以及介词短语等语言单位，因不适合本研究要进行的主语和谓语生命性判断与分析，都不纳

14. 中美大学生英语作文中无灵主语句使用情况对比分析
English sentences with inanimate subjects

入句位统计。因此，本研究将根据 Master（1991；2001），Low（1999）以及 Seskauskiene（2009；2010）等国外同类研究的做法，以主谓对子（subject-predicate pair），即具有显性主语的小句，作为句位统计单位。经过手工标注和句位统计，中国大学生49篇英语作文中小句总数2100个；美国大学生49篇英语作文中小句总数4120个。

为了方便对比分析，在本研究中，对无灵句与无灵主语句进行了区分。"无灵句"由无灵主语和无灵谓语构成，整个句子不存在明显的生命性，既没有主语在指称意义上的外显生命性（animacy in designation），也没有谓语在陈述意义上的内含生命性（animacy in assertion），如"Winter is cold. It often rains. Leaves have fallen."为三个无灵句。"无灵主语句"则由无灵主语和有灵谓语组成，或由虽在指称意义上不具外显生命性但在陈述意义上具有内含生命性的名词化主语（subject through nominalization）构成，即整个句子通过生命性概念的跨域映射而成为一种隐喻表达方式，如"Winter often sees cold rain and fallen leaves. Embarrassment stopped any more questions."为两个无灵主语句（何明珠，2012a）。此外，本研究还将中美大学生的各49篇英语作文区分为记叙文、描写文、说明文和论说文四类，以便对比分析。

14.3 英语无灵主语句的分布状况对比分析

14.3.1 中国大学生英语作文中无灵主语句的分布状况

表 14-1 各类小句的分布状况

作文类别	篇数	小句		无灵句		无灵主语句	
		总数	平均数	总数	平均数/百分比	总数	平均数/百分比
记叙文	15	781	52.1	107	7.1 / 13.7%	68	4.5 / 8.7%
描写文	5	194	38.8	38	7.6 / 19.6%	16	3.2 / 8.2%
说明文	19	681	35.8	153	8.1 / 22.5%	73	3.8 / 10.7%
论说文	10	444	44.4	87	8.7 / 19.6%	64	6.4 / 14.4%
合计	49	2100	42.9	385	7.9 / 18.3%	221	4.5 / 10.5%

(注：平均数=总数/篇数；百分比=无灵句或无灵主语句总数/小句总数。)

表 14-1 显示，中国大学生的 49 篇英语作文中共有小句总数 2100 个，篇均小句数为 42.9 个。其中，无灵句占 18.3%；无灵主语句占 10.5%。就四类作文而言，无灵句在说明文中所占比率最高，为 22.5%；在记叙文中的比率最低，为 13.7%。无灵主语句在论说文中所占比率最高，为 14.4%；在描写文中的比率最低，为 8.2%。

14. 中美大学生英语作文中无灵主语句使用情况对比分析

表14-2 无灵主语句的具体分布情况

作文类别	篇数	各篇无灵主语句个数	合计	平均数
记叙文	15	9;1;2;3;7;8;5;0;12;4; 3;5;3;2;4	68	4.5
描写文	5	4;3;5;3;1	16	3.2
说明文	19	7;0;5;3;5;3;1;4;4;3;0; 7;3;10;8;2;2;4;2	73	3.8
论说文	10	7;16;4;2;1;10;6;7;10;1	64	6.4
合计	49		221	4.5

表14-2显示,在中国大学生的49篇英语作文中,3篇没有无灵主语句,而最多的一篇却多达16句。其中含0至3句的作文,共有23篇,占总数的47.0%;含10句以上的共5篇,约占10.2%。

14.3.2 美国大学生英语作文中无灵主语句的分布状况

表14-3 各类小句的分布状况

作文类别	篇数	小句		无灵句		无灵主语句	
		总数	平均数	总数	平均数/百分比	总数	平均数/百分比
记叙文	11	1342	122	161	14.6 / 12.0%	74	6.7 / 5.5%
描写文	6	427	71.2	76	12.7 / 17.8%	34	5.7 / 8.0%
说明文	22	1753	79.7	335	15.2 / 19.1%	175	7.9 / 10.0%
论说文	10	598	59.8	150	15 / 25.1%	56	5.6 / 9.4%
合计	49	4120	84.1	722	14.7 / 17.5%	339	6.9 / 8.2%

(注:平均数=总数/篇数;百分比=无灵句或无灵主语句总数/小句总数。)

表14-3显示,美国大学生的49篇英语作文中共有小句总数4120个,篇均小句数为84.1个。其中,无灵句占17.5%,而无灵主语句仅占8.2%。就四类作文而言,无灵句和无灵主语句在记叙文中所占比率都最低,分别为12%和5.5%;无灵句在论说文中所占比率最高,为25.1%;无灵主语句在说明文中的比率最高,为10.0%。

表14-4 无灵主语句的具体分布情况

作文类别	篇数	各篇无灵主语句个数	合计	平均数
记叙文	11	5;4;11;12;3;17;1;10;2;3;6	74	6.7
描写文	6	6;8;8;4;6;2	34	5.7
说明文	22	6;10;1;2;6;4;6;8;12;3;19;9;7;26;5;11;10;9;2;3;8;8	175	8.0
论说文	10	7;3;5;4;10;8;11;4;2;2	56	5.6
合计	49		339	6.9

表14-4显示,美国大学生的英语作文,篇篇都有无灵主语句,最多的一篇多达26句。其中含1至3句的作文共13篇,占总数的26.5%;含10句以上的共12篇,占24.5%。

14.3.3 中美大学生英语作文中无灵主语句的分布情况对比分析

对比表14-1与表14-3可以发现:

第一,虽然已有研究(马广惠,2001)表明,美国大学生英语作文篇幅比中国大学生的长得多,前者平均长度约799个词,后者约456个词,均值差为343,但在本研究中,二者的小句总数差和篇均小句差却更大,分别是4120对2100和84.1对42.9,均值差分别为2020和41.2,前者几

14. 中美大学生英语作文中无灵主语句使用情况对比分析
English sentences with inanimate subjects

乎是后者的两倍。在篇幅不变的情况下,小句数与口语化程度成正比(Halliday,1992)。因此,美国大学生英语作文的口语化程度明显高于中国大学生。

第二,只有明确这一点,才能理解为什么美国大学生英语作文中无灵句和无灵主语句的篇均数(14.7和6.9)会高于中国大学生英语作文(7.9和4.5),而其所占百分比(17.5%和8.2%)却低于后者(18.3%和10.5%)。这是因为无灵主语句与书面语程度成正比(何明珠,2012b)。

第三,中美大学生英语作文中无灵句的百分比相差不大(18.3%与17.5%),仅0.8%之差,而无灵主语句的百分比却相差明显(10.5%与8.2%),有2.3%的差距,因而值得进一步对比分析。

第四,中美大学生英语作文中的无灵句和无灵主语句在记叙文和描写文中所占比率较低,在论说文和说明文中所占比率较高,这条分界线很一致,也很明确。但在论说文与说明文之间,以及记叙文与描写文之间,界限却不够分明。这一方面是因为记叙文和描写文比论说文和说明文的口语化程度更高,它们之间容易明确区分;另一方面则可能是因为论说文与说明文之间的书面语程度,以及记叙文与描写文之间的口语化程度都不太容易区分,导致作文分类出现了偏差。

第五,虽因语体差异无灵主语句在中国大学生英语作文中所占比率(10.5%)比在美国大学生英语作文中(8.2%)还高,但对比表14-2与表14-4还能清楚发现:无灵主语句在美国大学生英语作文中比在中国大学生英语作文中分布更均衡。美国学生含1—3个无灵主语句的作文仅占26.5%,含4—9句的占49.0%,含10句以上的占24.5%;而中国学生含0—3个无灵主语句的作文高达47.0%,含4—9句的占42.9%,含10句以上的仅占

10.2%。造成这种差异的原因可能是：英语是美国大学生的母语，是中国大学生的外语；恰当使用无灵主语句是美国大学生母语能力的自然体现，而对中国大学生来说，无灵主语句是一种与汉语完全不同的表达方式。中国大学生因个体英语水平差异而造成这种使用分布不均现象应是在情理之中。

14.4 英语无灵主语句的使用特征对比分析

英语无灵主语句的最大亮点是由其生命性概念跨域映射而产生的隐喻性表达效果（何明珠，2011），其核心则是谓语动词，因为"谓语动词能比句中其他任何词语表达更多信息"（Goldberg，1995）并能直接体现生命性特征。因此，本节拟对上述中美大学生各49篇英语作文中的221个和339个无灵主语句的谓语动词使用情况进行对比分析，从而探讨他们使用英语无灵主语句的共性和差异。

14.4.1 常用动词的使用情况对比

在中国大学生的221个无灵主语句中，共使用了148个不同谓语动词，比率为67.0%；在美国大学生的339个无灵主语句中，共出现了192个不同谓语动词，比率为56.6%。由此可见，美国大学生英语作文中无灵主语句谓语动词的重复率比中国大学生高10.4%，这是其口语化程度高和常用动词多的缘故。在中美大学生作文中用作无灵主语句谓语的动词中，只有47个同时出现在他们的作文里：add, arouse, affect, awaken, break, bring, beat, begin, cause, cast, come, change, create, depend, determine, divide, disappear, dawn, emerge, fall, force, give, go, grow, happen, help, hide, keep,

14. 中美大学生英语作文中无灵主语句使用情况对比分析

English sentences with inanimate subjects

lead, make, meet, measure, move, offer, occur, pass, play, provide, require, run, separate, serve, show, take, vary, work, win。这些同时在中美大学生作文中出现的动词中,重复使用用3次以上的只有19个。除这47个动词外,另外还有15个动词只在二者之一中出现,但都出现了3次以上。这34个常用动词的使用情况见表14-5。

为了深入考察中美大学生使用这些常用动词构造英语无灵主语句的具体情况,本节选取由 make, come, go, bring, take, give, provide 这7个动词构成的130个无灵主语句进行对比分析。

第一,make 是一个词义丰富的致使动词,最容易生成英语无灵主语句。因此,中美大学生英语作文中用 make 造出来的无灵主语句都很多,但按篇幅或小句总数的比率来计算,还是中国大学生的使用频率更高,但他们表达的内容和方式不如美国大学生那样丰富和自然。

如表14-6所示,中美大学生使用 make 的相同表达方式只有括号内的4种;中国大学生的用星号*标记的那4种表达方式不够自然或难以理解:make sb. satisfied or excited 不如 satisfy or excite sb. 自然;time has made several strokes 不合英语的拟人习惯;最后两句是汉语表达方式,不是地道的英语。对比分析显示:美国大学生能灵活运用 make 的习惯搭配和引申义造句,而中国大学生则只能坚守 make 的"制造"和"使"这两个本义。

第二,come 和 go 是英语中最常用的一对不及物行为动词,很容易生成无灵主语句,因而中美大学生用 come 和 go 造出来的无灵主语句差异不大。

表14-7显示,美国大学生使用由 come 和 go 组成的短语动词比中国大学生多。

表14-5 34个常用动词的使用情况对比

动词	美	中	动词	美	中	动词	美	中
make	30	24	keep	5	1	add	1	3	prevent	3	0
come	16	10	play	5	1	double	4	0	start	6	0
cause	12	1	help	4	2	do	3	0	benefit	0	3
require	8	1	offer	4	2	fade	3	0	catch	0	3
bring	7	7	change	4	1	get	3	0	hold	0	5
go	6	4	provide	3	3	increase	4	0	present	0	4
take	7	3	lead	3	2	improve	3	0	rise	0	4
affect	5	2	create	3	1	lie	4	0			
give	5	5	happen	3	1	mark	3	0			

14. 中美大学生英语作文中无灵主语句使用情况对比分析

English sentences with inanimate subjects

表 14-6 中美大学生 make 使用情况对比

中国大学生的使用情况	数量	美国大学生的使用情况	数量
(make a deep impression on sb.)	2	(make a lasting impression on sb.)	1
(make sb. angry, despondent, mad, etc.)	7	(make sb. healthier, sad, rich, etc.)	7
make sb. satisfied, excited, etc.*	3	make sth. popular, rough, difficult	3
(make sb. do sth.)	5	(make sb. do sth.)	8
(The marching made our legs ache.)	1	(Her hair made her look dynamic.)	1
make it possible to do sth.	1	make sb., sb.	2
make up an important part of sth.	1	make sth. sth.	2
Great hopes make great men.	1	make sth. do sth.	2
After his childhood, time has made several strokes.*	1	TV, movies, books etc. must make money	2
Montage makes the colorful flowers flash into a joyful crowd.*	1	make unusual noises	1
Could the two rough hands before me make such an exquisite thing?*	1	make any difference	1
合计	24	合计	30

表 14-7 中美大学生 come 和 go 使用情况对比

中国大学生的 come 使用情况	数量	美国大学生的 come 使用情况	数量
sth. comes from sth.	2	sth. comes from sth.	1
sth. comes only once.	1	sth. comes with sth.	3
A new day came.	1	sth. comes to mind or one's attention	3
Success seldom comes easily.	1	sth. does not come easy or easily	2
The chance finally came.	1	sth. comes into question	1
…, time of receding comes to pass	1	come true; come to life	2
A mingled feeling came over me.	1	come in; come around	2
A voice came into my ears.	1	The answer came to me the next day.	1
The moon came out slowly.	1	The pressures come crashing down.	1
合计	10	合计	16
中国大学生的 go 使用情况	数量	美国大学生的 go 使用情况	数量
Two years went by, …	1	Insurance rates would go down.	1
As a famous Chinese saying goes, …	1	Things have gone just a bit too far.	1
Only one path went to the school.	1	Things rarely go that way.	1
His name went from military camps to every corner of our country.	1	go through several stages; the money goes to the same place / to fund a radio station.	3
合计	4	合计	6

第三，bring 和 take 是英语中一对很常用的及物行为动词，因其多义性和习语性也常用来构建无灵主语句。表14-8 概括了这两个常用动词在中美大学生无灵主语句中的用法。

表14-8 显示，美国大学生使用 bring 和 take 构造无灵主语句比中国大学生更灵活。

第四，give 和 provide 两词在中美大学生作文篇幅不等的情况下使用次数相同，这说明中国学生的使用频率高于美国学生。

表14-9 显示，对于 give 这个典型双宾语动词，美国学生只将其用于"sth. gives sb. sth."这一句型中生成无灵主语句，而中国学生却造出了"The song gives confidence in life. The descending sun has given the world a transient gilded dignity and poetry."这样不太符合英语表达习惯的句子。关于 provide 这个词，美国学生都只把它用作带单宾语的及物动词，而中国学生却将其分别用在"provide sb. with sth.; provide sth. for sb.; provide sb. sth."等不同句型中。这种使用差异很可能是由我们的课堂教学或教材过度概括引起的。

14.4.2 特色动词的使用情况对比

这里所谓的特色动词是指能够反映中美大学生各自所造的无灵主语句中不同特点的动词。对比分析中美大学生英语无灵主语句中所使用的340个动词（含47个重复动词），除了发现上述常用动词的使用差异外，还发现他们常用两类不同特色的动词。中国大学生常用的一类特色动词是表意比较抽象或概括的正式书面语用词，包括 accompany, conquer, distinguish, determine, disappoint, enhance, inspire, integrate, merit, obscure, represent, remind, reinvigorate, summon, stimulate, signify, vivify, 等等。略举数例如下：

表 14-8 中美大学生 bring 和 take 使用情况对比

中国大学生的 bring 使用情况	数量	美国大学生的 bring 使用情况	数量
bring sb. together	1	bring sb. together	3
bring sb. sth.	2	bring sb. sth.	1
bring sth. back	1	bring about sth.	1
bring sb. to a place / back to consciousness	2	Acquiring a new culture and language brings many hardships	1
bring sth. home to sb.	1	bring sb. home	1
合计	7	合计	7
中国大学生的 take 使用情况	数量	美国大学生的 take 使用情况	数量
sth. takes on a different appearance.	1	It takes sb. a long time to do sth.	2
Time will take revenge on man.	1	sth. takes a long time before it …	
The train took me to my work place.	1	sth. takes place; sth. takes a lot of money	2
		sth. takes care of sth. sth. takes the risks out of sth. sth. takes sb. to or into sth.	3
合计	3	合计	7

14. 中美大学生英语作文中无灵主语句使用情况对比分析
English sentences with inanimate subjects

表 14-9 中美大学生 give 和 provide 使用情况对比

中国大学生的 give 使用情况	数量	美国大学生的 give 使用情况	数量
sth. gives sb. sth.	3	sth. gives sb. sth.	5
sth. gives sth.*	1		
sth. gives sth.*	1		
合计	24	合计	30
中国大学生的 provide 使用情况	数量	美国大学生的 provide 使用情况	数量
Activities on campus provide me with opportunities to use my talents.	1	Crayons provide the perfect "snap" to relieve pen-up irritation.	1
The two-day weekend can provide more time for sb. to do sth.	1	Both the nose and the yard fence provide fortification.	1
The information highway has provided us a new method of acquiring information.	1	Basketball provides an avenue from… to …	1
合计	24	合计	30

(1) The same ideas, interests and beliefs <u>summoned</u> us together.
(2) Optimistic music <u>stimulates</u> people to do more for the public.
(3) Friendship may <u>accompany</u> you all your life.
(4) Information highway has magically <u>enhanced</u> information sharing degree.
(5) The misty curtain of rain at once <u>obscures</u> and <u>vivifies</u> his features.
(6) The fresh color <u>reinvigorates</u> my numbed senses.

由于此类动词不涉及人的具体动作或行为，其生命性特征不够明显，因而这类无灵主语句的隐喻度也不高。中国学生能使用这类动词，可能是他们先想到这些汉语意思，然后查汉英词典而用上的。

中国大学生常用的另一类特色动词是无灵和有灵兼有的不及物动词，包括 alter, burst, explode, flow, float, glare, happen, jiggle, radiate, ripple, shine, splatter, vary, whistle 等。部分例句如下：

(7) After a while, our bowls on the desk <u>jiggled</u>.
(8) The summer sun was <u>glaring</u> over head.
(9) Suddenly, streaks of faint red hue <u>radiated</u> across the sky.
(10) The feeling <u>shone</u> again in my heart.
(11) The chilly wind <u>whistled</u> by.
(12) Laughter <u>rippled</u> cheerfully around the fire.

14. 中美大学生英语作文中无灵主语句使用情况对比分析
English sentences with inanimate subjects

由于此类动词处在有灵动词和无灵动词之间，加上都是不及物动词，其生命性特征较低，因而这类句子的隐喻度也较低，处在无灵句与无灵主语句的模糊分界线上。中国学生常用这类动词造句，可能是因为这种英语表达方式与汉语很相似。

相反，美国大学生常用的一类特色动词是表意具体的言语或感知动词，包括 ask, explain, insult, reply, know, see, mourn, wake, 等等。例如：

(13) Obnoxious commercials insult your intelligence.
(14) Good food knows no boundaries.
(15) Ever since that day, his paintings have mourned the loss of his crayons.
(16) Stress may explain the especially high burnout rate.
(17) The last part of the profile asked me questions about my opinion of job performance.
(18) The computer could see the difference in our opinions of job performance.

由于此类动词直接表达人的言语和感知等具体动作或行为，生命性特征十分明显，因而在无灵主语句中经生命性概念跨域映射所产生的隐喻性也很强。

美国大学生的另一类特色动词是生动形象的名动转用词，包括 birth, block, bond, challenge, dent, frame, lap, line, mark, profile, rate, result, signal, stem, skyrocket, 等等。例如：

(19) But in a way, our differences bonded our friendship even more.

(20) The survey rated such aspects as variety, quality and taste of the food.

(21) This birthed a whole new way of thinking, surrealism.

(22) Prices for everything have skyrocketed.

(23) The silence signaled the conclusion of our last meal.

(24) These inconveniences dent the overall voter turnout.

此类由名词转用为动词的词,在转用过程中由于增加了表达相关动作或行为的方式而变得更为具体,用在无灵主语句中其生命度更高,隐喻性更强。

动词所表达的动作或行为越具体,其生命性就越强;生命性越强的动词用在无灵主语句中,其隐喻度就会越高;隐喻度越高的无灵主语句,其生动形象性就越明显(何明珠,2011)。因此,对比中美大学生用各自两类特色动词所造的英语无灵主语句可以发现:中国大学生的英语无灵主语句不如美国大学生的生动形象。

14.5 结论

本节对中美大学生各 49 篇英语作文中无灵主语句的分布状况和使用特征进行了对比分析。研究发现:①中美大学生英语作文的篇均词差与篇均小句差对比表明,美国大学生英语作文的口语化程度高于中国大学生英语作文,这一结果支持了马广惠（2002）的观点。②中美大学生英语无灵主语句的篇均数与篇均百分比对比显示，中国大学生的英语无灵主语句使用比率高于美国大学生；中美大学生的英语无灵主语句在记叙文和描写文中所占比率都低于论说文和说明文，这些结果支持了何明珠（2012b）"无灵主语句与书面语程度成正比"的观点。③无灵主语句虽然在中国大学生英语作文中所占比率高于美国大学生英语作文，但在后者中分布更均衡。这说明英语无灵主语句对于美国大学生来说是一种普通而自然的表达方式，而对于中国大学生来说则是个体英语水平差异的体现。④中美大学生英语无灵主语句中常用动词使用情况对比分析表明，在共用的 47 个动词中，make 的使用频率最高、使用差异最大，美国大学生能灵活运用该词的习惯搭配和引申义造句，而中国大学生则只能坚守其本义，经常造出不够自然或难以理解的句子。此外，美国大学生比中国大学生更能灵活运用由 come 和 go，bring 和 take，以及 give 和 provide 等常用动词构成的惯用短语、固定搭配和常见句型来构造英语无灵主语句。⑤就中美大学生在英语无灵主语句中各自使用两类不同特色动词进行的对比分析显示，中国大学生英语作文中的部分无灵主语句因其生命性不够明显，隐喻度不够高，而不如美国大学生的无灵主语句生动形象。

第四章

探讨与商榷

English sentences with inanimate subjects

15. 论英语无灵主语句的分析与解释基础[①]
——与翁义明先生商榷

语言研究已从过去对语言现象的观察与描写发展到现在对语言现象的分析与解释。分析与解释必须建立在观察与描写的基础之上，但更重要的是必须找准适合支撑相关分析与解释的理论依据。只有这样，才能确保分析的全面性与解释的合理性。对英语无灵主语句这一语言现象的研究也是如此。以往的研究主要描写这种句子的语法、语义或语用特征以及相应的英汉互译方法，而近十年来的研究则集中分析与解释这一句式的生成机制及其存在理据。最近读到翁义明先生（2005）的相关研究（以下简称翁文），就属于后一类。笔者近年（何明珠，2003，2005，2007，2009，2011）对英语无灵主语句的研究兴趣也很浓厚，读了翁文很有启发，但也有一些不同看法，想与翁先生商榷并求教于方家。

隐喻性是英语无灵主语句的生动性与普遍性之根源，分析与解释英语无灵主语句必须建立在隐喻理论的基础上。语言事实表明：每一个生动形象、客观精练的英语无灵主语句都是隐喻句（何明珠，2003）。这一点与翁文所持的看法是相同的，因为文中讨论的正是这类句子。然而，翁文在术语

[①] 本节内容原载于《南京晓庄学院学报》2012年第2期。

15. 论英语无灵主语句的分析与解释基础
English sentences with inanimate subjects

的使用、理论依据的定位以及权威观点的引用这三方面存在值得商榷的地方。

15.1 术语使用的精确性问题

翁文的标题和正文都使用"无灵句"这一术语,却在引言部分大谈主语和主语与谓语的搭配关系,并专辟一节进行"无灵句的界定"。然而,依笔者之见,这些讨论都不得要领。因为"英语无灵句"与"英语无灵主语句"虽然只有两字之差,却不能同指一个概念。例如,"Winter is cold. It often rains. Leaves have fallen."是三个英语无灵句,而"Winter often sees cold rain and fallen leaves."则是一个英语无灵主语句。无灵句是指整个句子不存在生命性;而无灵主语句则只是主语不存在生命性,整个句子的生命度却很强。翁文在第2节中指出,"在语言中一般来说,有灵句由有灵名词+有灵动词构成,无灵句由无灵名词+无灵动词构成",并举四个英语句子为例。文章接着又说:"英语的语言事实表明,属于无灵主语类的主语与有灵动词配用的现象,就像有灵主语与有灵动词配用那样正常。"并举"The fifth day saw them at the summit."和"Life had never brought them a gloomier hour."这两个英语句子为例。这说明该文讨论的是"英语无灵主语句",而非"英语无灵句"。在细读这一节时,笔者发现作者一时用"名词+动词构成",一时又用"主语与动词配用",混淆了"名词与主语"及"动词与谓语"这两对术语中的不同概念,忽视了"无灵句"与"无灵主语句"这对不同术语的区别。然而,术语的混用可是学术研究的大忌。

15.2 理论依据的定位问题

既然英语无灵主语句的最大亮点就是其隐喻性,那么分析与解释英语无灵主语句的理论依据当然就是相关隐喻理论。翁文的第 3 部分是该文的主体,从三个方面对英语无灵主语句进行分析,其分析的理论依据实际上就是韩礼德的语法隐喻(grammatical metaphor),这是理所当然的事。然而,不知为什么作者在文章的正标题和第 3 部分的三个副标题中都未提及"语法隐喻"这个名称,而是分别使用其上义名称"功能语法"和下义概念"概念隐喻""及物性"与"主位信息结构"。细读原文可以发现,这不是简单的名称使用问题,而是作者缺乏对语法隐喻理论的全面了解,因而可能导致误解。第一,系统功能语法,又叫系统功能语言学,是一个完整的语言学理论体系,语法隐喻理论只是这一体系中的一个重要组成部分。韩礼德的系统功能语言学理论大致包括阶与范畴语法、系统语法和功能语法等内容,其中语言的三大元功能或纯理功能(metafunction)理论是其最重要的语言学理论。这三大元功能是指概念功能、人际功能和语篇功能,其中概念功能包括及物性系统、语态系统和归一性系统,人际功能包括语气系统、情态系统和基调系统,语篇功能包括主位系统、信息系统和衔接系统等(胡壮麟,1994:F14)。显然,英语无灵主语句的分析与解释不可能使用这一庞大的理论体系,而应该使用其中的具体隐喻理论作为论述依据。第二,韩礼德的"语法隐喻"这一概念与认知语言学中的"隐喻"概念没有直接的关系。在系统功能语言学中,语法隐喻根据纯理功能可分为三类:概念语法隐喻、人际语法隐喻和语篇语法隐喻。有时也把"语法"省去不说,直接

15. 论英语无灵主语句的分析与解释基础
English sentences with inanimate subjects

说概念隐喻（ideational metaphor）、人际隐喻（interpersonal metaphor）和语篇隐喻（textual metaphor）。但必须注意的是，这里所说的"概念隐喻"与认知语言学（如 Lakoff and Johnson，1980）中的"概念隐喻"（conceptual metaphor）是两个完全不同的概念，不能混淆（黄国文，2009）。为了将二者区分开来，侯建波（2008）特地把 conceptual metaphor 译为"观念隐喻"，把 ideational metaphor 译作"概念隐喻"。翁文在既没指出语法隐喻的三大类别，又没标出相应英语名称的情况下，直接使用"概念隐喻"这个中文名称，容易导致误解。第三，韩礼德（2004：56）认为语法隐喻涉及两种转移：①级的转移；②语法功能和语法类别的转换。他把语法隐喻分为概念隐喻和人际隐喻，其中概念隐喻包括名物化和及物性隐喻；人际隐喻主要包括情态隐喻和语气隐喻（侯建波，2008）。如此看来，翁文在其第 3 部分将"概念隐喻"和"及物性"这两个不同层次的概念并列使用欠妥，更不应该混淆名物化（nominalization）和及物性系统中的过程类型转换两者之间的差异，这都是没能把握概念隐喻的精神实质所致。第四，系统功能语言学中的语法隐喻是在词汇语法（lexicogrammar）层面上，而不是在句子或小句层面上建构起来的；是指小句的三种成分：过程（process）、过程参与者（participant）和与过程相关的环境（circumstance），分别由词汇语法中的动词词组（verb phrase）、名词词组（noun phrase）和副词词组（adverb phrase）来体现的情况。如这三者之间分别对应，就是一致式，否则，就是隐喻式。因此，不能说"有灵句"就是"一致式"，"无灵句"就是"隐喻式"。而翁文在其第 3 部分却就是这样说，也是这样举例的。请看例句：The notice tells you to be quiet. 对于系统功能语言学来说，这个句子是一致式，不存在语法隐喻，因为言语过程中的言语参与者,即言语者(sayer),既可以是生命体,也可以是非生命体。但对于认知语言学来说,这是一个地地道道的隐喻句,因为这里存在概念跨域映射和概念隐喻(conceptual metaphor)。如此看来,理论依据的正确定位直接影响语言分析的全面性和合理性。

15.3　权威观点的引用问题

　　进行学术研究,必须引用权威观点作为论述支撑,但引文内容必须完整,引文出处必须准确无误。这不仅体现学术研究的规范性,更能反映作者的社会责任感和治学态度。翁文引述颇丰但引文大多只有半句或一句话。更大的问题是,有些引述在标明出处的地方找不到原话。例如,在翁文第3部分的3.1节里,有三处引用了韩礼德《功能语法导论》(Halliday,1994)一书中的观点,并标注了页码,可是其中两处对不上号。第一处是"意义与表达的关系不是随意的,语法的形式与编码的意义之间存在着自然的联系"(Halliday,1994:107)。第二处是"我们假定任何一个隐喻式的表达都有一个或多个字面的——用我们的术语毋宁说是一致式的——表达方式"(Halliday,1994:321)。笔者手头正好有这本书,在107页和321页里怎么也找不到这两句话。因为107页讲process, participant 和 circumstance, 而321页讲ellipsis 和 substitution, 所讲内容与翁文所引内容可以说是风马牛不相及的。

　　写文章做研究难免出现小的疏忽或差错,但就语言研究而言,在术语的精确性、理论依据的适切性以及引用权威观点的准确性三方面不能出现大的差错。否则,分析与解释语言现象的基础就不能牢固建立。笔者愿就此与翁先生共勉,并欢迎批评指正。

16. 生命性与英语无灵主语句的拟人效果[①]

16.1 引言

"有灵"是指具有生命性,"无灵"就是说与生命体无关。由英语无灵名词充当主语和有灵动词充当谓语的英语无灵主语句,因其句式新颖独特、结构严谨、言洁义丰、生动形象,而受到国内英语研究者的广泛关注。最近读到陈勇等人(2004;2007)的相关研究(以下简称陈文1和陈文2),虽然没有使用英语无灵主语句这个名称,但研究的对象正是这一语言现象。笔者近年(何明珠,2003;2005;2007;2009)对英语无灵主语句的研究兴趣也很浓厚,读了陈文很有启发,但也有一些不同看法,想与陈教授等商榷并求教于方家。

生命性的跨域映射(cross-domain mapping of animacy)是英语无灵主语句生动形象和简洁精练的根源之所在。陈文抓住了这一点,并从拟人的角度对英语无灵主语句这一语言现象进行分析与解释,颇有新意。但陈文在术语的规范性、分析与解释的合理性以及语言表达的逻辑性三方面存在值得

[①] 本节内容原载于《湖南科技学院学报》2011年第6期。

商榷的地方。

16.2　术语的规范性

术语是学术研究的基础，它不仅体现研究者的学术思想和观点，还能反映研究者的学术修养和治学态度。术语的规范性直接关系着研究成果的品位和档次。陈文1在其标题和摘要中使用了"动词拟人"和"动词拟人转义"两个术语；陈文2却在其标题中又使用了"拟人动词"这一术语。前后两篇文章探讨的是同一语言现象，但指称同一概念的术语却发生了变化，这就明显地违背了术语的规范性原则。其实，需要指出的是，陈文中有些术语本身就很值得商榷。

首先，无论是"动词拟人"还是"拟人动词"似乎都不是恰当的术语。因为单独一个词，不管是动词或名词还是形容词或副词，都无法产生拟人效果。单词必须在句子中，（如"Money talks. Words may kill. Fear seized them all."等）或至少要在词组中，（如"an angry sky, a killing hour, a friendly river, laughing valleys"等）才能产生拟人效果。虽然在传统修辞学中，拟人作为一种修辞格，可能为了分类的方便，也许有人将其分别叫作动词拟人、名词拟人或形容词拟人，但在研究英语无灵主语句时，用"动词拟人"或"拟人动词"这样的术语来指称这种语言现象，无法揭示其本质和内在规律。其实，邵志洪等（2007）在对英汉拟人法使用对比研究中区分了词汇化拟人和修辞性拟人，基本揭示了英汉无灵主语句中拟人机制的内在规律。他们认为拟人可分成隐性和显性两类。前者是词汇化拟人（lexicalized personification），后者是修辞性拟人（rhetorical personification）；前者属 dead metaphor（死的隐喻），后者属 live metaphor

16. 生命性与英语无灵主语句的拟人效果
English sentences with inanimate subjects

（活的隐喻）。由于英汉两种语言在语法特征和语言心理等方面存在较大差异，因此各自在拟人方法的使用上也很不相同：英语动词系统中有十分丰富的词汇化拟人表达法，而汉语指称系统中有十分丰富的词汇化拟人表达法。但无论在汉语还是英语中，词汇化拟人都涉及词语的正常搭配问题。例如，在"以陈独秀为代表的一种思潮认为……"这一词汇化拟人表达法中，"认为"一词已经历了词汇化过程，与"思潮"等无灵主语形成了正常的搭配关系。这时，人们一般不会意识到自己在使用拟人表达法。而在"*The view represented by Chen Duxiu held…"中，held 未曾经历类似的词汇化过程，不能与 The view 形成正常搭配，所以不能被接受。同样，在"Winter often sees cold rain and fallen leaves."中，"sees"已经历了词汇化过程，与"Winter"这个无灵主语形成了正常搭配关系。而在汉语中，"看见"还未经历相应的词汇化过程，不能与"冬天"构成正常搭配。"冬天常常看见寒雨和落叶"这样的句子还不能被接受。如此看来，单独讨论"动词拟人"或"拟人动词"是没有意义的。

其次，"动词拟人转义"（verbal personification connotation）这一术语令人费解。读者无法知道陈文1到底是探讨"动词"的转义，还是"拟人"的转义，甚或是"动词拟人"的转义。虽然文章第一部分的最后一句有"'动词拟人'转义"字样，但通读全文之后，读者还是无法知道"'动词拟人'转义"到底指什么，因为文章根本没有清楚陈述这个概念。

最后，"原型人物"（prototype person）这一术语在陈文2中没有得到合理定义或充分解释，读者因而无法正确理解这一术语。虽然作者在文章的第一部分引用了赵艳芳（2001）第102页上的一句话来解释"原型"这个概念，但没有指明这里的"原型人物"就是"原型"。如果二者同指一个概念，那么术语中的"人物"一词和英语译文中的person一词就是多余的了。然而，本节探讨的是英语无灵主语句的拟人机制，必须涉及"人"。因此，"原型人物"这个术语一定要有明确的定义和确切的所指。否则，读者可以有多种理解：一是作者或说话者心目中的"人"；二是读者或听话者心目中的"人"；三是与动词相关的任何"人"。术语所指的不确定性同样违背术语的规范性原则。

16.3 分析与解释的合理性

对语言现象的分析与解释必须建立在恰当的理论基础之上，也就是说，要有可靠的理论依据。陈文1的目的实际上就是分析英语无灵主语句的语用特点和解释英语无灵主语句的汉译方法，但在分析与解释之前却未建立任何理论基础。虽然作者在文章的第一部分引用了李鑫华（2001）的一段话来说明语言中的拟人机制，但这段话，甚至文章的整个第一部分，都无法为后面的分析与解释提供理论依据。正因为如此，后面的分析与解释都很难到位：第二部分所列7个"语用特点"既无一致性又无连贯性，大都是对英语无灵主语句的描写或说明，与"语用特点"基本不搭界；第三部分的翻译方法解释也因缺乏理论指导而没有新意。陈文2的主要目的应该是分析与解释英语无灵主语句中"人"的潜意识体现方式，但也因缺乏可靠的理论依据，使得文章三个部分的内容不甚连贯与一致；第三部分所列的6种潜意识体现方式也是重复交叉，缺乏条理性，有时还举例不当。此外，如上文所述，术语的非规范性也影响分析与解释的合理性。例如，"拟人动词"这一术语既不规范又不合理。请看例句：When poverty comes in at the door, love flies out through the window.（贫穷进门来，爱情越窗飞。）如果"进门来"（come in）是"人的动作"，即"拟人动词"，那么"越窗飞"（fly out）则是"鸟的动作"，是否可以叫作"拟鸟动词"呢？而"Misfortune is creeping over the city."中的动词creep是否可以称为"拟虫动词"呢？

其实，如上文所述，生命性是无灵主语句的灵魂，也是拟人表达法的核心。语言事实表明：生命性越强，拟人效果就越明显；拟人效果越显著，无灵主语句就越生动。如果用认知语言学的概念映射理论（theory of cross-domain mapping）作为分析与解释依据，通过分析和解释生命性这一概念的跨域映射过程来阐释无灵主语句的拟人效果，论述应该会更合理并更有说服力。

16.4　语言表达的逻辑性

语言表达的逻辑性决定论文的可读性与研究结果的可信度。除了上文提到的部分术语缺乏合理性因而不合逻辑外，文章中还有不少语句缺乏逻辑性。这里略举数例并加以说明。

例1："日常英语特别是科技英语中，由于抽象名词能使概念表达准确清楚，不易产生歧义，而且作者在心理上和考虑问题时对过程、特征和结果较为关注，这类词也能贴切表达作者的这种愿望，因而抽象名词被大量用来做主语。"

这句话有多处不合常理，违背逻辑，难以让人理解：一是"日常英语"怎能与"科技英语"完全相同呢？二是

"抽象名词"怎能"使概念表达准确清楚，不易产生歧义"呢？三是抽象名词怎能贴切表达作者关注过程、特征和结果的愿望呢？作者在这句话的后面引用了刘光耀等（2000）的一句话，读者也许可以通过参考刘文帮助理解，但笔者细读刘文后还是不能理解上面这句话。因为刘文讲日常英语与科技英语存在表达差异，而上面这句话说日常英语与科技英语相同，都经常使用抽象名词；刘文说行为主语的理解和翻译必须借助谓语提供的语境，而上面这句话讲抽象名词能使概念表达准确清楚，不易产生歧义。这实在让人产生南辕北辙的感觉。

例2："此外，在含有 see, find, notice, discover, observe, take 等动词的拟人法翻译成汉语时，句子成分要作调整。"

这句话让人费解的是：拟人法怎能翻译成汉语？

例3："意译法。将英语动词拟人转义的比喻意义和语用目的翻译出来。"

与上例相同，语用目的怎能翻译出来？人们通常能明确目的或达到目的，没有人能翻译目的，更何况是语用目的。
以上三例来自陈文1的第三部分，下面的例子来自陈文2的第二部分。

例4："拟人动词中无灵名词主语的突显特点"

这个副标题里有两点让人琢磨不透：一是拟人动词中哪

16. 生命性与英语无灵主语句的拟人效果
English sentences with inanimate subjects

有无灵名词主语？二是除了无灵名词可作主语外，是否还有无灵动词或无灵形容词等可作主语？

例5："拟人动词中的主语一般都是无灵名词，即这些名词均指向无生命、无灵魂的东西或抽象概念等。"

与上例相同，"拟人动词中"哪有"主语"可言？世界上哪有"有生命""有灵魂"的东西？

16.5 结语

行文至此，有人可能会说，这样咬文嚼字，似乎有些过分吹毛求疵。的确，如果是学生习作或不公开发表的文章，这样挑剔可能有些过火。但对于在大学学报上发表出来的学术论文，这样的分析与评论是十分必要的，因为这些文章不仅会影响千千万万的莘莘学子，还会直接影响全社会的学术风气。当然，写文章做研究难免出现疏忽或差错，但就语言研究而言，在术语的规范性、分析与解释的合理性以及语言表达的逻辑性等方面不能出现大的差错。否则，不可能有效分析与解释语言现象。笔者愿就此与陈教授等共勉，并欢迎批评指正。

17. 年轻人做学问不可毛糙
（电子邮件三则）

邮件一

李老师，你好！

近读贵刊《滁州学院学报》2016年第1期贵校吴老师的文章《认知语言学意义观关照下的〈醉翁亭记〉句式英译比析研究》，受益匪浅，但感慨也良多。吴老师思路清晰，条理分明，语言流畅，但最令我惊异的是她敢于挑战大家译作，包括杨宪益与翟里斯等翻译名家的译作。

不迷信权威，敢于创新是年轻人的优点，但在挑战权威与大胆创新之前要有厚实的专业功底；在创新的过程中，还应谨小慎微，不可毛糙。

该文的核心内容是第二部分，关于三个汉语句式：无主句、骈句和"也"字句的英译对比分析。具体说来，就是从《醉翁亭记》中挑选了三个句子，找到对应的六种译文，分别进行对比分析。现就这三小节中的明显纰漏指正如下：

一、吴老师有文章（《内蒙古民族大学学报》2012年第1期《认知语言学视角下的汉语无主句英译》）指出：用英语的无灵主语句来翻译汉语的无主句是一种有效的翻译手段。这次想用实例来验证其主张。的确，"山行六七里，见

17. 年轻人做学问不可毛糙
English sentences with inanimate subjects

闻水声潺潺"的六种译文中有四种是英语无灵主语句。但问题是，吴老师没有对比分析这四种无灵主语句译文与另外两种有灵主语句译文的优劣，而是全部否定这六种译文，并大胆给出了自己的译文：A walk of six or seven Li will gradually hear the gurgling water. 事实上，这个译文不可能优于已有的四种英语无灵主语句译文，因为它本身就是不合英语造句要求的错句。英语造句十分讲究逻辑性，英语无灵主语句也概莫能外。表面上，英语无灵主语句似乎不合常理，但其内在隐喻机制（包括拟人与借喻等）能确保句子语义的逻辑性。这种隐喻机制就是生命性概念的跨越映射，即有灵谓语的生命性映射在无灵主语之上。我们可以说 The White House hears no excuses. 也可以说 The year 1976 saw great changes in China. 但就是不能说 A walk of six or seven Li will gradually hear the gurgling water. 原因在于主语 a walk of six or seven Li 与谓语 hear 都具有生命性，不能形成跨域映射。因此，生命性很强的感官动词 see, witness, hear, find, know 等在英语无灵主语句中做谓语时，其主语一般是表达时间或地点等抽象概念的无生命事物。其实，以英语为母语的汉学家翟里斯的译文 A walk of two or three miles on those hills brings one within earshot of the sound of falling water 才是地道的无灵主语句。其主语 walk 的生命性很强，谓语 bring 的生命性较弱，可以形成跨域映射。因此，当英语无灵主语句的主语是动作名词或动名词时，其谓语一般是 bring, show, indicate；appear, exist；proceed, follow 等表达因果、存在、时间先后等逻辑关系的弱生命性动词。

二、关于骈句"临溪而渔，溪深而鱼肥，酿泉为酒，泉香而酒洌"的六种译文对比分析，吴老师认为潘正英的译文 To angle at the stream where the stream is deep and the fishes are fat; to brew the fountain water into wine where the water is delicious and the wine is clear 比杨宪益的译文 The fish are freshly caught from the stream, and since the stream is deep and the fish are fat; the wine is brewed with spring water, and since the spring is sweet the wine is superb 更好。这一点，可以见仁见智，但决不可以把杨老的译文抄错！前半句多出一个 and，会使杨老的译文无法让人读懂。本人细读之后认为：无论从哪个方面看，杨译应该是这六种译文中最好的。妄评名家译作，又拿不出自己的译文，实不可取。

三、略有古汉语常识的人都会把"望之蔚然而深秀者，琅琊也"称为"者……也"句，而不会称之为"也"字句。这个句式的很强判断语气，不是一个位于句末的"也"字能独立产生的，而是通过"者""也"两个字构成固定句型来实现的。吴老师花了不少笔墨对"也"字和"也"字句进行阐述，依我看，不得要领。

因没有吴老师的联系方式，只好写信给学报编辑部的责编李老师您。我花时间和精力把上述看法写出来，一是想帮助年轻学者端正做学问的态度；二是本着对学术求真的责任心；三是出于保护贵刊学术质量的良好愿望。请将此信转给吴老师，她应该知道我，因为她读过我的文章并引用过我的观点。谢谢！

广州航海学院 何明珠

17. 年轻人做学问不可毛糙
English sentences with inanimate subjects

邮件二

尊敬的何老师：

您好！

我是晚辈吴××，今天打开邮箱看到您通过我校编辑部李老师转发给我的信件。晚辈仔细阅读了何老师的信件，何老师在信中指出的一些问题确实是晚辈不够谨慎造成的，比如把杨老的译文抄多了一个"and"。有一些问题，由于晚辈写这篇文章的大概时间是2015年9月份，还需查一下当时写这篇文章的一些原始材料，再给何老师一一答复。

此外，晚辈会谨记何老师的教诲，做学问要谨小慎微，千万不能毛糙。何老师的这封信件对于晚辈来说真的是场及时雨啊！！！

非常感谢何老师！

祝何老师身体健康，工作顺利，一切顺心！

晚辈吴××敬上

邮件三

小吴老师，你好！

很高兴，你能及时回信。因研究兴趣所致，最近在知网上浏览到你的这篇文章；因你也做英语无灵主语句研究，出于关心的愿望，写了你读到的那封信；因没有你的联系方式，只好通过贵校学报编辑部的李老师转交，望能理解。能否接受我提出的意见，需要时间思考，这很自然，请慢慢推敲。今天回信还想补充指出的是,你在抄写汉语原作时,弄错了三个汉字,请予核实:①"山行六七里,渐闻水声潺潺",不是"山行六七里,见闻水声潺潺"(是"渐",不是"见");②"临溪而渔,溪深而鱼肥",不是"临溪而鱼,溪深而鱼肥"(是"渔",不是"鱼");③"酿泉为酒,泉香而酒洌",不是"酿泉为酒,泉香而酒冽"(是三点水,不是两点水)。如此可见,做学问必须谨小慎微,不可毛糙。学者著述,犹如妇女怀胎。婴儿如何,全靠基因与母爱;论著如何,全凭学术功底与精力投入。不知这个比喻是否恰当?

顺致问候!

广州航海学院 何明珠

附:《醉翁亭记》原文

环滁皆山也。其西南诸峰,林壑尤美。望之蔚然而深秀者,琅琊也。山行六七里,渐闻水声潺潺而泻出于两峰之间者,酿泉也。峰回路转,有亭翼然临于泉上者,醉翁亭也。作亭者谁?山之僧智仙也。名之者谁?太守自谓也。太守与客来饮于此,饮少辄醉,而年又最高,故自号曰醉翁也。醉翁之意不在酒,在乎山水之间也。山水之乐,得之心而寓之酒也。

若夫日出而林霏开,云归而岩穴暝,晦明变化者,山间之朝暮也。野芳发而幽香,佳木秀而繁阴,风霜高洁,水落而石出者,山间之四时也。朝而往,暮而归,四时之景不同,而乐亦无穷也。

17. 年轻人做学问不可毛糙
English sentences with inanimate subjects

至于负者歌于途,行者休于树,前者呼,后者应,伛偻提携,往来而不绝者,滁人游也。临溪而渔,溪深而鱼肥。酿泉为酒,泉香而酒洌;山肴野蔌,杂然而前陈者,太守宴也。宴酣之乐,非丝非竹,射者中,弈者胜,觥筹交错,起坐而喧哗者,众宾欢也。苍颜白发,颓然乎其间者,太守醉也。

已而夕阳在山,人影散乱,太守归而宾客从也。树林阴翳,鸣声上下,游人去而禽鸟乐也。然而禽鸟知山林之乐,而不知人之乐;人知从太守游而乐,而不知太守之乐其乐也。醉能同其乐,醒能述以文者,太守也。太守谓谁?庐陵欧阳修也。

Appendix

English sentences with inanimate subjects

English Sentences with Inanimate Subjects: A Metaphorical Perspective[①]

Introduction

In the field of applied linguistics, particularly in comparative and contrastive studies between English and Chinese, considerable attention has been devoted to English sentences with inanimate subjects (ESWIS) (Chen, 1990; Wang, 1997; Zhang, 1999; Wu, 2002). However, few studies have so far dealt with this kind of sentences from the perspective of metaphor and still fewer have probed this language phenomenon from different approaches. The goal of the present thesis is, therefore, to study ESWIS from three different approaches: rhetorical, cognitive and systemic-functional, in hopes of discovering the causes for their abundance and their cognitive and grammatical mechanisms.

Within the category of applied linguistics, the present study concentrates on the metaphorical features, the classification, the

---

① 本节《隐喻视角下的英语无灵主语研究》是笔者早年用英语写成的硕士论文,就内容而言应该归入本书第 2 章,但因英语论文与其余各篇体例不同,故作附录单独呈现。

pragmatical characteristics and the mental properties of ESWIS. It also touches upon relevant translating strategies and techniques in this respect.

It is due to my teaching experience of many years in English writing and English-Chinese translating and thanks to my supervisor Prof. Tu Guoyuan's suggestions and encouragements that I venture to take up this study. My interest was further aroused when I read G. Lakoff & M. Johnson's *Metaphors We Live By* (1980) and M. A. K. Halliday's *An Introduction to Functional Grammar* (1994) and Fan Wenfang's *A Systemic-Functional Approach to Grammatical Metaphor* (2001). The methods of study in the present thesis mainly include comparison, classification and causal analysis. Comparisons are made between conceptual and grammatical metaphors and between English and Chinese thinking patterns. A tentative classification of ESWIS is conducted in keeping with the two approaches to metaphor. Causal analyses are carried out during the discussion of translating techniques from ESWIS into Chinese. The whole thesis consists of five chapters.

Chapter 1 presents a brief review of metaphor studies in three different fields: traditional rhetoric, cognitive linguistics and systemic-functional grammar. Theories of conceptual metaphor (CM) by cognitive linguists like G. Lakoff and M. Johnson and of grammatical metaphor (GM) by functional grammarians like M. A. K. Halliday are briefly introduced and illustrated with examples.

Chapter 2 studies the causes for the abundance of ESWIS from the metaphorical perspective. Rhetorical metaphors, conceptual metaphors and grammatical metaphors are analyzed one by one in connection with ESWIS.

Chapter 3 makes a tentative classification of ESWIS and analyzes their basic features respectively. The classification may be of little practical significance and the dividing line may be by no means clear, but it can help a lot in the process of discussion.

Chapter 4 is a comparative study between English and Chinese from the thinking perspective. This is done with hopes of discovering the mental properties behind ESWIS. The comparison is expected to serve as a further explanation of why ESWIS are so abundant in the English language and of why inanimate subjects are so rare in Chinese sentences.

Chapter 5 points out some effective ways of translating ESWIS into Chinese in accordance with their respective pragmatical features. In order to encourage a creative use, instead of a blind overuse, of these translating methods, a dialectical viewpoint of translating ESWIS into Chinese is put forward at the end of the chapter in connection with the two translating strategies: domestication and foreignization.

Chapter 1 Metaphor Studies: From Rhetorical Tradition to Cognitive and Systemic-Functional Approaches

1.1 Rhetorical Approach: Metaphor as a Figure of Speech

The study of metaphor dates back to Aristotle, who simply considers metaphor to be one of the eight different forms of a Noun (a strange word as it is called) and takes it as the transference of a word from one thing to another, the transference being either from genus to species, or from species to genus, or from species to species, or on grounds of analogy (Fan, 2001: 3). That is to say, Aristotle defines metaphor within the confinement of words and this idea of metaphor as words has led researchers from different fields in concentrating their minds on lexical metaphor for centuries. Because of this tradition, metaphor has ever since been regarded as a figure of speech, or as an ornamental device used in the rhetorical style, and within this tradition, the essence of metaphor is captured by the notion of a violation of a selection restriction, or a semantic deviation; i.e. one or more words for a concept are used outside their normal conventional meaning to express a "similar" concept. For example, words like "mother" in "Failure is the mother of success" and "a block of ice" in "Sally is a block of ice" are not used in their normal everyday sense. It is certainly wise of traditional metaphor theorists to discover the unusual use of words in metaphorical expressions, but the explanatory power of their theories is limited. That's why in rhetoric we have other figures of speech like metonymy, synecdoche and personification to explain such sentences as "Many people like reading Lu Xun", "You are not expected to talk about morality when you do not have enough bread to eat", and "The wind sighed in the tree tops".

1.2 Cognitive Approach: Conceptual Metaphor (CM)

As time goes on, Max Black finds, in a precognitive context, that metaphors act as "cognitive instruments" (1962: 37). This means that metaphors are not just a way of expressing ideas by means of language, but a way of thinking about things. In the same vein, George Lakoff and Mark Johnson co-authored in 1980 their famous work, a significant landmark in this respect, *Metaphors We Live By*, in which they no longer treat metaphor as a figure of speech but study it from the cognitive approach. They point out in the book, "Our conceptual system is largely metaphorical. The way we think, what we experience, and what we do every day is very much a matter of metaphor." (Lakoff & Johnson, 1980: 3) "The concept is metaphorically structured, the activity is metaphorically structured, and consequently the language is metaphorically structured" (Lakoff & Johnson, 1980: 5). By illustrating the abundance of metaphorical expressions in our daily communication from such metaphorical concepts as "TIME IS MONEY" and "ARGUMENT IS WAR", Lakoff and Johnson create the term "conceptual metaphor" and in the light of this theory, the metaphors they enumerate in their book are roughly classified into three kinds[①]:

A. Structural Metaphors like:
TIME IS MONEY

> You are wasting my time.
> This gadget will save you hours.
> I don't have the time to give you.
> We are running out of time.
> How do you spend your time?
> That flat tire cost me an hour.
> I have invested a lot of time in her.
> He is living on borrowed time.

ARGUMENT IS WAR

> Your claims are indefensible.
> He withdrew his offensive remarks.
> He attacked every weak point in my argument.
> She shot down all my arguments.
> I demolished his argument.
> I have never won an argument with him.

B. Orientational Metaphors like:
HAPPY IS UP; SAD IS DOWN

[①] See Zhao (2000: 106), with some of the examples substituted or modified accordingly.

I am feeling up.
That boosted my spirits.
You are in high spirits.
He is feeling down.
She is really low these days.

C. Ontological Metaphors like:
CONTAINER METAPHORS

The ship is coming into view.
Are you in the race on Sunday?
There is a lot of land in Kansas.
We are out of trouble now.

In fact, these conceptual metaphors are so pervasive and so deeply rooted in common human experience that 70% of our daily expressions are estimated to derive from them[①].

Later on, G. Lakoff moves a step forward on the cognitive theory of metaphor in his paper *The Contemporary Theory of Metaphor* (1993) by defining metaphor as "a cross-domain mapping in the conceptual system". Here he changes his definition of metaphor from "understanding and experiencing one kind of thing in terms of another" to "a cross-domain mapping in the conceptual system." The focus of metaphor is thus not on the language but on the way we conceptualize things in one mental domain in terms

---

① See Zhao (2000: 106), with some of the examples substituted or modified accordingly.

of another. In short, the idea of "cross-domain mapping in the conceptual system" becomes essential for us to understand the nature of metaphor.

1.3 Systemic-Functional Approach: Grammatical Metaphor (GM)

M. A. K. Halliday's famous work *An Introduction to Functional Grammar* was first published in 1985 and then its revised edition came out in 1994. In this book, Halliday devotes a whole chapter to GM. In fact his treatment of GM is regarded as the real beginning of conscious study of GM and his idea of GM serves as a great milestone in the history of metaphor study because he opens up a whole new realm of study on metaphor.

Halliday doesn't attempt to define GM in his book but he makes a statement like this: "There is a strong grammatical element in rhetorical transference; and once we have recognized this we find that there is also such a thing as grammatical metaphor, where the variation is essentially in the grammatical forms although often entailing some lexical variation as well." (Halliday, 1994: 342) From this statement we can see that Halliday studies GM in the rhetorical tradition rather than from the cognitive approach. Therefore, Fan (2001: 33) makes a definition like this: "GM is an incongruent realization of meanings involving transference of grammatical units from one domain to another, either from a basic domain to a sub-domain, or from one sub-domain to another sub-domain."

Within the framework of his functional grammar, Halliday first distinguishes two types of realization relationships between grammar and semantics: "congruent" and "metaphorical". Then, in accordance with his theory of metafunctions of language, Halliday classifies GM into two kinds: ideational metaphor and interpersonal metaphor. At this point, however, Fan (2001: 159) finds it possible and necessary to add another kind, i.e. textual metaphor, to match Halliday's theory of the three language meta-functions: ideational, interpersonal and textual.

As far as the present study is concerned, we have to confine our discussion here within ideational metaphor and nominalization, because they are closely related to our analysis of English sentences with inanimate subjects (ESWIS) in the following chapters.

According to Halliday's functional grammar, the ideational function of language is concerned with the meaning of the clause as representation.

> Language enables human beings to build a mental picture of reality, to make sense of what goes on around them and inside them. Here the clause plays a central role, because it embodies a general principle for modeling experience—namely, the principle that reality is made up of processes.
>
> "Our most powerful impression of experience is that it consists of 'goings-on', —happening, doing, sensing, meaning, being and becoming. All these goings-on are sorted out in the grammar of the clause. Thus, the clause is also a mode of reflection, of imposing order on the endless variation and flow of events. The grammatical

system by which this is achieved is transitivity. The transitivity system construes the world of experience into manageable set of process types."
......

The grammar distinguishes rather clearly between outer experience, the processes of the external world, and inner experience, the processes of consciousness. The grammatical categories are those of material, mental and relational processes. A process consists, in principle, of three components:
(1) the process itself;
(2) participants in the process;
(3) circumstances associated with the process.
(Halliday, 1994: 106-107)

Typically, process is realized by a verbal group, participant by a nominal group and circumstance by an adverbial group or a prepositional phrase. If this is the case, we call it the congruent realization. However, the realization relationship between semantics and grammar is not so simple. We may sometimes choose a nominal group to realize process, an epithet or a verbal group to realize participant, and a nominal group or a verbal group to realize circumstance. If this happens, we call it the incongruent realization, i.e. an ideational GM. Now, let's illustrate the point with two examples:

A. Congruent realization: They arrived at the summit on the fifth day.

Table 1.1 Congruent realization of grammatical categories illustrated with an example①

they	arrived	at the summit	on the fifth day
participant	process	circumstance	circumstance
nominal group	verbal group	prepositional phrase	prepositional phrase
Actor	Material	place	time

B. Incongruent realization or ideational GM: Their arrival at the summit happened on the fifth day.

Table 1.2 Incongruent realization of grammatical categories illustrated with an example②

their arrival	at the summit	happened	on the fifth day
participant	circumstance	process	circumstance
nominalized verbal group	prepositional phrase	verbal group	prepositional phrase
Actor	Attribute	material	time

From the above examples, we should come to see the following points:

(1) Through the congruent realization, an informal and colloquial clause is usually produced; whereas through the incongruent realization, we generally get an ideational GM, which always appears as a formal and semantically-dense clause.

---

① This figure is adopted from Halliday (1994: 345), with some adaptation and simplification.

② This figure is adopted from Halliday (1994: 345), with some adaptation and simplification.

(2) Nominalization seems to be a precondition for ideational GM. That's why Halliday clearly points out, "Nominalizing is the single most powerful resource for creating grammatical metaphor." (Halliday, 1994: 352)

(3) We must try to keep a balance between the two extremes, because "something which is totally congruent is likely to sound a bit flat; whereas the totally incongruent often seems artificial and contrived." (Halliday, 1994: 344)

Chapter 2 English Sentences with Inanimate Subjects (ESWIS): A Metaphorical Perspective

ESWIS abound in the English language, but the ESWIS we are discussing in this study refer to sentences not only with inanimate subjects but also with verbal groups of material or mental process (Halliday, 1994) as their predicates. That is to say, sentences like "1976 is an eventful year", "Moscow is a historic city", and "The camera is a machine for taking photos" are excluded because they seldom pose difficulty to Chinese learners of English. In this chapter, we'll concentrate the discussion on the metaphorical nature of ESWIS from three approaches in hopes of discovering the main causes of ESWIS.

2.1 ESWIS from Rhetorical Approach

Figures of speech in traditional rhetoric are mostly employed in formal written texts for the purposes of liveliness and vividness.

Some common figures like personification, metonymy and synecdoche are actually practical means of vivid expressions and they are all metaphorical①. Similarly, ESWIS frequently appear in the formal written style and they are typical ways of expressing ideas vividly. This coincidence of ESWIS with figures of speech is one of the causes of their abundance in the language. The following examples can illustrate this point:

(1) Dusk found the child crying in the street.
(2) Beijing has witnessed many changes in the past few years.
(3) White hair is crying for help.

"Dusk" in Example (1) refers to an abstract concept of time and "Beijing" in Example (2) is the name of a place. They are both inanimate. Logically speaking, they can't be the subjects of the two mental activities of "found" and "witnessed". However, speakers of English tend to personify them and by means of personification, the two sentences become not only acceptable but also vivid. Of cause, Example (2) can also be considered as a case of metonymy, in which "Beijing" is used to replace "people in Beijing", while Example (3) is commonly regarded as a case of synecdoche, in which a part (white hair) is used to mean a whole (people with white hair). The above

---

① The word "metaphorical" here is used in its broad sense. It actually means "figurative". In cognitive linguistics, metaphor includes such traditional figures of speech as metonymy, synecdoche, personification and so on. See also Zhao (2000: 207).

analysis indicates that ESWIS often go hand in hand with figures of speech and therefore they are highly metaphorical. The nature of liveliness and vividness is an immediate cause of the abundance of ESWIS in the English language.

2.2 ESWIS from Cognitive Approach

With the development of linguistics, people find the explanatory power of traditional rhetoric too limited. The classification of figures of speech often causes problems and rhetorical analysis is always superficial because it is chiefly concerned with the form of language itself. Therefore, people believe language must be studied in social and cognitive contexts. With this belief deeply rooted in people's mind, cognitive linguistics has become one of the most popular research fields and the study of metaphor has become a very important part in language studies. It is believed that metaphors are not just a way of expressing ideas by means of language, but a way of thinking about things. Contemporary cognitive linguists G. Lakoff and M. Johnson point out in their famous work *Metaphors We Live By*: "Our conceptual system is largely metaphorical. The way we think, what we experience, and what we do every day is very much a matter of metaphor." (1980: 3) "The concept is metaphorically structured, the activity is metaphorically structured, and consequently the language is metaphorically structured." (ibid. : 5) The essence of G. Lakoff's theory of "conceptual metaphor" is that in our conceptualization of the world, our concept in one cognitive domain (source domain, usually abstract and unfamiliar) is always mapped onto another (target domain, usually concrete and familiar). It is estimated that

70% of our daily expressions derive from conceptual metaphors[①]. Since conceptual metaphors are so pervasive, it is only natural for ESWIS, which are in fact derivatives of metaphorical expressions, to abound in the language. The following examples will suffice to illustrate this point.

(4) A good idea suddenly struck me. (IDEA IS PERSON)
(5) Nowadays, scientific ideas flow rapidly. (IDEA IS LIQUID)
(6) An evil idea is growing in his mind. (IDEA IS PLANT)
(7) Good ideas nurture good deeds. (IDEA IS FOOD)
(8) His idea of a bright future collapsed all of a sudden. (IDEA IS BUILDING)

2.3 ESWIS from Systemic-Functional Approach

As is discussed in the previous chapter, according to M. A. K. Halliday, father of grammatical metaphor (GM), there exist two kinds of realization relationship between semantics and lexicogrammar: congruent and metaphorical. The congruent realization refers to the congruity between (or among) semantics (represented by thing/entity, event, property or manner), lexicogrammar (represented by noun/nominal group, verb/verbal group, adjective or adverb) and function (represented by participant, process, attribute or circumstance). This can be illustrated

---

[①] See Zhao (2000: 106), with some of the examples substituted or modified accordingly.

English Sentences with Inanimate Subjects: A Metaphorical Perspective

by the following table:

Table 2.1 Congruent realization—experiential meaning①

Semantics	lexicogrammar	function
Thing/Entity	Noun/Nominal Group	Participant
Event	Verb/Verbal Group	Process
Property	Adjective	Attribute
Manner	Adverb	Circumstance

This kind of realization is a typical way of representing our experience and therefore is closest to our instinct. On the contrary, the metaphorical or incongruent realization (i.e. grammatical metaphor) refers to the discrepancy between semantics and lexicogrammar. This can be illustrated by the following figure:

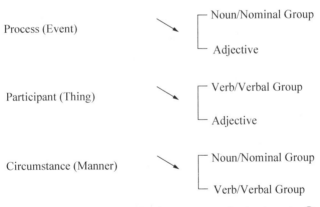

Fig. 2.1 Incongruent realization—grammatical categories②

---

① This table is adopted from Fan (2001: 38), with some change and supplementation.

② This figure is also adopted from Fan (2001: 38), with some change and supplementation.

Now, let's look at one of Halliday's classical examples for further illustration.

(9a) In the evening the guests ate ice cream and then swam gently.
(9b) The guests' supper of ice cream was followed by a gentle swim.

Apparently, Example (9a) is a congruent mode: (ⅰ) the two processes are represented by two verbs "ate" and "swam"; (ⅱ) the two participants are represented by two nominal groups "the guests" and "ice cream"; and (ⅲ) the three circumstances are represented by a prepositional phrase and two adverbial groups; while Example (9b) is a metaphorical mode (or a GM): (ⅰ) the process "ate" and the circumstance "in the evening" have been fused into the noun "supper" functioning as Head/Thing in a nominal group functioning as Identified; (ⅱ) the participants "the guests" and "ice cream" have been embedded as (a) Modifier/Deictic: Possessive and (b) Modifier/Qualifier: Appositive in this nominal group; (ⅲ) the process "swam" has been encoded as a noun "swim" functioning as Head/Thing in a nominal group functioning as Identifier; (ⅳ) the circumstance "gently" has been encoded as a Modifier/Epithet within this nominal group; and (ⅴ) the circumstance "then" has been encoded as a verbal group "was followed by", functioning as a relational process of the Circumstantial/Identifying type (Halliday, 1994: 344). After this series of adjustments, the semantic structure of Example (9b) has become more complicated, but its grammatical structure has been simplified and its lexical density has greatly increased. What's more, the animate subject in Example (9a) has become an inanimate one in Example (9b). That shows clearly: it is GM that brings about ESWIS. However, GM is, in turn, created by nominalization, which means turning verbs and adjectives into nouns. Halliday (1994: 352) points out in his book, "Nominalizing is the single most powerful resource for creating grammatical metaphor." As GM created by nominalization abounds in formal written English texts like scientific works, the abundance of ESWIS is undoubtedly a natural phenomenon in this kind of texts, too.

In the following, we have four more pairs as examples:

(10a) Two months after his mother died in 1921, he and Clementine lost their daughter. She was three years old. They loved her.

(10b) In 1921, the death of his mother was followed two months later by the loss of his and Clementine's lovely three-year-old daughter. (Dong, 2002)

(11a) I handed in my essay late, because my kids got sick.

(11b) The reason for the late submission of my essay was the illness of my children. (Eggins, 1994; Xiao & Wang, 2001)

(12a) We can improve its performance when we use super-heated steam.

(12b) An improvement of its performance can be effected by the use of super-heated steam.

(13a) We have noticed that the number of books in the library has been going down. Please make sure to obey the rules for borrowing and returning books. Don't forget that the library is for everyone's convenience. So from now on, we're going to enforce the rules strictly. You have been warned!

(13b) It has been noted with concern that the stock of books in the library has been declining alarmingly. The rules for the borrowing and returning of books are to be strictly obeyed and the needs of others duly met. Penalties for overdue books will be further enforced.

Chapter 3 Classification of ESWIS: Respective Features and Mechanisms

In Chapter 2, we have had a quick look at ESWIS from three approaches: rhetorical, cognitive and systemic-functional and we find that all ESWIS are metaphorical in one way or another. Since our concept, activity and language are all metaphorically structured, the abundance of ESWIS is obviously quite natural.

For the convenience of analyzing the features or characteristics of ESWIS, we are going to make a tentative classification of ESWIS in this chapter.

In the course of analysis, we find that ESWIS in the forms of figures of speech and ESWIS from the derivatives of conceptual metaphor are just two sides of the same coin. We therefore simply classify ESWIS, in accordance with CM and GM, into two types: rhetorical ESWIS and syntactical ESWIS[①].

3.1 ESWIS in Line with CM (Rhetorical ESWIS)

3.1.1 ESWIS with Nouns of Time or Place

When nouns of time or place serve as subjects in sentences, verbs of mental process are generally required as their predicates. For example:

(1) Dawn found him well along the way.
(2) Moscow believes no tears.

3.1.2 ESWIS with Nouns of Lifeless Entities

When nouns of lifeless entities are used as sentence subjects, both verbs of mental activity and verbs of action are applicable. For example:

(3) This medicine knows no bounds of effectiveness.
(4) Slow music encourages supermarket-shoppers to browse long but spend more.
(5) Poems lie at the tip of her tongue.

[①] I classify ESWIS into two types and name them in this way because of their different linguistic features and functions and in line with my discussion in the following chapters.

(6) Alarm began to take possession of him.

Rhetorically speaking, this type of ESWIS is regarded as figures of speech: personification or metonymy. However, from the cognitive point of view, they are all cases of metaphor because they are derivatives from relevant conceptual metaphors and a cross-domain mapping is obvious in each of them.

The typical characteristic or feature of this type of ESWIS is their liveliness and vividness. By using this type of ESWIS, people create an aesthetic effect, i.e. a linguistic beauty which is brought about by image schemata or by cross-domain mappings from unknown to known, or from unfamiliar to familiar, or from abstract to concrete. Another feature of this type of ESWIS is their objectiveness, with the help of which people sound fair and authoritative.

3.2 ESWIS in Line with GM (Syntactical ESWIS)

According to Halliday, ideational GM is always created by nominalization. When nominalized verbs and adjectives serve as subjects of sentences, GM and ESWIS come into being all at the same time.

3.2.1 ESWIS with Nouns Nominalized from Verbs

There are two ways to nominalize verbs: agnation and derivation. For example:

(7) A glance through his office window offers a panoramic view of the Washington Monument and the Lincoln Memorial.

(8) When something a little out of the ordinary takes place at the bar, the <u>sense</u> of it spreads quickly.
(9) A careful <u>comparison</u> of the two will show you the difference.
(10) <u>Rectification</u> of this fault is achieved by <u>insertion</u> of a wedge.

Here, the purpose of nominalization is to turn doings into things so as to pack the overt participant and the covert process into one form, thus creating a GM.

3.2.2 ESWIS with Nouns Nominalized from Adjectives

The nominalization of adjectives is usually carried out by derivation. For example:

(11) The <u>anxiety</u> and <u>jealousy</u> you apprehend from releasing the letter will be apt to increase by suppressing it.
(12) His <u>weariness</u> and the increasing <u>heat</u> determined him to sit down in the first convenient shade.
(13) The <u>fleetness</u> of his mare saved his life.
(14) By now, <u>optimism</u> had given way to doubt.

Here, the overt participant and the covert attribute are rolled into one form so as to create a GM.

From the above examples and the four pairs of examples at the end of Chapter 2, we can summarize the chief characteristics or features of ESWIS in combination with GM (i.e. syntactical ESWIS) like this:

(1) Like rhetorical ESWIS and CM, syntactical ESWIS and ideational GM are completely inseparable and they are also two sides of the same coin;

(2) Syntactical ESWIS are structurally compact, lexically dense and semantically implicit and complicated. They are, therefore, applicable and appropriate in the formal written style;

(3) Syntactical ESWIS are conducive to the prominence of theme or the thematization, which helps a lot in the cohesion and coherence of texts and the fluency of expression.

(4) Like rhetorical ESWIS, the most important feature, or the greatest advantage, of syntactical ESWIS is also their objectiveness, which brings more fairness and authority to the expression.

One more word must be said here is that the classification made in this chapter is in no way accurate. The two types of ESWIS do overlap from time to time and so an absolutely clear dividing line between them is, in fact, nonexistent. A tentative classification is made in this chapter only for the convenience of discussion.

Chapter 4 Mental Properties Behind ESWIS: With Chinese in Comparison

ESWIS are a unique linguistic phenomenon. It is unique because it is rare in languages like Chinese and this poses great difficulty to Chinese learners of English. As language phenomena are inseparable from mental attitudes and thinking habits, we'll in this chapter look at ESWIS from the thinking perspective with Chinese in comparison in order to pave the way for our discussion on translating ESWIS into Chinese in the next chapter.

A lot of studies (Pan, 1991; Liu, 1992; Hu, 1993; Jia, 1997; Zhang, 1999; Lian, 2002; Mao, 2002) have been recently carried out about the differences between the English and Chinese thinking patterns. Although they may seem to be either too general and lengthy or too specific and brief, the following two points are already in complete agreement: the English are rational while the Chinese perceptual; the English think in abstract concepts while the Chinese in concrete images.

4.1 Rational Thinking vs. Perceptual Thinking

There is a strong philosophical background behind the English rational thinking and the Chinese perceptual thinking. The English speakers have long been influenced by Aristotle's formal logic and the theory of rationalism which was very popular in Europe from the sixteenth to the eighteenth century. The influence of formal logic on the English mind can be seen from its reflection on the English language as the morphological strictness. For example, the only precondition for being the subject in English is the quality of being nominal; i.e. any English word that is in the noun form can serve as the subject in a sentence. That partly explains why ESWIS are so pervasive in the English language. Rationalism, on the other hand, holds that reason is the only prime source of knowledge and this belief has greatly encouraged the growth of scientific spirit, logical and analytical in particular, throughout the western world. The tradition of being logical and analytical is also reflected on the English language as being hypotactic. In a hypotactic language like English, therefore, the abundance of ESWIS is only natural.

Closely related to the English rational thinking is the object-consciousness of the English speakers. In the tradition of western philosophy, from the origin of the ancient Greek philosophers, nature has always been the target of cognition. Only by understanding nature can people control and conquer nature (Mao, 2002: 69). In the course of exploring nature, the westerners, including the English, have come to the realization that the natural object and the human subject are of equal significance. With this object-consciousness as their mental property, the English speakers tend to be very objective in their language. ESWIS are a case in point.

The Chinese speakers, on the contrary, have long been cultivated in the philosophical ideologies of Confucianism, Taoism and Buddhism.

Confucianism is in fact a combination of politics, ethics and philosophy[①]. Its essence is to teach people to be loyal and filial to their country and their family. Ever since ancient times, the Chinese people have been educated to be reserved and obedient. This mental property of the Chinese is reflected on their language as its semantic implicity. For example, in ancient Chinese written texts, there are no punctuation marks. Different people may read

---

① See Lian (2002: 42). The idea, instead of the exact words, is adopted here.

the same text differently and get different implications. Because of this tradition, the Chinese have always been solely concerned with the meaning of their language, paying little attention to morphology or syntax. Even in modern and contemporary Chinese, there is no morphological restriction for the subject or the predicate in a Chinese sentence. (Note: in English, the subject must be nominal and the predicate in its verb form.)

Another important philosophical idea from the three successive schools of ancient Chinese philosophers is "holism", which holds that man and nature form an organic whole in spirit (qi 气) and in principle (li 理) and that heaven and man respond to each other. Within this organic whole, heart and mind, form and spirit, mental and material, thinking and existing, subject and object are united into one respectively. The basic categories of this whole include "the Doctrine" (dao 道), "the Spirit" (qi 气), "the Supreme Ultimate" (taiji 太极) and "the Principle" (li 理) while "yin and yang" (the two opposing principles in nature, the former feminine and negative, the latter masculine and positive), "the five elements" (metal, wood, water, fire and earth, held by the Chinese ancients to compose the physical universe) and "the Eight Trigrams" (eight combinations of three lines—all solid, all broken, or a combination of solid and broken lines—joined in pairs to form 64 hexagrams, formerly used in divination) are the key elements of this whole. The Chinese holistic thinking derives from the symmetry of "yin and yang" into a dual structure of "the golden mean" and later develops into a plural structure like "the five elements" (Lian, 2002: 42). This holistic thinking approach has great impact on the Chinese mind: staying in the middle, keeping a good balance, giving equal consideration to both sides, finding interactive relationships between opposites, and attaining a harmonious unification. In sharp contrast to the English tradition of being logical and analytical, this mental property of the Chinese is reflected on the language as being paratactic. In a paratactic language like Chinese, inanimate subjects are quite unnatural and even unacceptable.

One more philosophical tradition from the Chinese ancients is the encouragement of instinctive perceptulization. According to Taoists, nature is a complete whole which can not be analyzed. You only perceive it, experience it and then comprehend it. Buddhists also encourage people to attain sudden enlightenment. They try their best to free their thoughts from the fetters of language and to transcend themselves and the worldly in an illogical, supertemporal and superspatial state of mind. This perceptual thinking approach is in close connection with the above two mental properties of the Chinese, but in direct opposition to the English rational thinking. Therefore, closely related to the Chinese perceptual thinking is the subject-consciousness of the Chinese speakers and with this subject-consciousness as their mental property, the Chinese speakers are quite subjective in their language. That also explains why inanimate or lifeless entities can never be used as sentence subjects together with verbs of action in Chinese. In this case, an animate subject is obligatory. As a result, in doing translation between English and Chinese, we must take this point into consideration. For example①:

(1) The remembrance of this incident will add zest to his life.
他想起这件事，就会更加感受到生活的乐趣。
(2) Astonishment, apprehension and even horror oppressed her.
她感到惊讶和忧虑，甚至有些恐惧不安。
(3) 他开车时心不在焉，几乎出了车祸。
His absence of mind when driving nearly caused an accident.
(4) 她疾病缠身，丧失了完成这项任务的信心。
Sickness robbed her of the confidence in accomplishing the task.

These four examples are provided here simply to show the different features of the English and Chinese subjects. Relevant translating methods in this respect will be discussed in detail in the next chapter.

4.2　Thinking in Concepts vs. Thinking in Images

Language is the outcome of human cognitive activities. As different peoples reflect the objective world in different ways, different languages actually reflect distinctive thinking patterns of different nations. English is an alphabetical language. The alpha-

---

① See Pan (1991: 364—381). The four examples here are quoted with some modification.

betical system of writing does not provide any imitation of natural phenomena. Instead, it is an artificial system of symbols. As these symbols are closely related to sounds instead of pictures, they can hardly produce direct images in the mind. Similarly, there is no immediate semantic relationship between the meaning and the alphabetical form of the word. Therefore, in order to carry across the meaning through the alphabetical form, there must be a fixed set of abstract concepts between a particular meaning and a particular form in the language. Furthermore, to define a certain conceptual meaning of a word, the exercise of reason and the power of inference is indispensable. As a result, speakers of alphabetical languages, speakers of English included, are quite advanced in their rational thinking. English, in the same way, is also a one-dimensional phonographic language, and so the meaning of an English word can only be comprehended from basically one single angle — abstract concept. Thus, speakers of English are used to thinking abstractly and analytically. This mental property is, in turn, reflected on the choice of the subject in the English sentence: nouns of abstract ideas can unexceptionally serve as subjects in English. That's an inherent cause for the abundance of ESWIS in the language. For example:

(5) Loneliness held the immigrants together and poverty kept them down (Pan, 1991: 381).
(6) Absence and distance make the overseas Chinese heart increasingly fond of the mainland (Mao, 2002: 69).

English Sentences with Inanimate Subjects: A Metaphorical Perspective

Written Chinese, on the contrary, is a pictographic language. Each pictographic character in ancient Chinese provides a clear imitation of a natural phenomenon and presents a picture or image to the mind. It is true that pictographic characters may also be an artificial system of symbols, but these symbols can produce direct images in the mind and therefore there is an immediate semantic relationship between the meaning of the character and the form of the symbol. Because of this directness between the meaning and the form, no abstract concepts are needed as a bridge in carrying across the meaning through the pictographic character. It is also true that pictographic characters are simultaneously phonographic, but Chinese philosophers believe that visual symbols are primary while audio symbols are secondary in transmitting meaning. This directness between the meaning and the form prevents speakers of pictographic languages, speakers of Chinese included, from thinking in abstract concepts. Instead, they are used to thinking in concrete images. Thus, the Chinese thinking process can be represented as "image—association—imagination" while the English one goes like this: "concept—judgement—reason". Within this thinking pattern, the Chinese are good at analogizing instead of analyzing. Because of this thinking habit, nothing abstract appears at the beginning of a Chinese sentence. In other words, the Chinese sentence always demands a concrete animate subject. For example:

(7) 她焦虑不安，心如刀绞。
Anxiety tore her into pieces.
(8) 他连日辛劳，已经瘦下好几磅了。

Successive exertion has already chipped a few pounds off him.

4.3 Summary

Language and mode of thinking are inseparable. In fact, different languages reflect different thinking approaches of different peoples. In this chapter, a brief comparison has been made between some chief English and Chinese mental properties behind their respective languages. The comparison shows that the English language reflects such thinking habits as being logical, analytical, cognitive, objective, rational and abstract while the Chinese language contrastively presents such thinking tendencies as being reserved, analogical, holistic, subjective, perceptual and concrete. The findings from this comparison serve to explain, in another respect, why ESWIS are so abundant in the English language and why inanimate subjects are hardly found in Chinese sentences. The comparison has also paved the way for the discussion in the next chapter.

Chapter 5 Ways of Translating ESWIS into Chinese

5.1 A Brief Overview

As is discussed in Chapter 4, diametrically different thinking approaches between the English and the Chinese bring about huge differences to the two languages in their forms and ways of expression, let alone cultural differences. Equivalent translation between these two languages seems, therefore, to be hardly possible. Liu (2000) has recently made a study on the question of translatability in accordance with language functions. He believes that there is a great correlation between the question of translatability and untranslatability and the three language functions. That is to say, the cognitive and expressive function of language forms the basis of general translatability between languages while the cultural and the aesthetic functions are the causes of untranslatability—the former produces relative untranslatability and the latter absolute untranslatability. He continues to point out that the unique formal features of the source language can not be translated into the target language. There are three kinds of untranslatable formal features of language: first phonic features, second graphical features and finally compositional characteristics of language units. Therefore, when the characteristics of the form of the source language are presented as rhetorical devices for the sake of aesthetic purposes, the translator has to find some other formal features of the target language to replace them so as to achieve similar aesthetic results. This is exactly the demonstration of the translator's creative ability. From this point of view, the translating of ESWIS into Chinese falls into the category of untranslatability. As a result, if ESWIS are unavoidably to be translated into Chinese, they have to be creatively done. Creative translating does not mean following fixed rules mechanically, but making appropriate choices according to specific situations and weighing up the advantages and disadvantages. Our analysis in Chapter 3 shows that rhetorical ESWIS from the perspectives of figures of speech and conceptual metaphor (CM) are rhetorical means to create aesthetic effects of liveliness and vividness through their formal features while syntactical ESWIS from the viewpoint of grammatical metaphor (GM) are technical ways to perform the expressive function of language through their structural features. The purposes and functions of these two types of ESWIS are different and therefore they should be differently treated in being translated into Chinese. In the following, translating methods are discussed respectively, though the dividing line is quite unclear.

5.2 Ways of Translating Syntactical ESWIS into Chinese

When syntactical ESWIS are translated into Chinese, attention should be attached to the following two aspects. On the one hand, finding the right nexus (in the sense of Otto Jespersen), analyzing the logical relationships, denominalizing the nominalized verbs and adjectives, and reconstructing the meaning of the sentence in Chinese are the necessary steps to take.

(1) The execution of the prisoner preceded the president's arrival.
总统尚未到达，囚犯已被处死。
(2) His acceptance of bribes led to his arrest.
他因受贿而被捕。
(3) His help will ensure my success.
他肯帮忙，我就一定会成功。
(4) His words and deeds showed his honesty.

English Sentences with Inanimate Subjects: A Metaphorical Perspective

他的言行说明他是诚实的。

As is shown by the above examples[①], by finding the right nexus, we mean that there is always a hidden logical "subject-predicate" or "predicate-object" relationship between the nouns which are nominalized from verbs or adjectives and the determiners and/or modifiers before and/or after them. A noun phrase with this kind of logical relationship in it is called a nexus, in terms of Otto Jespersen, a famous Danish linguist. A nexus in English can be translated into an independent "minor sentence" in Chinese. For example, in Example (1) "The execution of the prisoner" and "the president's arrival", in Example (2) "His acceptance of bribes" and "his arrest", in Example (3) "His help" and "my success", and in Example (4) "his honesty" are all nexuses, and they are all rendered into independent Chinese "minor sentences".

By "analyzing the logical relationships", we mean that special attention must be attached to the distinction between the "subject-predicate" relationship and the "predicate-object" relationship in each nexus. Ignorance of this distinction will cause misunderstanding and mistranslation. For instance, in Example (1) "The execution of the prisoner" falls into the "predicate-object" relationship (i.e. there is a passive sense in it), while "the president's arrival" belongs to the "subject-predicate" rela-

---

[①] Some of the examples in this chapter are quoted from the works listed in the references. For the sake of space, the author finds it inconvenient to set out the sources of the examples separately and feels greatly indebted to all those concerned.

tionship (i.e. there is an active sense in it). In Example (2), "His acceptance of bribes" consists of a "subject-predicate-object" relationship, while in "his arrest", there is a "predicate-object" relationship. Furthermore, the implicit logical relationship of time, cause or condition etc. between one nexus and another must also be clearly analyzed and understood.

By "denominalizing the nominalized verbs and adjectives", we mean that the participants (in the sense of M. A. K. Halliday) in the form of nominalized verbs or adjectives in ESWIS must be turned back into verbs or adjectives in the Chinese version. Only in this way, can the Chinese version conform to the Chinese way of expression. For example, the following participants in the form of nouns in the above examples: "execution", "arrival", "acceptance", "arrest", "help" and "success", are all translated into Chinese verbs, and "honesty" in Example (4) is turned back into a Chinese adjective.

After the above three steps, each ESWIS can be naturally rendered into two or more Chinese "minor sentences". However, another important step is not to be neglected. That is: the meaning of each ESWIS must be completely carried across into Chinese. By "reconstructing the meaning of the sentence in Chinese", we mean that the focus of translation is meaning transference and that meaning can be adequately reconstructed in the target language. That's why Eugene A. Nida, a famous American translation theorist, points out: "Translating means translating meaning" (Nida, 1993). For instance, in Examples (1) and (2) the words "preceded" and "led to" seem to have disappeared in the Chinese translation, but their meanings have been fully reconstructed in the Chinese function words "尚未……已" and "因" respectively.

On the other hand, retaining the formal style and objective tone deserves great efforts.

As is summarized at the end of Chapter 3, one of the outstanding characteristics of ESWIS is their formal style and objective tone which are exhibited by their structural compactness, lexical density and semantic implicity. For the sake of retaining this characteristic of ESWIS in the target language, a clever use of Chinese four-character idioms or expressions must be made in the Chinese version. For example:

(5) The cast's brilliant acting drew stormy and lengthy applause from the audience.
台上演员演技高超,台下观众掌声雷动,经久不息。

(6) The increase of interests rate owed something to the serious consideration of the present situation.
上调利率,是出于对当前形势的认真考虑。

The reason for doing so is that Chinese four-character idioms or expressions are also formal in style and objective in tone.

5.3 Ways of Translating Rhetorical ESWIS into Chinese

5.3.1 How to Find the Right Subject for the Chinese Version

As is discussed in Chapter 4, according to the Chinese way of expression, the subject of a Chinese sentence is generally required to be animate, and so the subjects in ESWIS can not continue to serve as subjects in Chinese versions. Generally speaking, there are three ways to find a new subject for the Chinese version. First, if there is a relevant personal pronoun or a noun of animate entity in an ESWIS, no matter whether it is used as an object or as an attributive in the sentence and no matter what case or form it is in, it usually can act as the subject of the Chinese version. Second, if an ESWIS is a general statement without any reference to a particular animate entity, the subject of the Chinese version can be any of such general Chinese expressions as "人们","我们","大家","你" and so on. Third, if the above two ways do not work, translate the ESWIS into a Chinese sentence without a subject, which is very common in Chinese. For instance:

(7) Pork has priced itself out of his dish.
猪肉太贵，他吃不起。

(8) Space does not allow us to further analyze this problem here.
限于篇幅，我们不能在此对这个问题作进一步分析。

(9) By now optimism had given way to doubt.
至此，人们不再盲目乐观，而是疑惑重重。

(10) When something a little out of the ordinary takes place in the bar, the sense of it spreads very quickly.
酒吧里稍有异常情况，大家很快就能感觉到。

(11) The exigency of the case admitted of no alternative.

情况紧急,别无选择。

(12) Pit closure sees violent protests.
关闭矿井,抗议强烈。

There are, of course, exceptions, in which subjects in ESWIS remain unchanged in Chinese versions. For example:

(13) Adversity and struggle lie at the root of evolutionary progress.
逆境和奋斗是进化与发展的根源。

5.3.2 How to Handle the Subject in an ESWIS

As a new subject is generally found for the Chinese version, the subject of an ESWIS has to be turned into another sentence member in Chinese. We usually have two ways out: (1) denominalizing the subject of a syntactical ESWIS and turning it into the predicate of the Chinese version, and (2) translating the subject of a rhetorical ESWIS into the adverbial or attributive of the Chinese version. For example:

(14) A careful comparison of the two will show you the difference.
你仔细比较二者,就会知道其间的差别。
(15) Bitterness fed on the man who had made the world laugh.
这位曾让世人欢笑的人自己却饱尝辛酸。
(16) Autumn finds a beautiful sunny Beijing.
秋天里,北京阳光灿烂,景色优美。

(17) History knows only two kinds of war, just and unjust.
历史上的战争，只有正义的和非正义的两类。

However, exceptions do exist, when the subject of an ESWIS is turned into the object of a Chinese sentence. For example:

(18) That word always slips my mind.
我总记不住那个词。

5.3.3　How to Cope with the Predicate of an ESWIS

Generally speaking, the predicate of an ESWIS performs two functions: to embody logical relationships and to create rhetorical effects. Verbs like "owe to", "ensure", "contribute to", "lead to", "bring about", "result in", "draw", "bring", "precede", "follow", "require" etc. often perform the first function and they are quite objective in sense. For the second function, there are such verbs as "find", "see", "witness", "know", "show", "offer", "tell", "determine", "decide" and so on. These verbs are rather subjective and, according to M. A. K. Halliday, realize mental processes.

As is mentioned in Section 2 of this chapter, the objective predicates in ESWIS, which embody logical relationships in English, are generally translated into Chinese function words, which embody logical relationships in Chinese. (For illustration, please refer to Section 2 of this chapter). However, in this way the English implicit logical relationships become explicit in Chinese. On the other hand, the subjective predicates in ESWIS, whose purpose is to create rhetorical effects, are often left out in translation. The rhetorical effects which they produce with their inanimate subjects have to be compensated for by other means in Chinese. Of course, this is not an ideal outcome, but translation often leaves something for regret.

Professor Wang Zongyan (1985: 219) points out: "To some extent, learning a language means absorbing the concepts, attitudes and beliefs embodied in the language. For example, speakers of English usually do not distinguish abstract things from concrete things. Therefore, there are in English a lot of such personifying and metaphorical expressions as 'a flight of fancy', 'in the grip of fear' etc. These are not exactly special figures of speech, but common expressions"[①]. ESWIS under discussion in this study are, in fact, also a case in point.

5.4 A Viewpoint in the Opposite Direction

Schleiermacher, a famous German philosopher and translator, holds that there are two ways of doing translation: one is that the translator leaves the author in peace as much as possible and moves the reader toward him, and the other is that the translator leaves the reader in peace as much as possible and moves the author toward him. Later on, L. Venuti (1995), a famous Ameri-

---

① The original in Chinese of this quotation goes like this: "学一种语言,在某种程度上得把这种语言所体现的观念、态度、信仰吸收过来。例如说英语的人常常把抽象事物和具体事物当作同类的东西,所以英语中有许多人格化和比喻说法,如 a flight of fancy, in the grip of fear 等。这些并不是什么特殊的修辞手法,而是常用的词句。"

can translator and translation theorist, in his book *The Translator's Invisibility* develops the idea into a pair of well-known technical terms: domestication and foreignization, which are now regarded as two different translation strategies (Liu & Yang, 2002). The techniques of translating ESWIS into Chinese discussed above in this chapter belong to the translation strategy: domestication, because by using these techniques we leave the Chinese reader in peace and move the English author toward him. That is to say, these translating techniques help the translator to keep apart the English and Chinese cultures and modes of thinking embodied in the two languages. Therefore, domestication as a translation strategy does not seem to be in keeping with the current rapid social development and progress, because cultural and ideological interchanges between different nations are greatly encouraged during the present process of globalization. Out of this consideration, we seem to have to turn back in the opposite direction—foreignization: to leave the English author in peace and move the Chinese reader toward him. To make this turn, we have the following three reasons. First, although the thinking approaches of a particular nation have their outstanding and distinctive characteristics or features, they are always in the process of change, either collectively or individually, because the economic and cultural interflow between nations will unavoidably cause changes in thinking approaches, and furthermore, thinking approaches without change and development will surely become ossified and cease to exist. With the current globalization of economy and culture in full swing, English has become or is becoming an international language and therefore the absorption of the English mode of thinking is inevitable. Second, the history of cultural and thinking evolution shows that the human thinking process itself has always been very creative, compatible and absorptive. Finally, in a sense, the introduction of a new expression from a foreign language means the absorption of a new thinking approach, and this will naturally enrich the expressive function and thinking patterns of the native language.

From the above point of view, or in accordance with the foreignization strategy, the methods of translating ESWIS into Chinese discussed in this chapter have to be employed creatively and flexibly. That is to say, appropriately retaining the English way of expression and the English mode of thinking in translating ESWIS into Chinese is not only possible but also necessary. For example:

(19) His departure brought to an end the long period of negotiations starting from January 1946.
Version A: 由于他已离去，这场从1946年1月开始的长期谈判只好告终。
Version B: 他的离去结束了从1946年1月开始的长期谈判。

(20) A close study of their short stories will lead to the conclusion that they have a striking resemblance in several aspects.
Version A: 仔细研读他们的短篇小说之后，人们将必然得出这样的结论：他们在有些方面很相似。
Version B: 仔细研读他们的短篇小说会得出他们在有些方面有惊人相似之处的结论。

(21) Absence and distance make the overseas Chinese

heart increasingly fond of the mainland.

Version A: 华侨离乡背井，远居国外，所以他们在感情上越来越向往大陆。

Version B: 离乡背井和远居国外使华侨在感情上越来越向往大陆。

（22） The whole devastating experience sharpened my appreciation of the world around me.

Version A: 经过这场灾难之后，我觉得人生更有乐趣了。

Version B: 整个这场灾难性经历使我对周围世界的观察更敏锐了。

The above examples show that all the four Version A's are provided by following the translating methods discussed in this chapter and they sound natural and fluent to the Chinese ear because the English way of expression and the English mode of thinking have been replaced by their Chinese counterparts. However, all the four Version B's are also becoming accepted by contemporary Chinese speakers because they sound novel and exotic. If this is the case, the translator is again in a situation of embarrassment, out of which he has to find his way by making clever choices. But two things are certain: the change of thinking patterns takes a long time and nothing in this world can go to extremes.

Conclusion

With G. Lakoff's conceptual metaphor （CM） and M. A. K.

Halliday's grammatical metaphor (GM) as theoretical bases, a comprehensive study of English sentences with inanimate subjects has been conducted in this thesis. To sum up, the main findings of the present study fall into the following four groups:

First, there are three causes for the abundance of ESWIS or constructing mechanisms for ESWIS.

(1) The coincidence of ESWIS with such figures of speech as personification, metonymy and synecdoche etc. is one of the causes for the abundance of ESWIS. In other words, metaphorical figures of speech like personification, metonymy and synecdoche etc. are one of the constructing mechanisms for ESWIS.

(2) The pervasiveness of conceptual metaphors in our daily expressions is another cause for the abundance of ESWIS. That is to say, conceptual metaphors serve as another constructing mechanism for ESWIS.

(3) Grammatical metaphors by means of nominalization make the abundance of ESWIS possible in formal written texts. Namely, ESWIS are often constructed with the help of grammatical metaphors.

Second, two types of ESWIS are identified with their respective features.

(1) ESWIS can be classified into two types: rhetorical and syntactical.

(2) Rhetorical ESWIS are lively and vivid while syntactical ESWIS are structurally compact, lexically dense and semantically implicit. All ESWIS are objective, which brings fairness and authority to the expressions.

Third, mental properties exist behind ESWIS.

(1) A comparison between English and Chinese from the thinking perspective shows that the English language reflects such mental properties as being logical, analytical, cognitive, objective, rational and abstract while the Chinese language presents such thinking tendencies as being reserved, analogical, holistic, subjective, perceptual and concrete.

(2) The respective thinking habits between the English and the Chinese serve to explain in another respect why ESWIS are so abundant in the English language and why inanimate subjects are so rare in Chinese sentences.

Fourth, some effective ways are found to translate ESWIS into Chinese:

(1) flexible adjustment of the grammatical functions of words, clear understanding of the logical relationships between sentence members, and clever division of phrases with the help of nexus;

(2) choosing the right subject for the Chinese version and properly handling the English subject and predicate so as to comply with the Chinese way of expression;

(3) making appropriate use of Chinese four-character idioms or expressions in order to represent the objectiveness and conciseness of ESWIS.

The application of the theories of both CM and GM to the study of ESWIS is a fairly new attempt. The practical value of the findings in the present study remains to be judged, evaluated and tested in future studies. However, it will be a great satisfaction to the author of the present thesis if this study provides some inspiration and stimulates some interest in this field of applied linguistics.

参考文献

1. 英文文献

Biber, D. *Variation across Speech and Writing*. Cambridge: Cambridge University Press, 1988.

Black, M. More about Metaphor. In Andrew Ortony (ed.) *Metaphor and Thought*. Cambridge: Cambridge University Press, 1993.

Black, Max. *Models and Metaphors*. Ithaca & New York: Cornell University Press, 1962.

Bloor, Thomas & Bloor, Meriel. *The Functional Analysis of English: A Hallidayan Approach*. London: Edward Arnold, 1995.

Chao, Yuenren. *A Grammar of Spoken Chinese*. Berkeley, Los Angeles & London: University of California Press, 1968.

Cohen, L. Jonathan. The semantics of metaphor. In Andrew Ortony (ed.) *Metaphor and Thought*. Cambridge: Cambridge University Press, 1993.

Comrie, Bernard. *Language Universals and Linguistic Typology*. Chicago: The University of Chicago Press, 1981.

Fan, Wenfang. *A Systemic-Functional Approach to Grammatical Metaphor*. Beijing: Foreign Language Teaching and Research Press, 2001.

Fergusson, Rosalind & Jonathan Law. *The Penguin Dictionary of Proverbs*. London: Market House Books Ltd. , 2000.

Foley, W. A. *Anthropological Linguistics*. Oxford: Blackwell Publishers, 1997.

Goatly, Andrew. Species of metaphor in written and spoken varieties. In Mohsen Ghadessy (ed.) *Register Analysis: Theory and Practice*. London: Pinter Publishers, 1993.

Goldberg, A. E. *Construction: A Construction Grammar Approach to Argument Structure*. Chicago & London: University of Chicago Press, 1995.

Halliday, M. A. K. & C. M. I. M. Matthiessen. *An Introduction to Functional Grammar* (3rd Edition). London: Edward Arnold, 2004.

Halliday, M. A. K. *An Introduction to Functional Grammar* (2nd Edition). Beijing: Foreign Language Teaching and Research Press; London: Edward Arnold, 1994.

Halliday, M. A. K. Some lexicogrammatical features of the *Zero Population Growth* text. In: William C. Mann and Sandra A. Thompson (ed.) *Discourse Description: Diverse Linguistic Analyses of a Fund-raising Text*. Amsterdam: John Benjamins, 1992: 327-358.

Halliday, M. A. K. *An Introduction to Functional Grammar*. London: Edward Arnold, 1985.

Halliday, M. A. K. On the language of physical science. In Mohsen Ghadessy (ed.) *Registers of Written English: Situational Factors and Linguistic Features*. London: Pinter Publishers, 1988.

Halliday, M. A. K. Written language: lexical density & Spoken language: grammatical intricacy. In *Spoken and Written Language*. Oxford: Oxford University Press, 1989.

He, Mingzhu. *Studies on English Sentences with Inanimate Subjects: A Metaphorical Perspective*. MA Thesis. Changsha: Central South University, 2003.

He, Mingzhu. Writing English the English Way. *Teaching English in China*, 2000 (4).

Jespersen, Otto. *Essentials of English Grammar*. London: George Allan & Unwin Ltd, 1933.

Jespersen, Otto. *Selected Writings of Otto Jespersen*. London: Allen & Unwin, 1960.

Jespersen, Otto. *The Philosophy of Grammar*. London: The University of Chicago Press, 1951.

Lakoff, George and Mark Johnson. *Metaphors We Live By*. Chicago: The University of Chicago Press, 1980.

Lakoff, George and Mark Turner. *More than Cool Reason: A field guide to poetic metaphor*. Chicago: The University of Chicago Press, 1989.

Lakoff, George. The contemporary theory of metaphor. In Andrew Ortony (ed.) *Metaphor and Thought*. Cambridge: Cambridge University Press, 1993.

Lakoff, George. *Women, Fire and Dangerous Things*. Chicago: The University of Chicago Press, 1987.

Langacker, R. *Foundations of Cognitive Grammar (vol. II): Descriptive Application*. Stanford, California: Stanford University Press, 1991.

Leech, G. & J. Svartvik. *A Communicative Grammar of English*. London: Longman, 1974.

Levin, S. R. *The Semantics of Metaphor*. Baltimore: John Hopkins University Press, 1977.

Lewis, Norman. *Word Power Made Easy*. London: Longman, 1949.

Low, Graham. "This paper thinks …": Investigating the acceptability of the metaphor AN ESSAY IS A PERSON. In: L. Cameron and G. Low (ed.) *Researching and Applying Metaphor*. Cambridge: Cambridge University Press, 1999.

Martin, J. R. *English Text: System and Structure*. Amsterdam: John Benjamins, 1992.

Master, Peter. Active verbs with inanimate subjects in scientific prose. *English for Specific Purposes*, 1991 (1): 15-33.

Master, Peter. Active verbs with inanimate subjects in scientific research articles. In: M. Hewings (eds) *Academic Writing in Context: Implications and Applications*. Birmingham: The University of Birmingham Press, 2001.

Newmark, Peter. *About Translation*. Clevedon: Mutilingual Matters Ltd., 1991.

Nida, Eugene A. & Charles R. Taber. *The Theory and Practice of Translation*. Leiden: E. J. Brill, 1968.

Nida, Eugene A. & Jan de Waard. *From One Language to Another*. Nashville: Thomas Nelsons Publishers, 1986.

Nida, Eugene A. *Language, Culture, and Translating*. Shanghai: Shanghai Foreign Language Education Press, 1993.

Pinkham, Joan. *The Translator's Guide to Chinglish*. Beijing: Foreign Language Teaching and Research Press, 2000.

Quirk, R. et al. *A Comprehensive Grammar of the English Language*. London: Longman Group Ltd, 1985.

Richards, I. A. *The Philosophy of Rhetoric*. Oxford: Oxford University Press, 1936.

Ricoeur, Paul. *The Rule of Metaphor*. Toronto: University of Toronto Press, 1977.

Searle, John R. *Expression and Meaning*. Cambridge: Cambridge University Press, 1979.

Seskauskiene, Inesa. The paper suggests: Inanimate Subject + Active Verb in English Linguistic Discourse. *Kalbotyra*, 2009 (3): 84-93.

Seskauskiene, Inesa. Who discusses: the paper or the author of the paper? Inanimate Subject + Active Verb in Lithuanian Linguistic Discourse as Compared to English. *Respectus Philologicus*, 2010 (23): 83-99.

Simpson, John & Jennifer Speake. *Oxford Concise Dictionary of Proverbs*. Oxford: Oxford University Press, 1998.

Talmy, Leonard. *How Language Structures Space*. In H. Pink & L. Acredolo (ed.) *Spatial Orientation: Theory, Research and Application*. New York: Plenum Press, 1983.

Taylor, John R. *Linguistic Categorization: Prototypes in Linguistic Theory*. Oxford: Oxford University Press, 1989/1995.

Thompson, G. *Introducing Functional Grammar*. London: Edward Arnold, 1996.

Ungerer, F. & H. J. Schmid. *An Introduction to Cognitive Linguistics*. London: Longman, 1996.

Venuti, Lawrence. *The Translator's Invisibility—A History of Translation*. London and New York: Routledge, 1995.

2. 英语正文中的中文文献

Chen, W. B.（陈文伯）Yinghan fanyi lianxi（英汉翻译练习

English – Chinese Translation Exercises）［J］. Yingyu shijie（英语世界, *The World of English.*）1990 – 1992,（1）–（6）.

Cheng, Q. L.（程琪龙）Yuyan renzhi he yinyu（语言认知和隐喻 Language Cognition and Metaphor）［J］. Waiguoyu（外国语, Foreign Languages.）2002,（1）.

Dong, H. L.（董宏乐）Gainian yufa yinyu yu yingwen xiezuo nengli de tigao（概念语法隐喻与英文写作能力的提高 Ideational Grammatical Metaphor and the Improvement of English Writing Ability）［J］. Guowai waiyu jiaoxue（国外外语教学, Foreign Language Teaching Abroad.）2002,（3）.

Hu, S. Z.（胡曙中）Yinghan xiuci bijiao yanjiu（英汉修辞比较研究 A Comparative Study of English – Chinese Rhetoric.）［M］. Shanghai：Shanghai waiyu jiaoyu chubanshe（上海：上海外语教育出版社, Shanghai：Shanghai Foreign Language Education Press.）1993.

Hu, Z. L.（胡壮麟）Yufa yinyu（语法隐喻 Grammatical Metaphor）［J］. waiyu jiaoxue yu yanjiu（外语教学与研究, Foreign Language Teaching and Research.）1996,（4）.

Hu, Z. L. Zhu, Y. S. & Zhang, D. L.（胡壮麟, 朱永生, 张德禄）Xitong gongneng yufa gailun（系统功能语法概论 An Introduction to Systemic Functional Grammar.）［M］. Changsha：Hunan jiaoyu chubanshe（长沙：湖南教育出版社, Changsha：Hunan Education Press.）1989.

Hu, Z. L.（胡壮麟）Ping yufa yinyu de hanlide moshi（评语法隐喻的韩礼德模式 A Review of Hallidian Geammatical Metaphor）［J］. waiyu jiaoxue yu yanjiu（外语教学与研

究, Foreign Language teaching and Research.) 2000, (2).

Jia, Y. X. (贾玉新) Kuawenhua jiaojixue (跨文化交际学 Cross-cultural Communications.) [M]. shanghai: Shanghai waiyu jiaoyu chubanshe (上海: 上海外语教育出版社, Shanghai: Shanghai Foreign Language Education Press.) 1997.

Jia, Z. G. (贾志高) Lun yinyu hudonglun he renzhi hudonglun de tongyi (论隐喻互动论和认知互动论的统一 On the Unification of Metaphorical Interaction and Cognitive Interaction) [J]. Sichuan waiyu xueyuan xuebao (四川外语学院学报, Journal of Sichuan International Studies University.) 2002, (2).

Li, L. (李力) Yinghan yupian zhong hexin chengfen de zhuanyi chengyin (英汉语篇中核心成分的转移成因 Causes of the Transference of Core Elements in English and Chinese Texts) [J]. Waiyu yu waiyu jiaoxue (外语与外语教学, Foreign Languages and Their Teaching.) 2001, (4).

Lian, S. N. (连淑能) Lun zhongxi siwei fangshi (论中西思维方式 On Chinese and Western Thinking Modes) [J]. Waiyu yu waiyu jiaoxue (外语与外语教学, Foreign Languages and Their Teaching.) 2002, (2).

Liu, Y. L. & Yang, Z. J. (刘艳丽, 杨自俭) Yetan "guihua" yu "yihua" (也谈"归化"与"异化" "Domestication" and "Foreignization" Revisited) [J]. Zhongguo fanyi (中国翻译, Chinese Translators Journal.) 2002, (6).

Liu, M. Q. (刘宓庆) Yinghan duibi yanjiu de lilun wenti (英汉对比研究的理论问题 Theoretical Issues in English and

Chinese Contrastive Studies.) [A]. Wang Fuxiang zhubian (王福祥主编 in Wang, F. X. eds.) Duibi yuyanxue lunwenji (对比语言学论文集 A Collection of Contrastive Linguistic Papers.) [C]. Beijing: Waiyu jiaoxue yu yanjiu chubanshe (北京: 外语教学与研究出版社, Beijing: Foreign Language Teaching and Research Press.) 1992.

Liu, Z. D. (刘重德) Wenxue fanyi shijiang (文学翻译十讲 Ten Lectures on Literary Translation.) [M]. Beijing: zhongguo duiwai fanyi chuban gongsi (北京: 中国对外翻译出版公司, Beijing: China Translation and Publishing Corporation.) 1991.

Liu, Z. Q. & Shi, Y. (刘振前, 史煜) Richang yingyu zhong yinyu de pubianxing jiqi renzhi de guangxi (日常英语中隐喻的普遍性及其与认知的关系 Universality of Metaphor in Daily English and Its Relationship with Cognition) [J]. Waiyu jiaoxue (外语教学, Foreign Languages Education.) 2002, (1).

Liu, Z. Q. (刘振前) Yinyu de wenhua renzhi benzhi yu waiyu jiaoxue (隐喻的文化认知本质与外语教学 Essence of Cultural Cognition in Metaphor and Foreign Language Teaching) [J]. Waiyu yu waiyu jiaoxue (外语与外语教学, Foreign Languages and Their Teaching.) 2002, (2).

Liu, Z. Z. (刘传珠) Keyixing wenti de yuyan gongnengguan (可译性问题的语言功能观 Translatability from the Perspective of Language Functions) [J]. Zhongguo fanyi (中国翻译, Chinese Translators Journal.) 2000, (1).

Mao, Z. M. (毛忠明) Yingyu zhuyu de siwei yanjiu ji hanyi (英语主语的思维研究及汉译 On the Mentality of English

Subjects and Their Translation into Chinese) [J]. Waiyujie (外语界, Foreign Language World.) 2002, (5).

Pan, W. G. (潘文国) Han ying yu duibi gangyao (汉英语对比纲要 An Outline of Chinese – English Contrastive Study.) [M]. Beijing: Beijing yuyan wenhua daxue chubanshe (北京: 北京语言文化大学出版社, Beijing: Beijing Language and Culture University Press.) 1991.

Shu, D. F. (束定芳) Lun yinyu de yunzuo jizhi (论隐喻的运作机制 On the Mechanism of Metaphor) [J]. Waiyu jiaoxue yu yanjiu (外语教学与研究, Foreign Language Teaching and Research.) 2002, (2).

Wang, Z. Y. (王宗炎) Yuyan wenti tansuo (语言问题探索 An Exploration of Some Language Issues.) [M]. Shanghai: Shanghai waiyu jiaoyu chubanshe (上海: 上海外语教育出版社, Shanghai : Shanghai Foreign Language Education Press.) 1985.

Wang, Y. (王寅) Ying yi han: jufa jiegou bijiao (英译汉: 句法结构比较 A Comparison of Sentence Structures: From English into Chinese) [J]. Zhongguo fanyi (中国翻译, Chinese Translators Journal.) 1993, (5).

Wang, Y. (王寅) Renzhi yuyanxue de zhexue jichu: tiyan zhexue (认知语言学的哲学基础: 体验哲学 Embodied Philosophy: Philosophical Basis for Cognitive Linguistics) [J]. Waiyu jiaoxue yu yanjiu (外语教学与研究, Foreign Language Teaching and Research.) 2002, (2).

Wang, Z. (王竹) Yinghan biaoda fangshi chayi ji dui zhongguo xuesheng fanyi yu xiezuo de yingxiang (英汉表达方式差异及对中国学生翻译与写作的影响 Differences in English and Chinese Expressions and Their Influence on Chinese Students in Translating and Writing）[J]. Zhongguo fanyi（中国翻译, Chinese Translators Journal.）1997，(3).

Wen, X.（文旭）Renzhi yuyanxue de yanjiu mubiao, yuanze he fangfa（认知语言学的研究目标、原则和方法 Research Goals, Principles and Methods of Cognitive Linguistics）[J]. Waiyu jiaoxue yu yanjiu（外语教学与研究, Foreign Language Teaching and Research.）2002，(2).

Wu, Q.（吴群）Yuyi guantong, yuju biantong：bawo "rencheng" he "wucheng" de zhuanhuan（语义贯通，语句变通——把握"人称"和"物称"的转换 "Personal" and "Impersonal" Shift through Coherence in Meaning and Change in Sentence Structure）[J]. Zhongguo fanyi（中国翻译, Chinese Translators Journal.）2002，(4).

Xiao, J. A. & Wang, Z. J.（肖建安，王志军）Mingwuhua jiegou de gongneng ji bianti tezheng（名物化结构的功能及变体特征 Functions of Nominalization and Its Variety Features）[J]. Waiyu yu waiyu jiaoxue（外语与外语教学, Foreign Languages and Their Teaching.）2001，(6).

Xie, Z. J.（谢之君）Yinyu：cong xiucige dao renzhi（隐喻：从修辞格到认知 Metaphor：From Rhetorical Devices to Cognition）[J]. Waiyu yu waiyu jiaoxue（外语与外语教学, Foreign Languages and Their Teaching.）2000，(3).

Zhang, H. T.（张海涛）Yinghan siwei chayi dui fanyi de yingxiang（英汉思维差异对翻译的影响 Effects of the Differences in English and Chinese Thinking on Translation）[J]. Zhongguo fanyi（中国翻译, Chinese Translators Journal.）1999，(1).

Zhao, Y. F.（赵艳芳）Renzhi yuyanxue gailun（认知语言学概论 An Introduction to Cognitive Linguistics.）[M]. Shanghai：Shanghai waiyu jiaoyu chubanshe（上海：上海外语教育出版社, Shanghai：Shanghai Foreign Languages Education Press.）2001.

Zhu, L.（朱玲）Yinyu：dui xiangsixing de shuangxiang rentong（隐喻：对相似性的双向认同 Metaphor：Two-way Identification of Resemblance）[J]. Xiuci xuexi（修辞学习, Contemporary Rhetoric.）2002,（1）.

Zhu, Y. S.（朱永生）Yuyan, yupian, yujing（语言、语篇、语境 Language, Text and Context.）[M]. Beijing：qinghua daxue chubanshe（北京：清华大学出版社, Beijing：Tsinghua University Press.）1993.

Zhu, Y. S.（朱永生）Yufa yinyu de gengju jiqi gongxian（语法隐喻的根据及其贡献 Foundations and Contributions of Grammatical Metaphor）[J]. Waiyu jiaoxue yu yanjiu（外语教学与研究, Foreign Language Teaching and Research.）2000,（2）.

3. 中文文献

蔡基刚. 英语教学与英语写作中的汉式英语 [J]. 外语界, 1995（3）.

蔡基刚. 英语写作对比研究 [M]. 上海：复旦大学出版社, 2001.

蔡金亭. 汉语主题突出特征对中国学生英语写作的影响 [J]. 外语教学与研究, 1998（4）.

曹军. 从《呼啸山庄》两个中译本看英语文学文本汉译的结构转换 [D]. 南京：南京航空航天大学, 2010.

曾东京, 姜华. 综合性英汉词典英谚收译的三大问题 [J].

四川外语学院学报, 2003 (5): 157 - 160.

曾东京. 对英谚汉译问题的再思考 [J]. 上海科技翻译, 1998 (1): 5 - 8.

曾东京. 浅论《综合英语成语词典》与《英语成语词典》 [J]. 外语教学, 1991 (1): 75 - 82.

曾文华. 英汉语篇衔接手段的差异与翻译策略 [D]. 武汉: 华中师范大学, 2004.

常虹. 基于大学英语英汉对比教学的实证研究 [J]. 湖州师范学院学报, 2012 (6): 122 - 126.

陈定安. 汉英比较与翻译 [M]. 北京: 中国对外翻译出版公司, 1991.

陈腊春. 中西思维差异对中学生英语写作句法的影响 [D]. 武汉: 华中师范大学, 2006.

陈文伯. 关于英汉谚语的对译 [J]. 外国语, 1987b (6): 38 - 43.

陈文伯. 关于英谚介绍的几个问题 [J]. 现代外语, 1987a (2): 21 - 28.

陈晓静, 李英垣. 汉英有灵句与无灵句言语方法对比研究 [J]. 湖州师范学院学报, 2000 (2): 62 - 65.

陈勇. 英语动词拟人转义的语用特点及翻译 [J]. 湖南文理学院学报 (社会科学版), 2004 (2).

程晓堂, 崔荣佳. 连接性词语的功能新解 [J]. 外语教学, 2004 (2).

楚建伟, 高云. 概念语法隐喻与英语书面语语体意识的培养 [J]. 西安外国语大学学报, 2014 (3): 65 - 67.

丁玉伟. 英语无灵主语句的汉译 [J]. 山东外语教学, 1995 (2): 59 - 60.

樊亮亮. 非意愿性论元双及物构式之构式语法研究 [D]. 南

昌：江西师范大学，2011.
范武邱. 英语，你美在哪里［J］. 科技英语学习，2004（4）.
冯捷. 主体性还是客体性——二语习得中句式运算与语用意义接口的一项研究［D］. 广州：广东外语外贸大学，2008.
冯庆华. 实用翻译教程. 上海：上海外语教育出版社，2002.
冯树鉴. 谈谈无灵主语句的汉译［J］. 大学英语，1990（4）：64-66.
冯树鉴. 无灵名词作主语时的汉译［J］. 科技英语学习，1995（1）：9-11.
冯树鉴. 无生命名词作主语时的译法［J］. 英语知识，1991（1）：10-15.
桂清扬. 英语谚语分类初探［J］. 上饶师专学报（社科版），1988（1）：94-98.
何明珠. 论英语无灵主语句的分析与解释基础［J］. 南京晓庄学院学报，2012a（2）：54-56.
何明珠. 生命性与英语无灵主语句的类型分析［J］. 湘潭师范学院学报（社会科学版），2005b（4）：87-90.
何明珠. 英语书面与口头语篇中的无灵主语句对比分析——以韩礼德一项相关研究中的实例为语料［J］. 英语研究，2012b（3）：1-7.
何明珠. 英语无灵主语句的汉译策略与方法探索［J］. 中南大学学报（社会科学版），2005c（3）：403-409.
何明珠. 英语无灵主语句的理解与翻译［J］. 外语教学，2003a（5）：51-55.
何明珠. 英语无灵主语句的认知突显分析［J］. 外语教学，2009a（5）.
何明珠. 英语无灵主语句的生产机制与表现形式再探［J］.

外语与外语教学，2005a（7）：11-14.

何明珠. 英语无灵主语句的隐含逻辑语义关系分析［J］. 湖南工业大学学报（社会科学版），2009b（3）：88-91.

何明珠. 英语无灵主语句的隐喻性与生命性认知探源［J］. 外国语文，2011b（5）：39-43.

何明珠. 英语无灵主语句研究综述［J］. 西安外国语大学学报，2011a（2）：10-13.

何明珠. 英语无灵主语句与汉式英语［J］. 西安外国语大学学报，2007（4）：26-29.

何明珠. 英语无灵主语句与英汉思维特征对比［J］. 株洲师范高等专科学校学报，2003b（4）：75-77.

何自然. 语用学探索［M］. 广州：世界图书出版公司，2000.

侯建波. 语法隐喻：新解与反思［J］. 外语教学，2008（5）.

胡明涛. 许渊冲古诗英译中的意境美和无灵主语翻译法探究［J］. 六盘水师范学院学报，2013（6）：64-66.

胡壮麟.《功能语法导论》导读［A］. Halliday, M. A. K. *An Introduction to Functional Grammar* (2nd Ed). Beijing: Foreign Language Teaching and Research Press/ London: Edward Arnold, 1994.

黄伯荣，廖序东. 现代汉语［M］. 兰州：甘肃人民出版社，1983.

黄国文. 电子语篇的特点［J］. 外语与外语教学，2005（12）.

黄国文. 语法隐喻在翻译研究中的应用［J］. 中国翻译，2009（1）.

黄昆海. 英汉主语使用差异述略［J］. 外语与外语教学，2002（9）：26-28.

黄文静. 英语无灵主语双及物构式的认知研究［D］. 湘潭：湖南科技大学，2013.

霍明杰. 英语无灵主语句研究的意向性视角 [J]. 外文研究, 2014 (4): 19 - 23.

贾德霖. 思维模式与线性序列 [J]. 外国语, 1990 (5).

简庆闽, 等. 大学英语书面表达的连贯性评价和缺陷分析 [J]. 外语教学与研究, 2003 (5).

金其斌. 中英谚语对比五题 [J]. 云南师范大学学报（对外汉语教学与研究版）, 2006 (1): 80 - 85.

赖余. 《英语谚语选译》若干译例质疑 [J]. 江西师范大学学报, 1984 (1): 86 - 89.

蓝纯. 认知语言学与隐喻研究 [M]. 北京: 外语教学与研究出版社, 2005: 116 - 119.

李发根. 小句经验功能与翻译 [J]. 外语与外语教学, 2004 (7).

李金姝, 张国勇, 陈勇. 英语拟人动词中原型人物的潜意识性 [J]. 湖南科技学院学报, 2007 (8).

李文中. 中国英语与中国式英语 [J]. 外语教学与研究, 1993 (4).

李鑫华. 英语修辞格详论 [M]. 上海: 上海外语教育出版社, 2001.

连淑能. 英汉对比研究 [M]. 北京: 高等教育出版社, 1993

连淑能. 英语的"物称"与汉语的"人称" [J]. 山东外语教学, 1993 (2): 29 - 32.

连淑能. 英语含非人称主语句子的汉译 [J]. 翻译通讯, 1983 (6).

梁茂成. 英语谚语的理解与翻译 [J]. 中国翻译, 1995 (5): 36 - 39.

刘光耀, 姜玲. 从语境看行为主语译为状语从句的技巧 [J]. 中国科技翻译, 2000 (4).

刘锦. 中英思维方式的差异对翻译的影响［J］. 重庆科技学院学报（社会科学版），2012（6）：153－157.

刘礼进. 生命性对英汉语 NP 用法的作用——一项语料考察［J］. 外语教学与研究，2003（2）：111－119.

刘巧民. 论英语无灵主语句的汉译［D］. 长沙：湖南师范大学，2011.

刘树阁. 英语无生命主语句子的理解与翻译［J］. 现代外语，1995（3）：65－66.

刘树阁. 有灵动词与无生物主语——浅析英语无生物主语句子的理解与翻译［J］. 郑州工学院学报（社科版），1994（2）：68－72.

刘云波. 英谚汉译的几点看法［J］. 外国语，1995（6）：43－45.

卢卫中. 人体隐喻化的认知特点［C］./束定芳. 语言的认知研究——认知语言学论文精选. 上海：上海外语教育出版社，2004：470－485.

马秉义. 英汉主语差异初探［J］. 外国语，1995（5）：55－59.

马广惠，文秋芳. 大学生英语写作能力的影响因素研究［J］. 外语教学与研究，1999（4）.

马广惠. 中美大学生英语语篇对比修辞分析［J］. 解放军外国语学院学报，2001（6）：5－8.

马广惠. 中美大学生英语作文语言特征的对比分析［J］. 外语教学与研究，2002（5）：345－349.

毛荣贵，D. S. Houston. 中国大学生英语作文评改［M］. 上海：上海交通大学出版社，1997.

毛荣贵. 英语写作纵横谈［M］. 上海：上海外语教育出版社，1998.

牛保义. 英汉语工具主语句的象征关系研究 [J]. 外语教学, 2008 (1): 1-6.

牛保义. 英汉主语对比 [J]. 外语教学, 1994 (2): 49-53.

钱歌川. 英文疑难详解 [M]. 北京: 中国对外翻译出版公司, 1981.

钱冠连. 语言: 人类最后的家园——人类基本生存状态的哲学与语用学研究 [M]. 北京: 商务印书馆, 2005.

乔曾锐. 译论 [M]. 北京: 中华工商联出版社, 2000.

丘巧珍. 探讨无灵主语句的英译汉——《家园》(节选) 翻译实践报告 [D]. 广州: 广东外语外贸大学, 2014.

邵志洪, 邵惟韺. 词汇化拟人和修辞性拟人——英汉拟人法使用对比研究 [J]. 解放军外国语学院学报, 2007 (2): 1-5.

申连云. 形合与意合的语用意义及翻译策略 [J]. 外国语, 2003 (2)

盛莉敏. 英汉对比视角下英语无灵主语的汉译 [D]. 兰州: 兰州大学, 2016.

束定芳. 隐喻学研究 [M]. 上海: 上海外语教育出版社, 2000.

宋志平. 英谚望文生"译"八例 [J]. 大学英语, 1996 (6): 78-80.

孙勉志. 汉语环境与英语学习 [M]. 上海: 上海外语教育出版社, 2001.

孙敏. 生命度及认知视角下的隐喻性无灵主语句研究 [D]. 天津: 天津工业大学, 2016.

孙锐. 英语无灵主语句修辞特色的认知阐释 [J]. 湖南农业大学学报 (社会科学版), 2008 (1): 97-99.

孙兴文. 英语隐喻性无灵句: 生命特征与汉译策略 [J]. 云

南师范大学学报（哲学社会科学版），2006（6）：125 - 130.

孙致礼. 再谈文学翻译的策略问题［J］. 中国翻译，2003（1）.

覃修桂. "眼"的概念隐喻——基于语料的英汉对比研究［J］. 外国语，2008（5）：37 - 43.

唐青叶. Like 类与 please 类心理动词的视角研究［J］. 外语教学，2004（3）：39 - 43.

唐青叶. 视角与意义的建构［J］. 外语学刊，2009（3）：62 - 65.

童斯琴. 无灵主语句在《红楼梦》双译本中的使用分析［J］. 海外英语，2013（12）：280 - 282.

王桂珍. 主题、主位与汉语句子主题的英译［J］. 现代外语，1996（4）.

王晋军. 名词化在语篇类型中的体现［J］. 外语学刊，2003（2）.

王珏. 汉语生命范畴初论［M］. 上海：华东师范大学出版社，2004.

王力. 中国现代语法［M］. 北京：商务印书馆，1985.

王立非，等. 母语水平对二语写作的迁移：跨语言的理据与路径［J］. 外语教学与研究，2004（3）.

王满良. 英汉主语比较［J］. 外语教学，1999（1）：87 - 95.

王秋海. 美国大学生作文选［M］. 北京：世界知识出版社，1999.

王仁强. 论异化与归化的连续体关系［J］. 现代外语，2004（1）.

王书亭，王建敏. 英语流行谚语［M］. 北京：石油大学出版社，2004.

参考文献

王素娥. 翻译中的反客为主 [J]. 黑河学刊, 2016 (6): 70 -73.

王文斌. 论汉语"心"的空间隐喻的结构化 [J]. 解放军外国语学院学报, 2001 (1): 57-60.

王晓均. 101对汉英常用谚语对照 [M]. 北京: 北京语言大学出版社, 2008.

王晓俊. 英汉译本中的主语对比分析 [J]. 河南理工大学学报 (社会科学版), 2014 (1): 67-72.

王雪莹. 英语无灵主语的意象翻译 [J]. 外文研究, 2014 (4): 24-29.

王燕华, 黄培希. 中国学生二语写作中无灵主语句的产生机制 [J]. 东华大学学报 (社会科学版), 2010 (4): 316-320.

王耀敏. 文化思维模式的差异在汉英语言中的体现 [D]. 长春: 长春理工大学, 2004.

王寅. 英语语言宏观结构区别特征 (续) [J]. 外国语, 1992 (5).

魏在江. 从中西思维方式看翻译中静态与动态的转换 [J]. 山东外语教学, 2006 (6): 92-96.

魏志成. 英汉时间主语比较及翻译 [J]. 外国语, 1997 (1): 48-55.

魏志成. 英汉语比较导论 [M]. 上海: 上海外语教育出版社, 2003.

文秋芳, 等. 中国大学生英语书面语中的口语化倾向 [J]. 外语教学与研究, 2003 (4).

翁义明. 英语无灵句的功能语法分析 [J]. 四川外语学院学报, 2005 (1): 87-89.

吴显友. 小议无生命主语的英译汉 [J]. 大学英语, 1998

(10).

吴小芳. 认知语言学意义观关照下的《醉翁亭记》句式英译比析研究［J］. 滁州学院学报, 2016 (1).

吴小芳. 认知语言学视角下的汉语无主句英译［J］. 内蒙古民族大学学报, 2012a (1): 29–30.

吴小芳. 认知语言学视角下的英语无灵主语句新解［J］. 鸡西大学学报, 2012b (10): 85–86.

吴雨田. 英谚管见［J］. 外国语, 1987 (5): 37–42.

席建国, 马苏勇. 英语无灵句与汉语有灵句的句法对比及翻译［J］. 四川外语学院学报, 2002 (3): 126–132.

熊力游. 简单句的隐性因果功能与翻译研究［J］. 外语与外语教学, 2007 (7).

徐盛桓, 李淑静. 英语原因句的嬗变［J］. 外语学刊, 2005 (1).

徐通锵. 徐通锵自选集［M］. 郑州: 河南教育出版社, 1993.

阎佩衡, 孙迎春, 马小文. 建立一个逻辑语法范畴——试论语言形式的内部转换问题［J］. 山东师大外国语学院学报, 2001 (4).

燕南. 英语谚语的理解和翻译［J］. 中国翻译, 1987 (3): 20–23.

杨炳钧. 渐变群在非限定小句中的体现及其意义［J］. 外语学刊, 2007 (3).

杨永林. 言简意赅, 含蓄隽永——也谈英语非人称主语句［J］. 山东外语教学, 1986 (1): 21–26.

于心荟, 卫洁. 翻译共性视角下汉英同声传译中的主语转换［J］. 现代交际, 2019 (8): 89–91.

喻家楼, 胡开宝. 析汉、英语中的有灵、无灵和动态、静态句［J］. 外国语, 1997 (5): 52–54.

张法科,仇伟.处所主语句的认知研究[J].外语教学,2006(6).

张寒冰.生命度等级与英语无灵主语句研究[J].金陵科技学院学报(社会科学版),2019(2):1-4.

张杰.基于语料库的学术论文结论部分的情态序列研究[D].新乡:河南师范大学,2012.

张今,陈云清.英汉比较语法纲要[M].北京:商务印书馆,1981.

张京鱼,等.有生性在中学生英语心理谓词习得中的认知作用[J].外语教学与研究,2004(5).

张梅岗,李光曦.科技英语中因果动词的作用与译法[J].中国翻译,1994(5).

张梅岗,杨红,张建佳.英汉翻译教程[M].北京:国防工业出版社,2008.

张瑛.英语无灵主语句的翻译策略——以《翻译研究百科全书》的翻译实践为例[D].太原:山西大学,2018.

张哲.从英语无灵主语句的角度谈如何培养英语思维[J].长春理工大学学报,2012(2):98-99.

张志祥.语言结构顺应视域下的涉外导游词翻译[J].语言与翻译,2018(2):51-55.

长孙馥蓉.名词化与大学英语写作探究[J].陕西教育(高校),2011(7-8):45-46.

赵桂华.英语非生物主语结构分析及其翻译[J].齐齐哈尔大学学报,2002(2).

赵景梅.汉英语言映射下的中西文化思维差异[J].安徽科技学院学报,2015(5):80-83.

赵明.论英汉翻译中的"有灵"与"无灵"[J].中国科技翻译,1999(2):14-16.

郑雅. 有灵主语与无灵主语转换 [J]. 新余学院学报, 2015 (3): 90-92.

钟小佩. 从认知的角度看汉英"世界是人"的隐喻概念 [C]./束定芳. 语言的认知研究——认知语言学论文精选. 上海: 上海外语教育出版社, 2004: 487-499.

朱正键. 4500双解英语谚语 [M]. 上海: 上海译文出版社, 2006.

朱中都. 英语写作中的负迁移 [J]. 解放军外国语学院学报, 1999 (2).

卓勇光. 等式主位与信息对应的功能分析 [J]. 现代外语, 2004 (3).

左自鸣. 英汉思维差异与英语无灵主语句 [J]. 广西师范学院学报（哲学社会科学版）, 2004 (4): 107-120.